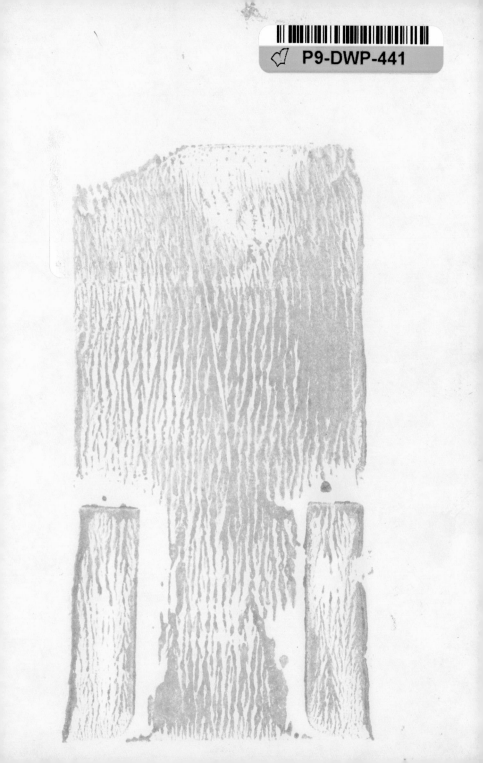

TWENTIETH CENTURY VIEWS

The aim of this series is to present the best in contemporary critical opinion on major authors, providing a twentieth century perspective on their changing status in an era of profound revaluation.

Maynard Mack, *Series Editor*
Yale University

STEPHEN
CRANE

A COLLECTION OF CRITICAL ESSAYS

Edited by

Maurice Bassan

Prentice-Hall, Inc. *Englewood Cliffs, N.J.*

A SPECTRUM BOOK

Current printing (last number):
10 9 8 7 6 5 4 3 2

Contents

III

Discussions of Individual Works

STEPHEN
CRANE

Introduction

by Maurice Bassan

I

"Art, in the splendor of her processional toward the everlasting altars, does not disclose those of her train who hobble in tatters, their mouths filled with goblin-laughter, their hands making ironical gestures toward the fat and complacent public." So writes a young artist in one of Stephen Crane's early fragmentary narratives. The poverty, the goblin-laughter, and the ironical gestures define with uncommon clarity Crane's own physical and spiritual state when he was pursuing a lonely, impoverished, yet dedicated existence in the nether regions of New York City during the early 1890s. This was the Stephen Crane who, in search of "the real thing," slept in Bowery flophouses and stood in blinding snowdrifts with the unemployed; who was eating, after he managed to sell a few newspaper sketches, "with charming regularity at least two times per day"; who, finally, was writing in his own slow and deliberate way some of the most remarkable stories and poems of the decade and of our entire literary history. The splendid processional went its way, elevating in its van such figures as Thomas Bailey Aldrich and Richard Watson Gilder, suffering the presence of Mark Twain and William Dean Howells, and casting into its train not only Stephen Crane but other "disreputable" figures like Theodore Dreiser and Edwin Arlington Robinson.

This Stephen Crane—the lonely artist just out of his teens and working at times in an obscurity like that of Nathaniel Hawthorne in his solitary chamber—had developed out of an ancestral and moral chemistry that might have produced a minister, a soldier, or a ballplayer rather than a writer. He had, however, abandoned the letter, though not the spirit, of his minister father's gentle Methodism (his mother too, Crane declared, "was always more of a Christian than a Methodist"). Or, if we remember Crane's conscious

1

pride in his military heritage that dated back to the Revolutionary War and his performances as drill captain at Claverack, we can easily see how he might have become a soldier. Or, despite his frail constitution soon weakened by incessant smoking, he might have played professional baseball (his goal at fifteen) after his display of skill at varsity shortstop while attending Syracuse. Like most occupations, the ministry, the military, and sports had in common the ideal of a code of moral or physical perfection against which men measured their individual worth. This was true as well of the splendid processional of Art, which Crane approached gingerly as a reporter of Jersey shore news for the New York *Tribune*. The tension between ideal code and individual performance defines the limits and makes clearer the ironical gestures of Crane's art. Crane never abandoned the somewhat romantic conception of the code, retaining a singularly pure vision of the truth of "primitive" Christianity, of the nobility of military behavior, of the excellence of the sportsman's code, of the high purpose of art. From the beginning, in fact, he measured himself, other men, and the whole of society against such standards, and was equally aware of his own deficiencies and of the failure of most men through their overweening vanity, their childish or psychopathic delusions, or their failure of magnanimity. At Claverack, a friend recalled, he was "rather given to holding aloof, especially if the human animal was manifesting its capacity for collective action." The insight that man was more given to collaboration in the destruction of others than to brotherhood was an early one, long sustained.

Once chosen, the career was agonizing in the extreme, as Crane's remarks to Willa Cather at the end of his first phase in 1895 indicate. "Of all human lots for a person of sensibility," he wrote an editor in the same year, "that of an obscure free lance in literature or journalism is, I think, the most discouraging." Yet the rewards too were great—the admiration of fellow bohemian artists and the support in 1893 (after the publication of *Maggie*) of men who had made their mark such as Howells, Hamlin Garland, and B. O. Flower. Like Keats at approximately the same age, Crane passed through a relatively short period of apprenticeship, most notably marked by the writing of the eleven fantastic and clever *Sullivan County Sketches* (1892), several imitative of the moods and styles of Poe, Twain, and Kipling. Here he is the sportsman turning fabulist. Then, as with Keats, the apprenticeship was succeeded by a dazzling year and more of extraordinary performances. *Maggie: A Girl of the Streets, The*

Red Badge of Courage, perhaps most of *George's Mother,* two-thirds of all his poems, several superb stories—all were written between Crane's birthday late in 1892 and mid-1894, though several of these works were not published in book form until later.

The studies of society like *Maggie* (which had to be published privately, for no respectable house or periodical would print it) and "An Experiment in Misery" are works of a curiously sardonic tenderness. Crane's major target was the nature of man himself, his hypocrisy, his weakness, his pitiful capitulation before the gods of respectability. *Maggie,* later acclaimed as the first dark flower of American Naturalism, a novel which emphasizes the oppressiveness of the slum environment and focuses on the basic drives of hunger, sex, and fear, yet was undoubtedly meant by Crane as a testament to those ideals of magnanimous human conduct that in the Bowery environment, and in society as a whole, are defined by their absence or impotence. Wounded in perhaps his deepest part—the minister in him—by the failure of society and the church, the failure of men to measure up to ideal codes of Nobility and Human Kindness (the latter "the final wall of the wise man's thought," he said), he could respond only negatively. Hence the bitter tone coupled with the submerged pity, hence the ironical gestures. But there was more to Crane's vision of society than this. In "An Ominous Baby" the allegory starkly proclaims the inevitability of class warfare; this is one extreme, one response to the turpitude and injustice of the monied. "No doubt," he declared at the end of "An Experiment in Luxury," the rich "would dispense their dollars like little seeds upon the soil of the world if it were not for the fact that since the days of the ancient great political economist [Christ], the more exalted forms of virtue have grown to be utterly impracticable." At the other extreme Crane seems moved, metaphysically, by the image in Melville's famous "Mat-Maker" chapter in *Moby Dick*: Chance "has the last featuring blow at events." In this aspect of Crane's view "the eternal mystery of social condition" becomes the mystery of the Fate that rules our lives.

The minister in Crane is apparent also in *The Black Riders,* the first and more important of the two volumes of "lines" (Crane also called his poems "pills") published in his lifetime. To be sure, Crane attacks a few ministerial figures who exhibit the same contemptuous indifference as the preachers in *Maggie,* and sometimes we seem to be in the presence of American *fleurs du mal,* diabolic, intense, savage. But despite the sense of doomed love, despite the futility, the self-mockery, and the attack on the Old Testament Yahweh, the poems display again the wounded spirit of the true believer, skeptical but with an idealistic faith in courage, truth, and virtue. Some of the little allegories—such as the Beckettian desert landscape with a man consuming his heart—are unforgettable, and unlike anything in poetry before or since. A spirit of macabre comedy plays over the surreal desert and mountain scenes, with their pitiful, absurd, doomed figures engaged in dramatic confrontations with a terrible fate. These strange poems appeared in a unique free-verse form that anticipated but probably did not influence the Imagists of some twenty years later.

The Red Badge of Courage, which belongs to the year 1893 though it was not published in book form until the fall of 1895, was Crane's first investigation of war. Crane employed battle imagery compulsively even earlier, however, as *Maggie* attests. Again "naturalistic" in the depiction of its subject (Crane declared that he intended "a psychological portrayal of fear"), the novel was strikingly original in attempting to determine precisely, from the point of view of an individual soldier—alert, sensitive, childishly vain—the effects of the old ceremonial code now obscured by the din and brutal horror of battle. The meaning of Crane's answer has been debated ever since: as everything from glorification of the heroics of war or the solidarity of the group to a dramatization of meaninglessness and the absurdity of the attempt to discover meaning in war or, indeed, life. Whether Henry Fleming is, then, a hero or a kind of existential antihero rests pretty much with the individual reader, for Crane at one time or another undercuts almost every value proposed in the book. Yet the effect is not one of incoherence, as if Crane himself could not decide. Hence the debate based on the attempt to trace the sources, the patterns, the structure, and the imagery of this still most remarkable of war novels has become very exciting in the last decade.

The early career of Stephen Crane is scarcely exhausted by these remarks. Working in his impoverished and solitary condition, he produced other important sketches and tales. But a paradox asserts itself. On the one hand, as Larzer Ziff argues, Crane seemed to be imposing his views upon his material, dramatizing predetermined assessments of man and society; thus we detect most clearly in his early work the outlines of the Christian minister and gentleman, of the Claverack drill captain, of the sportsman, and moreover, of the arraigner of man's postures of significance in the face of the immensities of Nature and Fate. On the other hand, it is also in this period that Crane seems most sensitive to literary influences—from Twain and Howells, from Tolstoy (his favorite writer), from Zola and Flaubert, from a dozen others, even from Homer, as Warren D. Anderson notes. Perhaps the resolution of the paradox is that Crane read the classics—the "enormous repudiations" of tradition and the past of which H. G. Wells speaks in his essay on Crane have been rather overstressed—and read his contemporaries, but always with some distrust of that grand processional from which he seemed to be excluded. He took what he needed from the past and its literature; what he needed and often found was the confirmation of his private vision.

II

Crane's first and major phase ended during 1895, though earlier the publication of *Maggie* in 1893 and the public reading of his poems in 1894 had provoked vague rumblings of the fame, or at least notoriety, that was to mark his second phase. A shortened version of *The Red Badge* was given magazine publication and created a stir in December, 1894; the following month Crane set off for the West as a syndicate feature writer. He found himself deeply sympathetic to the suffering of Nebraska farmers and of the poor Indians of Mexico who, to Crane's amazement, did not feel "the modern desperate rage at the accident of birth." During the trip, moreover, he was exposed to the sort of personal danger that attracted and haunted him all his life. This journey to the "great honest West" gave Crane the materials out of which some of his finest stories were to be wrought three years later; it is even possible that he sketched these stories as he wandered about Mexico City, observing sharply, like Ernest Hemingway later in Paris, the life of American expatriates. As John Berryman has noted, the trip did something else for Crane: it introduced a less deterministic view of the relation of man to nature into his fiction and confirmed for him those imperatives of endurance and courage that had been treated earlier with occasional uncertainty.

The Red Badge of Courage was published in October, 1895, and brought to Crane the sort of fame most writers dream of all their lives and never achieve—as Keats, for example, never did. In England it caused an explosion, to use Joseph Conrad's figure; in Amer-

ica, it was a triumph. Crane was immediately conscious of his problem; when the adulation began, he wrote to Nellie Crouse, he "perceived that the fight was not going to be with the world but with
myself." The fight with the world was in one sense over—the tatters,
the goblin-laughter, and the rest. What Crane was referring to, of
course, was his fight to remain true to the principles that had sustained him in New York, to remain true to his "quality of personal
honesty." But no partisan of Crane's immense total achievement
can deny that this second half of his career is, on the whole, rather
less distinguished than the first. For one thing, he wrote too much:
his productivity tripled, at least. For another, he began writing
somewhat pale imitations of himself, such as several of the "episodes" in *The Little Regiment*. He immersed himself in war journalism in Greece and Cuba, an enterprise that, despite several memorable sketches that resulted, was wasteful of his talent. As A. J.
Liebling has postulated, in his last year in England it was the dollars that damned him, as they had Melville, for he was driven to
churn out potboiling stories only one or two of which were up to
his early mark. And Crane knew all this, knew (like F. Scott Fitzgerald later) that there was a commercial side to his talent. The
shift in standards is abruptly marked in 1895, when Crane allowed
the "easy writing" of *The Third Violet* to be published, though he
knew it was "pretty rotten work." "People may just as well discover
now," he said, "that the high dramatic key of *The Red Badge* cannot be sustained." But this was not as honest as it should have been.

What happened, in short, was that Crane became a public writer
rather than a private one. He was famous, as well as infamous in
some circles that passed around with glee tales of his consorting
with low women, of his scandalous marriage (if it was a marriage)
to the madam of a Jacksonville house of assignation, of his taking
dope and of his being perpetually drunk. His public demanded war
stories and he wrote them; they wanted a "big book" of popular
romance and he obliged with the inferior *Active Service*. He became a popular journalist. He acted the role of "Baron Brede" at
his Surrey estate. This outline of Crane's later career is not meant
to disparage it; as Eric Solomon has convincingly shown in *Stephen
Crane in England*, on the basis of his art Crane moved easily and
with authority, despite his youth, among such makers of modern
fiction as Conrad and Ford and James. The private visions and agonies of the early years had not by any means disappeared. But there
was a distinct shift from the very poor, very obscure artist writing

solely for himself and for Fame, the artist making ironical gestures at the fat and complacent public, to the scandal-marked, very self-conscious, and more than slightly commercial author of the last half-decade of the century, coincident with the last five years of Crane's life.

There is no trace of commercial intent, however, in "The Open Boat," an indirect result of the ill-fated filibustering expedition to Cuba that Crane joined late in 1896. His sober journalistic report of the sinking of the *Commodore* was succeeded some months later by one of his most perfect tales. The careful control of the point of view—that of "the correspondent"—the clarity and precision of the prose as it dips and swells with the horizon and with the anxieties of the men, and the muted symbolic atmosphere all cohere in a story that at several points offers Crane's maturest vision of man's role in the cosmos. The position of man, isolated from God and Nature, becomes charged with a kind of existential dread and with the necessity, in order to survive, of challenging what remains with gestures of authenticity. But it appears that these gestures cannot be authentic except as validated by the isolated personality himself. For "there are no bricks and no temples" in this world; man is without weapons or targets for his rage. As James B. Colvert suggests, the figure of the "deeply hurt" individual exemplifies "the little man upon the mountain," the archetypal comic pilgrim of Crane's tiny odysseys. In the face of the fearful and monstrous indifference of the cosmos, men still attempt to make their gestures of defiance, still insist shrilly on the possibility of meaning. In "The Open Boat," then, we have a microcosm of Crane's world, which, in its distance from the old Romantic optimism and affirmation, quite clearly anticipates our world of the twentieth century.

The height of this second half of Crane's career was perhaps reached in 1897-98, while Crane was living in Surrey and writing such tales as "Death and the Child," "The Bride Comes to Yellow Sky," "The Blue Hotel," and *The Monster*. The last, together with a few of the more heavyweight *Whilomville Stories* later, shows that Crane's eye for the savageness of the societal pressure to conform was as sharp as ever, though the presentation was more sober and less sardonic than in the narratives of the early '90s. The two great Western tales, in which the violator-outcast appears in both comic and tragic guises, are complementary in color and in emotional effect: "The Bride" explodes the myths of the Wild West, "The Blue Hotel" confirms them. Because Crane's model continued to be the

minister's vision of primitive Christianity, it is not surprising that
the Swede in the latter story has seemed a Christ-figure to many
readers. But as in Faulkner's work, Crane's Christ-figures are all
ironically presented and there is little or no possibility of redemption. "Death and the Child," based on Crane's experiences in
Greece, presents an ironic hero not unlike Henry Fleming in *The
Red Badge*, one who postures and dances as an observer through
the war while the seemingly undistinguished peasants fight stolidly
on. Something very like a mystique of the veteran emerges more
clearly in this story than ever before, and is confirmed in the later
"Timothy Lean" stories as well as in the tales and sketches of Cuba
—again based on Crane's experiences—collected in *Wounds in the
Rain*. It is in this respect, at least, that we can detect the continuity
of Crane's imagination from his earliest work to the latest.

III

Despite Crane's glittering reputation during his second phase, it
was only two decades after his death that readers and critics began
to understand more clearly the nature of his achievement. Crane
was sensitive to the early stirrings of the severe cultural panic that,
according to F. J. Hoffman, began to be felt more definitely at the
end of World War I, when "there was little or no moral security
to be found in any American institution." It was this sense of abiding loss that gave Crane's work (like Henry Adams's *Education*)
the peculiarly pessimistic flavor that was so congenial to the '20s.
Standard formulations of conduct and piety were widely questioned
and widely abandoned, and writers sought to make sense of what
remained either, like Edith Wharton, by using the past as a fixed
point from which to judge the present, or by creating a romantic
discipline of the self. Fitzgerald moves in this latter direction, and
Hemingway apotheosizes it. But despite the impressive connections
one can indicate between Crane's sensibility and Hemingway's—
first pointed out by Philip Young and since expanded by critics who
have compared particular stories—we cannot in all fairness say
that Crane "anticipated" Hemingway, for the apotheosis of the self
was distinctly alien to Crane's nature, as the numerous deflated
"little men" of his stories prove. Crane is harder at the core, and in
one sense more deeply skeptical than his later admirer. And it was
this very sense of disaffiliation in Crane, of a profound question-

ing of social verities, of the isolated figure facing a retreating cosmos, above all of the brutality and senselessness of war that made
this strange rebel of the '90s seem very relevant to the spirit of the
'20s and to its major literary figures.

It was in 1923 that Thomas Beer published his impressionistic
biography of Crane, calculated more to clear away the miasma of
vicious personal rumors than to present a rounded picture of the
man and artist. Joseph Conrad's personal memoir that served as an
introduction to the book, while touched with his obvious affection
for the young man he had known, conveyed perhaps too much the
impression that Crane's work had been quite fragmentary, unfin-
ished, too "brilliant" without solidity and depth. The twelve-volume
Work of Stephen Crane, which appeared in the mid-'20s, created
the very different impression that Crane had written much more—
specifically, much more of worth—than anyone had suspected; he
was not, after all, a one-book man. The introductions to this edition—which itself remained an incomplete record of Crane's total
output—by such writers as Sherwood Anderson, Willa Cather, Joseph Hergesheimer, Amy Lowell, and H. L. Mencken were enthu-
siastic but all somewhat irrelevant to Crane's work, as if enthusiasm
and a sense of rediscovery were a substitute for criticism. In general,
Crane was seen as embodying one of two archetypes: the Chatter-
tonian "marvellous boy," or the Poe-esque, demonic, drug-driven
writer—hardly as the serious, mature, responsible artist he was.

The 1950s saw a second, much more authentic revival. Books by
R. W. Stallman and John Berryman attempted to trace the larger
patterns in Crane's life and art and emerged with theories over
which critical debate persists. For Stallman, whose *Omnibus* edition
of 1952 was a landmark in Crane studies, Crane was a highly conscious artist skillful in arranging apparently incoherent structures
and in charging images with complex symbolic meanings. Berryman's *Stephen Crane* (1950) sought to elevate Crane's stature as a
writer by carefully defining literary influences upon him and the development of his ideas as well as by discussing the significance of
terms widely applied to Crane such as *impressionist, ironist,* and *naturalist.* While Berryman's effort to explain Crane's psychic makeup
has struck some readers as amateurish, the psychoanalytic approach
of recent critics such as Daniel Weiss has produced more satisfactory
results. Daniel Hoffman's *The Poetry of Stephen Crane* (1957) was
another landmark, for the first time establishing the influence of
Crane's Methodist heritage upon his themes and craft, and tracing

relationships between Crane's poems and the poetic traditions of his time and our own.

Much of the criticism of the past decade, including the very close readings that Crane's major novels and stories have received, has been in the form of intelligent footnotes to the work of Berryman, Stallman, and Hoffman. In addition, there have been many studies exploring in depth the antecedents of *Maggie* and *The Red Badge of Courage*. More recently, Edwin H. Cady's excellent *Stephen Crane* (1962) examined Crane in a number of perspectives, variously considering the claims of the usual labels and discussing the metaphor of sports (used in a critique by George W. Johnson), the archetype of the gentleman *déclassé*, and Crane as experimenter and "youthful pluralist." Eric Solomon's critical study, *Stephen Crane: From Parody to Realism* (1966), established a species of continuity between Crane's art and the forms of contemporaneous literature and subliterature. Meanwhile, other scholars like Thomas A. Gullason and Olov W. Fryckstedt have gradually brought the entire Crane corpus within our reach, including short stories long out of print, local-color sketches, and journalistic pieces from the Asbury Park days down to the long months in Cuba. English and Continental critics, too, have been progressively more interested in Crane's achievement, and there have been useful surveys by scholars such as Sergio Perosa and Georges Remords.

Despite the good quality and the reach of recent Crane criticism, much remains to be done. One would like to see commentaries on relatively neglected works such as *George's Mother, The Monster*, and "Death and the Child." Crane's poems have been little explored, and indeed his technical development in writing both poetry and prose narrative has been little more than sketched. His journalism, now fully available, and his short plays (not yet so) remain to be appraised and related to the whole of his work. His extraordinary connections to Mark Twain, his deep kinship with the dark writers of the Transcendental period, his role as a writer of the '90s—all these fields, and many more, are invitingly green. Like the work of the great modern European writers, like that of Hemingway and Faulkner, Crane's art belongs to that realm defined as "active" by Lionel Trilling. The unconscious minds of Hemingway and Faulkner, Trilling writes in words that are applicable to Crane as well,

> have wisdom and humility about themselves. They seldom make the attempt at formulated solution, they rest content with the "negative capability" [Keats's famous phrase]. And this negative capability, this

willingness to remain in uncertainties, mysteries, and doubts, is not, as one tendency of modern feeling would suppose, an abdication of intellectual activity. Quite to the contrary, it is precisely an aspect of their intelligence, of their seeing the full force and complexity of their subject matter.

It is for this reason that Stephen Crane, like all great writers, remains a challenge for readers today—remains inexhaustible.

I have tried to compress into the limits of this volume most, if certainly not all, of the best, most representative, and most influential studies of Crane; perhaps, I should add, "most recent," since over half of the selections date from the 1960s. The bibliography at the end of the book offers a more comprehensive view of major editions, biographical studies, and critical commentaries. I have reproduced texts as faithfully as possible, although errors of fact have been corrected and, in a number of cases, abridgements have been made, either by the writers themselves or by the editor. Asterisks indicate that long passages have been omitted; ellipses mark the deletion of a paragraph or less.

I am pleased to record my indebtedness to Dominic J. Bazzanella who typed a large section of the manuscript. For other assistance I wish to thank Bernice Slote and Pietro L. Iaccarino.

I

Portraits

When I Knew Stephen Crane

by Willa Cather

It was, I think, in the spring of '94 [actually February, 1895], that a slender, narrow-chested fellow in a shabby grey suit, with a soft felt hat pulled low over his eyes, sauntered into the office of the managing editor of the *Nebraska State Journal* and introduced himself as Stephen Crane. He stated that he was going to Mexico to do some work for the Bacheller Syndicate and get rid of his cough, and that he would be stopping in Lincoln for a few days. Later he explained that he was out of money and would be compelled to wait until he got a check from the East before he went further. I was a Junior at the Nebraska State University at the time, and was doing some work for the *State Journal* in my leisure time, and I happened to be in the managing editor's room when Mr. Crane introduced himself. I was just off the range; I knew a little Greek and something about cattle and a good horse when I saw one, and beyond horses and cattle I considered nothing of vital importance except good stories and the people who wrote them. This was the first man of letters I had ever met in the flesh, and when the young man announced who he was, I dropped into a chair behind the editor's desk where I could stare at him without being too much in evidence.

Only a very youthful enthusiasm and a large propensity for hero worship could have found anything impressive in the young man who stood before the managing editor's desk. He was thin to ema-

"When I Knew Stephen Crane." From *The Library* (Pittsburgh), I (June 23, 1900), 1718.

ciation, his face was gaunt and unshaven, a thin dark moustache straggled on his upper lip, his black hair grew low on his forehead and was shaggy and unkempt. His grey clothes were much the worse for wear and fitted him so badly it seemed unlikely he had ever been measured for them. He wore a flannel shirt and a slovenly apology for a necktie, and his shoes were dusty and worn grey about the toes and were badly run over at the heel. I had seen many a tramp printer come up the *Journal* stairs to hunt a job, but never one who presented such a disreputable appearance as this story-maker man. He wore gloves, which seemed rather a contradiction to the general slovenliness of his attire, but when he took them off to search his pockets for his credentials, I noticed that his hands were singularly fine; long, white, and delicately shaped, with thin, nervous fingers. I have seen pictures of Aubrey Beardsley's hands that recalled Crane's very vividly.

At that time Crane was but twenty-three, and almost an unknown man. Hamlin Garland had seen some of his work and believed in him, and had introduced him to Mr. Howells, who recommended him to the Bacheller Syndicate. *The Red Badge of Courage* had been published in the *State Journal* that winter along with a lot of other syndicate matter, and the grammatical construction of the story was so faulty that the managing editor had several times called on me to edit the copy. In this way I had read it very carefully, and through the careless sentence-structure I saw the wonder of that remarkable performance. But the grammar certainly was bad. I remember one of the reporters who had corrected the phrase "it don't" for the tenth time remarked savagely, "If I couldn't write better English than this, I'd quit."

Crane spent several days in the town, living from hand to mouth and waiting for his money. I think he borrowed a small amount from the managing editor. He lounged about the office most of the time, and I frequently encountered him going in and out of the cheap restaurants on Tenth Street. When he was at the office he talked a good deal in a wandering, absent-minded fashion, and his conversation was uniformly frivolous. If he could not evade a serious question by a joke, he bolted. I cut my classes to lie in wait for him, confident that in some unwary moment I could trap him into serious conversation, that if one burned incense long enough and ardently enough, the oracle would not be dumb. I was Maupassant mad at the time, a malady particularly unattractive in a Junior, and I made a frantic effort to get an expression of opinion from him on

"Le Bonheur." "Oh, you're Moping, are you?" he remarked with a sarcastic grin, and went on reading a little volume of Poe that he carried in his pocket. At another time I cornered him in the Funny Man's room and succeeded in getting a little out of him. We were taught literature by an exceedingly analytical method at the University, and we probably distorted the method, and I was busy trying to find the least common multiple of *Hamlet* and greatest common divisor of *Macbeth*, and I began asking him whether stories were constructed by cabalistic formulae. At length he sighed wearily and shook his drooping shoulders, remarking:

"Where did you get all that rot? Yarns aren't done by mathematics. You can't do it by rule any more than you can dance by rule. You have to have the itch of the thing in your fingers, and if you haven't,—well, you're damned lucky, and you'll live long and prosper, that's all."—And with that he yawned and went down the hall.

Crane was moody most of the time; his health was bad and he seemed profoundly discouraged. Even his jokes were exceedingly drastic. He went about with the tense, preoccupied, self-centered air of a man who is brooding over some impending disaster, and I conjectured vainly as to what it might be. Though he was seemingly entirely idle during the few days I knew him, his manner indicated that he was in the throes of work that told terribly on his nerves. His eyes I remember as the finest I have ever seen, large and dark and full of lustre and changing lights, but with a profound melancholy always lurking deep in them. They were eyes that seemed to be burning themselves out.

As he sat at the desk with his shoulders drooping forward, his head low, and his long, white fingers drumming on the sheets of copy paper, he was as nervous as a race horse fretting to be on the track. Always, as he came and went about the halls, he seemed like a man preparing for a sudden departure. Now that he is dead it occurs to me that all his life was a preparation for sudden departure. I remember once when he was writing a letter he stopped and asked me about the spelling of a word, saying carelessly, "I haven't time to learn to spell." Then, glancing down at his attire, he added with an absent-minded smile, "I haven't time to dress either; it takes an awful slice out of a fellow's life." . . .

I have heard other people say how difficult it was to induce Crane to talk seriously about his work, and I suspect that he was particularly averse to discussions with literary men of wider education and better equipment than himself, yet he seemed to feel that this fuller culture was not for him. Perhaps the unreasoning instinct which lies deep in the roots of our lives, and which guides us all, told him that he had not time enough to acquire it. . . .

The hoped for revelation came unexpectedly enough. It was on the last night he spent in Lincoln. I had come back from the theatre and was in the *Journal* office writing a notice of the play. It was eleven o'clock when Crane came in. He had expected his money to arrive on the night mail and it had not done so, and he was out of sorts and deeply despondent. He sat down on the ledge of the open window that faced on the street, and when I had finished my notice I went over and took a chair beside him. Quite without invitation on my part, Crane began to talk, began to curse his trade from the first throb of creative desire in a boy to the finished work of the master. The night was oppressively warm; one of those dry winds that are the curse of that country was blowing up from Kansas. The white, western moonlight threw sharp, blue shadows below us. The streets were silent at that hour, and we could hear the gurgle of the fountain in the Post Office square across the street, and the twang of banjos from the lower verandah of the Hotel Lincoln, where the colored waiters were serenading the guests. The drop lights in the office were dull under their green shades, and the telegraph sounder clicked faintly in the next room. In all his long tirade, Crane never raised his voice; he spoke slowly and monotonously and even calmly, but I have never known so bitter a heart in any man as he revealed to me that night. It was an arraignment of the wages of life, an invocation to the ministers of hate.

Incidentally he told me the sum he had received for *The Red Badge of Courage*, which I think was something like ninety dollars, and he repeated some lines from *The Black Riders*, which was then in preparation. He gave me to understand that he led a double literary life; writing in the first place the matter that pleased himself, and doing it very slowly; in the second place, any sort of stuff that would sell. And he remarked that his poor was just as bad as it could possibly be. He realized, he said, that his limitations were absolutely impassable. "What I can't do, I can't do at all, and I can't acquire it. I only hold one trump."

He had no settled plans at all. He was going to Mexico wholly uncertain of being able to do any successful work there, and he seemed to feel very insecure about the financial end of his venture. The thing that most interested me was what he said about his slow method of composition. He declared that there was little money in story-writing at best, and practically none in it for him, because of the time it took him to work up his detail. Other men, he said, could sit down and write up an experience while the physical effect of it, so to speak, was still upon them, and yesterday's impressions made today's "copy." But when he came in from the streets to write up what he had seen there, his faculties were benumbed, and he sat twirling his pencil and hunting for words like a schoolboy.

I mentioned *The Red Badge of Courage*, which was written in nine days, and he replied that, though the writing took very little time, he had been unconsciously working the detail of the story out through most of his boyhood. His ancestors had been soldiers, and he had been imagining war stories ever since he was out of knickerbockers, and in writing his first war story he had simply gone over his imaginary campaigns and selected his favorite imaginary experiences. He declared that his imagination was hide bound; it was there, but it pulled hard. After he got a notion for a story, months passed before he could get any sort of personal contact with it, or feel any potency to handle it. "The detail of a thing has to filter through my blood, and then it comes out like a native product, but it takes forever," he remarked. I distinctly remember the illustration, for it rather took hold of me.

I have often been astonished since to hear Crane spoken of as "the reporter in fiction," for the reportorial faculty of superficial reception and quick transference was what he conspicuously lacked. His first newspaper account of his shipwreck on the filibuster *Commodore* off the Florida coast was as lifeless as the "copy" of a police court reporter. It was many months afterwards that the literary product of his terrible experience appeared in that marvellous sea story "The Open Boat," unsurpassed in its vividness and constructive perfection.

At the close of our long conversation that night, when the copy boy came in to take me home, I suggested to Crane that in ten years he would probably laugh at all his temporary discomfort. Again his body took on that strenuous tension and he clenched his hands, saying, "I can't wait ten years, I haven't time."

The ten years are not up yet, and he has done his work and gathered his reward and gone. Was ever so much experience and achievement crowded into so short a space of time? A great man dead at twenty-eight! That would have puzzled the ancients. Edward Garnett wrote of him in *The Academy* of December 17, 1898: "I cannot remember a parallel case in the literary history of fiction. Maupassant, Meredith, Mr. James, Mr. Howells, Tolstoy, all were learning their expression at the age where Mr. Crane had achieved his, achieved it triumphantly." He had the precocity of those doomed to die in youth. I am convinced that when I met him he had a vague premonition of the shortness of his working day, and in the heart of the man there was that which said, "That thou doest, do quickly."

At twenty-one, this son of an obscure New Jersey rector, with but a scant reading knowledge of French and no training, had rivaled in technique the foremost craftsmen of the Latin races. In the [five] years since I met him, a stranded reporter, he stood in the firing line during two wars, knew hairbreadth escapes on land and sea, and established himself as the first writer of his time in the picturing of episodic, fragmentary life. His friends have charged him with fickleness, but he was a man who was in the preoccupation of haste. He went from country to country, from man to man, absorbing all that was in them for him. He had no time to look backward. He had no leisure for *camaraderie*. He drank life to the lees, but at the banquet table where other men took their ease and jested over their wine, he stood a dark and silent figure, sombre as Poe himself, not wishing to be understood; and he took his portion in haste, with his loins girded, and his shoes on his feet, and his staff in his hand, like one who must depart quickly.

The Dollars Damned Him

by A. J. Liebling

[Crane's] letters clearly show us that [he] was the victim not of self-indulgence or a death wish, as it has been popular among critics to assume, but of his situation, which was banal. He died, unwillingly, of the cause most common among American middle-class males—anxiety about money. This fear expresses itself most often now through thromboses and cerebral hemorrhages, but it operates just as lethally with tuberculosis, which Crane had. Maladies, like breeds of dogs, move in and out of favor, but money worry is constant in societies wherein the western Nonconformist Protestant culture sets the pattern. (In England and the United States, Catholics, Jews, and non-believers take the same impress early in life as Presbyterians.) It is the fuse within the somatic bomb.

Artists are neither more nor less susceptible than Wall Street men or haberdashers. It is a matter not of temperament but of anthropology. Old Osawatomie John Brown, who feared no bullet, wrote to a friend that his creditors made him feel like "a toad under the harrow." Bankruptcy saddened the early life of Ulysses S. Grant, the otherwise imperturbable, and then the terror of bankruptcy came again and got him after his second term in the White House. He wrote his memoirs while dying of cancer of the throat, as Crane, twenty years later, was to grind out stories for magazines as he lay dying of tuberculosis. Crane, for all his irregular life and beliefs, was the son of a clergyman and the brother of a grasping lawyer. He was therefore peculiarly liable to the disease of his kind.

The turn of the century was a time when expenditure was accepted as the outward sign of Divine Grace. The steam yacht was the nimbus, reserved for millionaires, and while the author of *The Red Badge of Courage* did not set himself so high, he had an un-

"The Dollars Damned Him." From *The New Yorker*, XXXVII (August 5, 1961), 48-72 (abridged). © 1961 by The New Yorker Magazine, Inc. Reprinted by permission of *The New Yorker*.

realistic view of how he rated. Cora Crane, it is plain from her biography, shared his illusions. A handsome woman, adept at hospitality, she complemented her moody writer husband perfectly. Writers' consorts are of two kinds—those who are indignant at society's treatment of their husbands, and those who are indignant at their husbands for being writers. Cora was of the first sort. She shared Crane's justified conviction that he was a great man, and another, related but beside the point, that a first-class writer had a right to live on the same scale as the second-biggest brewer in Nottingham, Notts., or the best obstetrician in Tacoma, Washington. This shared heresy was so radical that not even the daredevil Crane dared express it, but it was implicit in his train of life. He did not say he was as good as a stockjobber, but he acted as if he thought he might be. He could hardly be blamed for wanting to live like a member of a profession that society took seriously. His mistake was thinking he could afford it. . . .

Crane left [Cora in 1898] while he went to Cuba to cover the Spanish-American War, and when he rejoined her in England they leased—at a bargain rental, because the place was in such disrepair —a great rambling old country house called Brede Place, in Sussex, which they operated with a scratch staff of eccentric servants. Crane was broke, although the public thought that as the author of *The Red Badge*, published three years earlier and already a classic, he was wealthy. He should have been, but he wasn't. American first-serial rights had brought him ninety dollars. The Cranes were, in effect, worse than broke. Cora had run up bills in England, and so they were seriously in debt, to the tune of nearly two hundred pounds—at the old rate of exchange, almost a thousand dollars. This, and not a patch on his lungs, was the first lesion of Crane's terminal disease. Leasing Brede, in the opinion of Crane's contemporaries, was asking for trouble. Cora, in excusing the Cranes' presumption, wrote to the critic Edward Garnett, "I hope that the perfect quiet of Brede Place and the freedom from a lot of dear, good people, who take his mind from his work, will let him show the world a book that will live." The dear, good people, as events turned out, followed Crane to Brede and sponged on him, for his public condition, in contrast to his private one, glittered. His comings and goings were chronicled in headlines. He was the ascendant literary star; the theory that he was already all through was not born until after his death. It was pure hindsight.

Crane was also the star war-correspondent of Hearst's *Journal*, then in its most flamboyant period of self-advertisement, and Mr. Hearst was supposed to shower his stars with the wealth of the Homestake Mine. Crane had written that great book *The Red Badge*—and the critics had been right in calling it great—in 1893, when he was twenty-two, but it had not been published until 1895. The reverberations of its success were still in the air. When he was twenty-one, he had written *Maggie: a Girl of the Streets*, which he published at his own expense and which had no sale at all. Brought out in 1896, after *The Red Badge*'s triumph, *Maggie* had added to his fame. And, in the few years since, he had shown that he could grow. In stories like "The Blue Hotel," "The Bride Comes to Yellow Sky," and "The Open Boat" he had written better than ever before. He had questionable lungs, but Dr. Edward Livingston Trudeau, a famous American specialist of the day, had examined him a year earlier and declared that his mild case of tuberculosis was arrested. Worry and work reactivated it, and at the end of a heartbreaking struggle of eighteen months to reduce his thousand-dollar debt by writing too much, he expired, owing five thousand dollars.

The disease, the bad doctors of the period, and the anxiety, acting synergetically, got him. The treatment for tuberculosis was so ineffective that even people without a worry in the world died of it in droves. The Duchess of Manchester lost two daughters to therapy; her experience made her, in the Cranes' circle, an authority on the disease. Crane, with his anxiety, was a pushover. Even a general practitioner could have killed him, but Cora exposed him to specialists. They aggravated the illness and increased his need of money, his efforts to get the money to pay them further aggravated the malady, and as he declined, his wife sent for increasingly costly consultants, who prescribed more outrageously destructive therapy. Had he in fact "burned himself out," as some of his literary biographers insist, or had he cared to die, he would have succumbed more rapidly. Only his will to survive and his tough baseball-player's constitution kept him alive. . . .

The letters reflect the progress of the uneven conflict—Crane against skewed values. . . . There is still outward confidence in Crane's letter of February 16, 1899, to his London agent, James B. Pinker, although it contains evidence that he could hear footsteps behind him:

Dear Pinker:
   I send you a rattling good war story—I think 5330 words. Please

send me a cheque for £40 so that I will get it on Sunday morning.
[He was already financing by the day.] . . . How am I going? Strong?

By February 19th, he had done another story, but the situation
had deteriorated:

Dear Pinker:
    I am mailing you at this time a whacking good Whilomville story—
4000 words—and I am agitatedly wiring you at the same time. . . .
I must have altogether within the next ten days £150, no less, as the
Irish say. But, by the same token, I am going to earn it. . . . £40 of
my £150 have I done yesterday and today, but for all your gods, help
me or I perish.

Translated into statistics, this meant that Crane had sent up on
February 16th a story potentially worth fifty-three pounds—he usually got ten pounds, or fifty dollars, for a thousand words. Simultaneously, he had wired for an advance of forty. This would leave
him, after Pinker sold the story and deducted his commission
(five pounds six shillings), about seven pounds to the good. With
the second letter, he sent on a story worth forty, but requested an
advance of a hundred and fifty. He was consequently at least a hundred and three pounds farther behind than when he started writing
the first story. But since he had written the forty-pound story in two
days (he did not count the days of gestation that must have pre-
ceded writing), he flattered himself that, if he buckled down to
work, he could do a forty-pound story *every* two days, and in ten
days catch up with the deficit, except for what he might have to
borrow to live the ten days. He knew, although he refused to admit
it to himself, that while a man may write a story in two days, or
even in one, the writing is only the final stage of production. It is
impossible to maintain such a pace over any considerable period.
His optimism, therefore, was a typical example of a writer's gift for
economic self-delusion. . . . There was no more time for "Blue
Hotels," for which three years intervened between germ and finished
tale. . . .

Cora's letters to Pinker become more frequent than Crane's; he is
too busy trying to write the Cranes out of the hole. The letters show
that Pinker was an angel among agents. He let the Cranes get into
him for two hundred and thirty pounds, a vast sum in the literary
world. Pinker sold a stupendous number of the words Crane wrote,
and even of those he contracted to write. (Crane was fluent to the
end, writing in his bed when he was too weak to sit up, although

the force of the tide diminished as he sank and his need became more acute.) The insuperable difficulty was the gap between the prices, which were scaled to support writers in lodging-houses, and Crane's American inner need to keep up a prosperous front. He complained constantly about the "Comanche braves" who descended uninvited upon Brede in platoons—Americans unknown to him or, at best, acquaintances of acquaintances—but he turned none away. He had a double American fear—that he might be thought to have a swelled head or no money.

* * *

A creature of another culture, an Elizabethan or a Regency gent, would have a hard time understanding why the Cranes did not slip their cables. It would have been wiser even from the point of view of their creditors if they had abandoned Brede. With a few months of complete rest, body and mind lying equally fallow, Crane might have recovered his health and his form, in which case he would have attacked the accumulated debts. His compulsion would have forced him to it. Melville, finding himself in a similar cul-de-sac, had solved *his* problem by abjuring writing. Consequently, he had managed to die solvent, and at the expense to posterity of only nineteen years' production. "Dollars damn me!" old Ishmael had written to Hawthorne in 1851, after a week spent trying to get in the potatoes at Arrowhead while he finished *Moby Dick* and to finish *Moby Dick* while he got in the potatoes.

* * *

The run-of-the-mill critic is a Linnaean; he likes to pop his specimens into plainly labeled phials, and Crane, genus Doomed Genius, went into the one labelled "Edgar Allan Poe." Because of the brief span between his late birth, in 1871, and his early death, in 1900, he became the least in focus of American masters, like a man seen through binocular lenses with one set for short distance and the other for long. He was born in the same year as Theodore Dreiser and Samuel Hopkins Adams, his contemporaries on Park Row, who survived him by forty-five and fifty-eight years, respectively. But he has been dead longer than Tolstoy or Ibsen and almost as long as Melville himself, who was born in 1819. Because of Crane's youth, much of the writing about him has a patronizing tone, as if he were eternally junior to discoverers born from ten to twenty years after his death. It has become standard procedure to reproach him for his limitations—although death allowed him little time in which to explore his limits—and to demand why he accomplished so little, although he accomplished a prodigious amount for his age. His legacy of viable masterwork is more considerable than those combined of all the provincial *petits-maîtres* who condemned him when he died. [Thomas] Beer, a slick-fiction writer turned informal (another way of saying careless) biographer, picked up and continued the pair of unfounded suppositions—that Crane was "unfulfilled" and that it didn't matter, because he lacked the capacity to improve. Beer was sympathetic, in the sloppy fashion of the early twenties. He made Crane a romantic figure, like Dick Diver.

Reforgotten, Crane drifted, a sitting duck for the new, Freudian-critical rediscovery. (The reason that a man doesn't write more than he does is that he never wanted to write more than he did. If he dies before he does, it proves that he didn't.) John Berryman said in his biography of Crane that he had an obsessive interest in women older than himself that gravely affected his subliminal retrospective intentions toward his mother, and an interest in horses that showed him pregnant with violence, of which the horse is a symbol. It had not occurred to Berryman that a man whose "idea of happiness" is a saddle might just like horses, or that if a man is much with horses, rides horses, covets horses, and thinks a good deal about horses, a high percentage of the images in his prose and verse are likely to be horse images. Or that most very young men spend a lot of time thinking about women older than they are, because the women younger than they are are still children. . . . When he left America with Cora, in 1897, he was twenty-six and she thirty-two. (She said, incidentally, that she was twenty-nine.) This is scarcely a monstrous discrepancy. . . .

"Sadism grinds strong in Crane's work," Berryman writes, "and its counterpart, masochism, does." He explained that Crane's overt bravery betrayed his inner fear (just as, to the initiate, abject cowardice reveals inner security, because it is not afraid of ridicule). "Death ends the terrible excitement under which he is bound to live—death is a way out, a rescue." *Bref,* Crane scared himself to death.

"Crane wasted his genius," Professor [R. W.] Stallman wrote nine years ago [in 1952]. "What killed Crane was . . . his own will to burn himself out, his Byronic craving to make his body 'a testing ground for all the sensations of life.' " Stallman adds, like a sensible uncle, "He could have retreated from life to calculate it at a

distance, as Hawthorne and James did. Instead, he got as close to
life as possible." *Bref,* Crane died because he neglected to put on his
overshoes—a truly academic mode of suicide. Professor Stallman,
incidentally, in his otherwise valuable *Omnibus,* descants inter-
minably on the benefits, for an author, of personal inexperience.
To describe well, he implies, nothing is so essential as not to have
seen. . . . "Was there any need for Crane to experience a blizzard
in order to write 'Men in the Storm'? Would not an imaginary rather
than an actual blizzard have served just as well, the germinal idea
of the story being a *symbolic* storm?" or, again, "The locality of
'The Blue Hotel' has symbolic import and could have been painted
with no first-hand knowledge of it. . . . The fight that he witnessed
and tried to stop during an incident in Lincoln, Nebraska, became
the fight depicted in 'The Blue Hotel,' but the germinal idea for
the story might just as well have had a literary source." (The heresy
of the monks—good wine from a second pressing.) For a clincher, he
advances the argument that "Crane reproduced the immediacies of
battle in *The Red Badge of Courage* long before he had seen and
suffered actual shellfire." This is to argue that if a man can tie his
shoelaces with one hand he couldn't do it better and faster and more
easily with two. . . .

Crane did not "reproduce the immediacies of battle"; he made a
patterned, a rhetorical, war such as never existed, to test the heart
of his hero. The readers who wasted their admiration on his backdrop were the ones who raved over the scenery in David Belasco's
productions of Civil War plays—"so natural you would have
thought it was real"—and who bought paintings because the Spanish dancers' mantillas made you think that if you touched them they
would feel like lace. The luxurious detail was a concession to the
only taste, besides his own, that Crane knew then. It is extraneous
to the true merit of the book, which is about a boy in a dragon's
wood, and timeless. After Crane had seen war, he drew more spar-
ingly, as in "The Upturned Face." He could, I suppose, have later
worked up other vicarious subjects as convincingly, except that he
never again had ten years to spare.

*   *   *

If he had lived on, even if he had not "developed" beyond the
point already reached in his best stories (a point that few others
have ever reached), he could hardly have failed to write others as
good. We have seen in our time that the best writers as they mature

become journalists—Sartre, Camus, Mauriac, Hemingway. Crane might have been the great correspondent that the First World War failed to produce. It fascinates me to speculate on the kind and quality of the work Crane would have done if he had recovered, even partially, and gone through with his escape to Texas. I cannot agree with Professor Stallman's opinion, expressed in 1952, that Crane's "death at twenty-eight resulted in no loss to literature. He had exhausted his genius." Stallman supported this by quoting [Hamlin] Garland, an older man who was in the beginning kind to Crane but became resentful when outstripped by him. Garland, a congenital stuffed shirt, couldn't write for free seeds. It is perhaps unfair to tilt against the Stallman of 1952. His researches show such devotion to Crane that he may well have shifted his attitude on the young author's capacity for growth. But he wrote then, "He produced too much, he kept repeating himself, and he never developed."

As a workman, Crane developed sharply between *The Red Badge*, written in 1893 and published in 1895, and "The Blue Hotel," which was conceived during his Western trip of 1895 and written in 1898. The only period of his brief life during which he produced too much, kept repeating himself, and so on, was in 1899 and 1900, the time of Brede. Even a baseball player is not ruled through because he has one bad season, and that under dreadful circumstances, and a tenor's high C is not judged by how he performs with one leg in a bear trap. The quality of the work admittedly fell off. As a beginner, Crane had had to cure himself of writing pastiches of Kipling, and at Brede he began to write pastiches of Crane. He had no time to let themes ripen in his mind. Once he began, he always wrote swiftly, but now when he began wrong he could not afford to tear up his work and start on a better line. I think, myself, that Crane might have written long novels of an originality as hard to imagine, in retrospect, as *Maggie* and *The Red Badge* would have been to anticipate. His chief problem would have been to keep free of another syndrome of advances and effort to catch up with them.

Dostoevski said that not one of his novels was two-thirds as good as it would have been if he had not had to hurry it in order to extract another advance. In the years leading up to his exile, in 1849, he wrote to the publisher Kraevski, "I struggle with my small creditors like Laocoön with the serpent!" (or Crane with the wine merchant at Brede), and, again, "To keep my promise and get the work

in on time, I forced myself, and wrote things as bad as 'The Lodger';
I was stupefied and humiliated by having written it, and for a long
time afterward could not concentrate on more serious work. Each
of these botched jobs brings on an attack of my illness"—an "inflam-
mation of the brain," later identified as epilepsy. Relief came from
an unexpected quarter—he was exiled to Siberia for eight years,
during which he was forbidden to publish. Crane had no such luck.

II

General Discussions

Crane's Art

by John Berryman

I

Since Dr. Johnson observed that a century was the term commonly fixed as the test of literary merit, authors have crowded each other out of sight more and more rapidly. The term cannot be now so long. An English critic says the present point is to write a book that will last just ten years; but a decade must be too short—fashion can catch up older trash than that. For Johnson, remember, the "effects of favour" must have ended. Under our industry of literary scholarship, having to be kept supplied with subjects, "survival" is a more ambiguous condition than it used to be: one may stand to gain by overvaluing his author however meager, or his author's toe. Other conditions make a term difficult to fix. But Crane has been dead half a century, academic interest has avoided him as both peculiar and undocumented, and some of his work is still decidedly alive. This is long enough. We are not dealing with absolutes: the questions of interest with regard to an author remembered at all are how, and what part, and why, and whether justly. Perhaps a question more general arises too in connection with Crane. American genius has not been literary. The executive idealism of a few men like Washington represents our spirit at a higher level, prob-

"Crane's Art." From *Stephen Crane* (New York: William Sloane Associates, 1950). © 1950 by William Sloane Associates, Inc. Reprinted by permission of William Sloane Associates.

ably, than can any of our literary masters. It may be merely our
failure so far to have produced a national author that creates this
impression, though we have to reckon also with a kind of national
commitment as different as possible from, say, French cultural commitment. At any rate the fact is certain: we have had little genius in
literature. The question is this: whether we have not in Stephen
Crane a genius very formidable indeed, an artist of absolute and
high vision—the sort of writer before whom most of our imposing
earlier authors utterly shrivel away—a national glory, if the nation
cared.

Let us lay aside at the outset matters of influence. Enough has
been mentioned in passing, of influences felt by Crane (Tolstoy,
Mark Twain, Goethe, Emerson, Whitman, Olive Schreiner, others),
to rescue him from the status of a "sport." He concentrates tend-
encies and powers already tentatively in play. At the same time
these influences certainly tell us very little about him; Crane was
perhaps as original as an author can be, and be valuable. We shall
have to study him by himself. More interesting by a good deal is the
influence he exerted, great and distinct upon Conrad, Willa Cather,
Ernest Hemingway, very decided upon others of his contemporaries
and then upon Theodore Dreiser, Sherwood Anderson, Carl Sandburg, even Sinclair Lewis, as well as T. E. Lawrence, F. Scott Fitzgerald, more recent figures. Strong and lasting despite interruptions
in his fame and availability, this influence is part of his importance.
"The stones he put in the wall"—as Anderson said it—"are still
there. . . ." But critics have read him so little that the source of this
whole aspect of recent English and American literary art has gone
mainly unrecognized and must remain matter for special study.
Crane's influence will be found no simple affair, traced through
these authors: it affected vision, technique, material. Whether, however, it has ever been commensurate with the degree of revolution
Crane effected is doubtful. I think it has not, and look for an explanation to the fact that his work of characteristic power has not
yet been isolated from his inferior, ugly, and trivial work.

I ought to say where this power is. It is in "The Open Boat" above
all, and "The Blue Hotel"; in the single long work *The Red Badge
of Courage* and short war-studies from "A Mystery of Heroism"
through "Death and The Child," "The Price of the Harness,"
"Virtue in War," to "The Clan of No-Name," "An Episode of War,"
"The End of the Battle," "The Upturned Face"; in the early and
late companion studies of society's ferocity, *Maggie* and *The Mon-*

ster; in two singular visions of happiness, "The Pace of Youth"
and "The Bride Comes to Yellow Sky"; in other prose constructions
delicate, dreadful and humorous, from "A Dark Brown Dog," "The
Reluctant Voyagers," "An Experiment in Misery," through "The
Veteran" to "Shame" and "An Illusion in Red and White"; in
two dozen poems from "Once I Saw Mountains Angry" through
the title-poem of *War Is Kind* to the posthumous marvelous "A
Man Adrift on a Slim Spar." The list by no means exhausts
Crane's excellence—very little behind some of this work come a
number of other stories, such as "The Little Regiment" and "Three
Miraculous Soldiers," the three Mexican stories, chapters even in
George's Mother and "War Memories," passages scattered everywhere. But at any rate not much less than this list will do in instance of where this author remains vivid, living.

You need very little to live. With *Wuthering Heights* and some
verses one woman is with us always. But my display of Crane's work
will certainly surprise both in bulk and variety most readers and
critics. The truth is that Crane sprang into fame amid a storm of
excited bewilderment and has passed into permanence in almost
perfect silence. The occasional critic or historian who looks at him
is just puzzled. A few are not comfortable yet about his being here
at all, and among the majority who accept him there is no agree-
ment about what kind of author he is. The most considerable attempts to account for him are still those by two of his English
friends: first the very able ten pages written by H. G. Wells for the
North American Review just after Crane's death in 1900. Wells
spoke of his "persistent selection of the elements of an impression,"
of his ruthless exclusion of mere information, of the direct vigor
with which the selected points are made; distinguished calmly the
perfect restraint of "The Open Boat" from overinsistence in "Death
and the Child" (then the critical favorite in England among Crane's
stories); and concluded with a prophecy brilliantly fortunate: "It
seems to me that, when at last the true proportions can be seen,
Crane will be found to occupy a position singularly cardinal. . . .
In style, in method and in all that is distinctively *not* found in his
books, he is sharply defined, the expression in literary art of certain
enormous repudiations. . . . It is as if the racial thought had been
razed from his mind and its site ploughed and salted. He is more
than himself in this; he is the first expression of the opening mind
of a new period, or, at least, the early emphatic phase of a new in-
itiative—beginning, as a growing mind must needs begin, with the

record of impressions, a record of a vigour and intensity beyond all precedent." Crane's position sank for a generation nearly to zero, and for forty years Wells's essay was never reprinted. Meanwhile Edward Garnett, whose "Appreciation" in *The Academy* (December 17, 1898) was the most acute view taken during Crane's lifetime, added some remarkable sentences when he extended it in 1921 for *Friday Nights.* Two qualities in especial, he said, combined to form what is unique in Crane, "viz., his wonderful insight into and mastery of the primary passions, and his irony deriding the swelling emotions of the self. It is his irony that checks the emotional intensity of his delineation, and suddenly reveals passion at high tension in the clutch of the implacable tides of life. It is the perfect fusion of these two forces of passion and irony that creates Crane's spiritual background, and raises his work, at its finest, into the higher zone of man's tragic conflict with the universe." I do not feel sure of the meaning of the impressive middle sentence here, but the other two show that Garnett understood Crane better than everyone since taken together and would form a happy point of critical departure for us if we had not some elementary difficulties to encounter.

There is first the question, baffling to most of his friends, his critics, and his age, of whether Stephen Crane did not write almost entirely from *inspiration.* His work seemed to come from nowhere, prose and poetry alike. The word "dream" is recurrent in comment on him—even Hemingway, vouching for the authority of *The Red Badge,* uses it when he calls that book "a boy's long dream of war." When Crane told an interviewer that it was a product of labor, the man was not less but more astonished, that Crane should have "kept this story in hand for nearly a year, polishing and bettering it. Perhaps this is the most amazing thing about a thoroughly amazing book. If he had said he wrote it in three days (as he wrote *The Black Riders*) one might understand such a *tour de force."* Crane's rejection of the notion of "inspiration" is irrelevant. Of course he *did* write from inspiration, and of course he wrote also from close long observation, inquiry, study, and then he rewrote. He was like other men of genius, in short, often inspired and immensely deliberate. Yet this double explanation does not really account for the impression his work has always given, which might be put as follows: one is surprised that it exists at all—and one's surprise, if it diminishes, does not disappear with familiarity. Hamlin Garland tells us indeed that Crane just "tapped" his brain for his poems. He cer-

tainly went through no apprenticeship in poetry; he just began—
began, we shall see, at a very high level—and if *The Black Riders*
was not, evidently, written in three days, it was written abruptly
and with effortless rapidity. As for prose, we have discovered an
early development there, but so early and masterly that the prodigy
remains. All this is thoroughly exceptional.

At the same time, Crane looks like a polar type of modern self-
consciousness. He copied into his notebook—whether as program
or as confirmation is unknown—a sentence from Emerson which
comprehensively defines one effect of this art which lighted the
nineties: "Congratulate yourselves if you have done something
strange and extravagant and have broken the monotony of a decorous age." Literary ambition unusually deliberate and powerful is
manifest all through his early life. "I began the war with no talent
but an ardent admiration and desire. I had to build up." Readers
and critics have recognized an effort in his work, and it forms a large
basis for critical objection. They see affectation, strain. A word applied nearly as frequently as "dream" is its converse: "trick." Just
before his death, a feminine critic put the objection as established:
"Men of intelligence yawn. The trick is too easily seen through."

Impressions more contradictory are hard to imagine, and a third
must be mentioned. Crane's work ever since it appeared has struck
readers as "barbaric." His poems were "crazy," and they still—in
standard anthologies—look very weird. The ferocity of his prose,
whether intended or casual, seems primitive. His animism is like
nothing else in civilized literature. Mountains, trees, dogs, men,
horses, and boats flash in and out of each other's identities. The
sun "had its hat over one eye" and one man's voice makes another
man "wish that he was a horse, so that he could spring upon the
bed and trample him to death." This is characteristic and frequent.
A disappointed boatman has a "face like a floor." If Crane lulls you
into safety for a minute, wait only. He is examining the electric
chair in Sing Sing: "the comfortable and shining chair . . . waits
and waits and waits" for "its next stained and sallow prince . . .
an odor of oiled woods, a keeper's tranquil, unemotional voice, a
broom stood in a corner near the door, a blue sky and a bit of moving green tree at a window so small that it might have been made by
a canister shot." The sentence concludes like an electrocution, and
when the keeper is quoted he might be a friendly aesthetician describing Crane's effect on the reader: "We calculate that the whole
business takes about a minute from the time we go after him." These

images come all from early, negligible, unreprinted newspaper stories; assaults in his important work may be more violent still. Crane's humor, finally, and his irony are felt as weird or incomprehensible. When he began a book of poems with the line,

> Do not weep, maiden, for war is kind,

the reviewers treated him, reasonably, as an *idiot*.

A dream, a trick, a savage or imbecile attack: any account of his work which hopes for assent will have to try to reconcile these views with each other, and with still other views. All we need agree yet is that it seems to display an essential, *obvious* coherence, originality, and authority, such as will justify any care we may take to appreciate it.

II

Let us begin with his poetry. The poetry and the prose show difference as well as unity, but an understanding of the poetry, if we can arrive at one, will help us with the prose. Since Crane is the important American poet between Walt Whitman and Emily Dickinson on one side, and his tardy-developing contemporaries Edwin Arlington Robinson and Robert Frost with Ezra Pound on the other, it has interest that he perhaps drew on both of his predecessors. He does not sound much like them.

> I saw a man pursuing the horizon;
> Round and round they sped.
> I was disturbed at this;
> I accosted the man.
> "It is futile," I said,
> "You can never—"
>
> "You lie," he cried,
> And ran on.

This does not sound much like a poem either. Here is another one:

> On the horizon the peaks assembled;
> And as I looked,
> The march of the mountains began.

> As they marched, they sang,
> "Ay! we come! we come!"

A conflict here between the sense of terror communicated and a suggestion of desire ("Ay!" answers as it were a question or entreaty)
produces more appearance of a poem. But both look rather like *impressions of fatal relation* than poems. They are a world away from
Whitman, an includer, an accumulator; these pieces would plainly
do with even less if they could, though less is inconceivable. They
differ too from Emily Dickinson, who as R. P. Blackmur has shown
tried always to write regular verse, in that there is obviously no attempt to write regular verse, or even, perhaps, verse at all. On the
other hand, no immaturity can be heard in them. Whatever it is
they try to do they do; they are perfectly self-possessed. Very odd is
the fact that in the first piece, despite its smallness, the rhymes are
almost inaudible. There they are: sped-said-cried, horizon-man-on.
Quite a set of rhymes for eight lines; yet even after you know they
are there, you can scarcely hear them. It opens indeed with a regular heroic, but this effect is destroyed so rapidly that it scarcely affects the ear as regular. Now it does not appear to be deliberately
destroyed, just as it does not appear to have been deliberately ar-
rived at. So with the rhymes: the writer does not appear to fight
their effect but seems to have come into the rhymes themselves by
accident, and simultaneously, by instinct, arranged for their muting.
The famous color and style of Crane's prose are absent, blankly absent.

All this is peculiar. Let us try a technical approach to two other
pieces, which stand at opposite limits of Crane's poetry. The first
is tiny:

> A man feared that he might find an assassin;
> Another that he might find a victim.
> One was more wise than the other.

The other is one of the major lyrics of the century in America and
I must quote it all.

> Do not weep, maiden, for war is kind.
> Because your lover threw wild hands toward the sky
> And the affrighted steed ran on alone,
> Do not weep.
> War is kind.

Hoarse, booming drums of the regiment,
Little souls who thirst for fight,
These men were born to drill and die.
The unexplained glory flies above them,
Great is the battle-god, great, and his kingdom—
A field where a thousand corpses lie.

Do not weep, babe, for war is kind.
Because your father tumbled in the yellow trenches,
Raged at his breast, gulped and died,
Do not weep.
War is kind.

Swift blazing flag of the regiment,
Eagle with crest of red and gold,
These men were born to drill and die.
Point for them the virtue of slaughter,
Make plain to them the excellence of killing
And a field where a thousand corpses lie.

Mother whose heart hung humble as a button
On the bright splendid shroud of your son,
Do not weep.
War is kind.

There is nothing to approach in the first piece, though, technically.
For a moment you don't hear it, then you do, with a little fear, as if
a man had put his face suddenly near your face; and that's all. The
indifference to craft, to *how* the thing is said, is lunar.

The second poem is based on the letter *i* in the word "kind."
There are rhymes "die" and "lie" in the set-in stanzas; wild, sky,
affrighted, flies, bright; just these, and they ought to make a high
lament. But of course they do nothing of the sort. The author is
standing *close* to one, not off on some platform, and the poem takes
place in the successful war of the *prose* ("unexplained," "gulped,"
and so on) *against* the poetic appearance of lament. It takes some
readers a while to hear this poem. Once heard, it is passionately
moving; and it is moving then exactly in the lines where ordinarily
a poet would not be moving,—not at all in the "bright splendid
shroud" line, but in the beautiful and *i*-less line before it. A domestic, terrible poem, what it whispers is: "I would console you, how I
would console you! *If I honestly could.*" In all its color and splendor, this is really not much more like an ordinary poem than the

other three; its method is theirs. The four pieces have in common also cruelty and pity, their nakedness, a kind of awful bluntness; and contemptuous indifference to everything that makes up "poetry" for other people. What shall we do with them?

The poems have an enigmatic air and yet they are desperately personal. The absence of the panoply of the Poet is striking. We remember that their author did not like to be called a poet nor did he call them poetry himself. How unusual this is, my readers will recognize: most writers of verse are merely dying to be called poets, tremblingly hopeful that what they write is real "poetry." There was no pose here in Crane. His reluctance was an inarticulate recognition of something strange in the pieces. They are not like literary compositions. They are like things just seen and said, *said for use*. The handwriting of doctors is not beautiful; the point of their prescriptions is just to be made out. (It is very remarkable, I have noticed since the present chapter was written, that Crane used the peculiar word "pills" for his poems. He had often a mysterious and even dreadful exactness of terminology. "Some of the pills," he said in New York when *The Black Riders* was under attack, "are pretty darned dumb, anyhow. But I meant what I said." He had in mind no doubt their lack of sugar-coating.) Robert Graves, one of the shrewdest, craziest, and most neglected students of poetry living, laid out a theory of the origin of poetry once. A savage dreams, is frightened by the dream, and goes to the medicine man to have it explained. The medicine man can make up anything, anything will reassure the savage, so long as the manner of its delivery is impressive; so he chants, perhaps he stamps his foot, people like rhythm, what he says becomes rhythmical, people like to hear things *again*, and what he says begins to rhyme. Poetry begins—as a practical matter, for *use*. It reassures the savage. Perhaps he only hears back again, chanted, the dream he just told the medicine man, but he is reassured; it is like a spell. And medicine men are shrewd: interpretation enters the chanting, symbols are developed and connected, the gods are invoked, poetry booms. Now Crane's poetry is like a series of primitive anti-spells. Sometimes he chants, but for the most part on principle he refuses to (no coating). He has truths to tell. Everybody else in the nineties is chanting and reassuring and invoking the gods. So Crane just says, like a medicine man *before* chanting or poetry began. And what he says is savage: unprotected, forestlike. Man's vanity and cruelty, hypocrisy and cowardice, stupidity and pretension, hopelessness and fear, glitter through the

early poems. God may exist; if so, He rolls down and crushes you.
Part of the irony in Crane's poetry results from the imposition of
his complex modern doubt upon a much stronger primeval set of
his mind.

> A man saw a ball of gold in the sky;
> He climbed for it,
> And eventually he achieved it—
> It was clay.
>
> Now this is the strange part:
> When the man went to the earth
> And looked again,
> Lo, there was the ball of gold.
> Now this is the strange part:
> It was a ball of gold.
> Ay, by the heavens, it was a ball of gold.

The first four lines were written by a minister's son and intellectual
of the nineties, the rest by a bushman.

   Now I wish to be more serious and explode some errors. Crane
has a textbook fame for his "experimentation" and for his "anticipation" of the free-verse movement. The notion of writing irregu-
larly Crane probably got from Whitman; possibly the notion of very
short short-line poems came to him after hearing Howells read Emily
Dickinson; W. E. Henley's free verse may have affected him, the
English Bible certainly did. There is no evidence in the poetry or
outside it that he ever experimented in verse. Instinct told him to
throw over metrical form, visions were in his head, and he wrote
them down. Some of the poems were no doubt more consciously
composed than others, and he revised some of them; their parable
and proverbial form they owe in part to the Bible and to Olive
Schreiner's *Dreams*; but "experiment" is not the word. As for "anticipation": some of the later people probably learned from him
(Pound mentioned him early, and it was Sandburg who introduced
Sherwood Anderson to his verse), and more would have if his
books had been more available; but his work is quite different from
theirs. A comparison of any of the short poems of Pound or H. D.
with the piece of Crane last quoted will make this clear. The later
poets are deeply interested in manner; Crane is deeply uninterested
in manner. In order to appreciate Crane's poetry, you must understand that it differs in intention and mode from the poetry both of

his period and of ours. It is primitive; not designedly so, but naturally primitive.

Some assistance for this view, which may perhaps need it, turned
up recently. T. S. Eliot in his paper on Poe and Valéry distinguishes
three stages in the development of poetry: a middle stage in which
the auditor or reader is interested in both the subject and the way
it is handled (the style), an earlier stage in which attention is directed entirely upon the subject, and our stage, in which the subject has become "simply a necessary means for the realization of the
poem. At this stage [Mr. Eliot goes on] the reader or listener may
become as nearly indifferent to the subject matter as the primitive
listener was to the style." This account is less incompatible with
Mr. Graves's than it may appear, for the savage is not aware that
he is worked upon by the chanting: he thinks he is attending wholly
to the matter. So Crane's phrasing and pausation affect us insensibly,
and the subject appears naked. One conclusive aspect of this whole
analysis will be considered fully when we come to the prose, but the
curious ground of Crane's personal preference of *The Black Riders*
to *The Red Badge* (expressed in a letter to Hilliard) must have a
word. Though absolutely opposed to "preaching" in literature, he
nevertheless preferred his poetry as "the more ambitious effort," attempting "to give my ideas of life as a whole, so far as I know it,"
while the novel was "a mere episode."

Crane as a poet, in fine—a poet is the only thing we can call him
—I take to represent an unexampled reversion. I take the steady
drift of our period toward greater and greater self-consciousness, an
increasing absorption in style, to be what has obscured the nature of
his work and delayed its appreciation. How far its point of view
really is from ours can be seen as well in a comparatively conventional, gentle piece as in the others:

> Ay, workman, make me a dream,
> A dream for my love.
> Cunningly weave sunlight,
> Breezes, and flowers.
> Let it be of the cloth of meadows.
> And—good workman—
> And let there be a man walking thereon.

He writes as if this presence of the man were inconceivable. "War is
kind" is perhaps his finest poem. The phrase is so repeated and

with such pity that in the face of reason one cannot learn to believe
he does not mean it; the poem may be compared to Webster's great
dirge in *The White Devil*, actually a nightmare of horror behind
the consolation, and contrasted with Hart Crane's *Voyages* (*II*), a
serious beautiful desperate poem less mature than these others. But
a considerable number of Stephen Crane's poems, once their range
is found, will be remembered. They do not wear out and there is
nothing else like them. It is said by Thomas Beer and others that
Crane lost his poetic faculty several years before his death; but not
all the poems have been collected, and the dating is very uncertain.
Fewer, certainly, of the more personal poems in the second book
(1899) are valuable. One first printed long after his death, and presumably late, is one of his best, "A man adrift on a slim spar"—

> . . . A pale hand sliding from a polished spar.
>   God is cold.
>
> The puff of a coat imprisoning air:
> A face kissing the water-death,
> A weary slow sway of a lost hand
> And the sea, the moving sea, the sea.
>   God is cold.

The poetry, then, *has* the character of a "dream," something seen
naïvely, in a new relation. It *is* barbaric, and so primitively blunt
that one sees without difficulty how it can be thought a trick. But
tricks are not this simple. And tricks can be learned; whereas none
of his innumerable parodists could simulate either the gleam or the
weight of his true work—they hang out at the edges of Crane's tone.
Neither

> The sea was blue meadow,
> Alive with little froth-people
> Singing

nor

> A horse,
> Blowing, staggering, bloody thing
> Forgotten at foot of castle wall

would ever be seen again. Crane was not only a man with truths to
tell, but an interested listener to this man. His poetry has the in-
imitable sincerity of a frightened savage anxious to learn what his
dream means.

III

Moving from Crane's poetry to his prose, we recognize the same sincerity, the same bluntness, the same hallucinatory effect, the same enigmatic character, the same barbarity. There is a formal difference, however; and before taking it up, I want to say something of an aspect of his art Garnett correctly thought fundamental, namely, his irony.

This word has spread and weakened until it scarcely means anything, or it means whatever we like in the general direction of difference-from-appearance. Accepting it seriously so, as *abdita vis quaedam* or "a certain hidden force"—the phrase quoted by Saintsbury from Montaigne who quoted it from Lucretius—Crane's work is a riot of irony of nearly every kind. A baby, consumed with grief for the killing of his dog (Crane does not say so), is so small that he can go downstairs toward its body only very slowly, backwards. Henry Fleming hands back the packet to his shamefaced friend (who has *not* run away the day before) with sentiments equally generous and self-congratulatory. A Swede, crazy with fear of Western aggression, gets drunk and stirs it to life. Examples plunge for citation and classification. But Crane is strong enough, as will appear, to bear any weight; we want the force of a concept.

Suppose we take two modern impressions of irony: as a comment downward, the expression, that is, of a superior man, antisocial; and as a refuge of a weak man. Both are trivial, but the first is more debased than the second. A refuge is a serious matter, and no human is very strong. The careful student J. A. K. Thomson observes that, tracing the Ironical Man to his beginnings, we "find him, not the remote and fastidious Intellectual, but someone far more elemental, simple, grotesque, and pitiful." This habit of mind—which one possesses by nature or not at all; it cannot be learned—is a form of *lying low* before the Divine Jealousy. Thomson associates it with man's development away from animism. Under the gradual growth of the recognition that Nature is inanimate, man learns to distrust the universe and pretends that he is nothing so as not to be an object of destruction. So long as trees and brooks were like him, he could understand them; once he cannot, the way is open to general fear: he had better hide. Thrusting back through this recognition, as Wordsworth had to and Crane, the exceptional modern man—animistic—is opened to both the primitive and the ironic.

Specifically, early Greek comedy presented a contest between the
Alazon (Impostor) and the *Eiron* or Ironical Man: after vauntings
and pretensions, the *Alazon* is routed by the man who affects to be
a fool. The Impostor pretends to be more than he is, the Ironist pretends to be less. Now in most of the criticism of Stephen Crane
that displays any sensitivity, whether outraged or not, one nearly
makes out a nervous understanding that this author is simultaneously *at war with* the people he creates and *on their side*—and
displays each of these attitudes so forcibly that the reader feels he is
himself being made a fool of; so that Crane's position is still dis-
proportionate with his achievement, and people after his death were
so eager to forget him that it took a World War, and later another
World War, to recall him generally to attention. I wonder whether
explanation will ease this feeling; for the truth is that, in a special
and definite sense, the reader *is* being made a fool of. Who are the
creations Crane is most at war with? His complex ones, his "heroes"? or his simplest ones, his babies, horses, dogs, and brooks?
With the first class his art is a Greek comedy, a contest with the impostor. Not even Maggie escapes this: "At times Maggie told Pete
long confidential tales of her former home life, dwelling upon the
escapades of the other members of the family and the difficulties
she had had to combat in order to obtain a degree of comfort." God
knows these distresses are real enough; one feels them, and at the
same time one is made to feel even more strongly that the character
has to run a gauntlet to the author's sympathy. So far as his creations
of the first class are striving to become members of the second class,
they become candidates for pathos or tragedy; so far as they fail,
they remain figures of (this deadly-in-earnest) comedy. Crane never
rests. He is always fighting the thing out with himself, for he contains both *Alazon* and *Eiron*; and so, of course, does the reader; and
only dull readers escape. As comedy, his work is a continual examination of pretension—an attempt to cast overboard, as it were, im-
pediments to our salvation. With creations of the second class, his
work is much more simply an irony of talisman, a prayer to Heaven
for pity; and it *technically* resembles Greek tragedy, in which the
theme is the Jealousy of Heaven.

There is regularly an element of pathos, therefore, in his ironic
(oppositional) inspection, and an element of irony regularly in his
pathos. A Crane creation, or character, normally is *pretentious* and
scared—the human condition; fitted by the second for pathos, by
the first for irony. If the second feeling can save the first, as in Henry

Fleming, the first can doom the second, as in the Swede. This pattern in his work seems hardly to have been perceived at all and is worth some insistence. The received account of Crane depends heavily upon the Gratuitous. He was bored by "plots," he drew "maps of accident," he emphasizes and ends in the "senseless," or he just brutalizes both his characters and the reader. The gratuitous is certainly very prominent, *outside* the central fate by which either one is lost or one is saved. Everything else—but only everything else—spins in irrelation; why pretend otherwise? in effect he says. And when he pretended himself, as he did sometimes, he was craftless as a sore thumb.

Let us look at this "fate" a little. It is against it that Crane's irony is most complex and energetic, and yet there is always one standpoint from which the product of this irony is not ironic at all. The Gordian example in his work would be the dreadful legend upon which the Swede's dead eyes rest, over the cash-machine: "This registers the amount of your purchase." But this death does. The Swede begged for it, *bought* it with his excess of fear and then his pretentiousness and even his over-protest against a boy's cheating in a game where no money was at stake. There is nothing accidental in the murder of this Swede except that it was the gambler who committed it and he gets a light sentence. Collins, in "A Mystery of Heroism," pretentiously gets himself into the position of taking an extreme risk to get a drink of water; he takes it, and finds out that this is what heroism is—not so much; but then the water is spilt. But that the water is spilt is the point, one way. He pretended that he could be a hero, he found that he could, and he found that it got him nothing, that nothing was changed; or, that everything was changed. The elimination of the water sends our eyes straight to the mysterious fate. In "The Open Boat" the community of the four men is insisted on, and Higgins is given special attention throughout, so that he is specially fit to be the price the others pay for their rescue: a sacrifice. Nothing of Crane's seems more gratuitous than the chapters devoted to the self-pity of her persecutors after Maggie's death. But besides serving as ironical distribution of the remorse that society ought to feel, this self-pity *is* suffering. Pete suffers agonies of drunken self-abasement and is fleeced. The mother's final scream is one of "pain"—she invents it, as we know, revels in it, but then she actually suffers it. If the author's tacit contempt here is intense, so is a (carefully guarded from pretentiousness) passion for retribution.

Carefully guarded—and the pattern of justice in his art has to manifest itself as best it can under the dreadful recognitions of honesty. Life is what it is. The consequences of these recognitions, bitterness and horror, disguise themselves in his grotesquerie of concept and style, his velocity, his displacements of rage. Open, they would be insupportable; and this will bring us in a moment to the difference between Crane's prose and his poetry. But I am afraid his use of grotesquerie will not be clear without illustration. I take two of its great strokes, one verging towards this author's wonderful humor, the other towards horror. "Many a man ought to have a bathtub larger than the boat which here rode upon the sea." This dry, gay, senseless remark enables him to contrast like lightning, with the sinister wilderness of water, isolation, and danger where the men toil, the most domestic, sheltered, comfortable home-situation imaginable: with the painfully moving, the stationary; with the effort for salvation, the pleasant duty of washing oneself. Note the mock-heroic outset—"Many a man . . ."—at once abandoned. Many a man is to *own* a bathtub—these men own nothing but, precariously, their lives. Instead, the boat is alive, it "rides," running the risks of a rider. And then the point of a bathtub is to have water in it, water rising in it—and with this ominous flash of the tiny dinghy shipping water, the little sentence has done its work and is superseded by: "These waves were most wrongfully and barbarously abrupt and tall. . . ." Clearly, an artist able to give such compact expression to such complexly bitter alternative reflection, with an air of perfect good nature, will not easily be found at the mercy of bitterness. My other illustration is the famous ninth chapter of *The Red Badge*, where the death of the tall soldier occurs in a prolonged uncanny ecstasy. Several million readers have been appalled by this and perhaps no reader has ever explained to himself what Crane was doing, as perhaps Crane never to himself named it: the Dance of Death.

Between the verse and the prose of an author who has written both successfully we expect to find a relation of a certain kind. Poetry, as the more highly organized form of communication, requires and evinces more art. The interminable verse of various nineteenth century novelists (Dickens, Thackeray, George Eliot) is indeed artless but this is not successful verse. The relation I am speaking of appears clearly in Keats, in Gray, even in Swift, even in Shakespeare. The greater nervousness of Meredith in his prose, for instance, is not the nervousness of art but the nervousness of temperament; his poetry is more artful. Hardy is a better craftsman in prose than critics allow. When young Jude is described as walking carefully over plowed fields lest he tread on earthworms and not liking to see trees lopped from a fancy that it hurt them: "This weakness of character, as it may be called, suggests that he was the sort of man who was born to ache a good deal before the fall of the curtain upon his unnecessary life should signify that all was well with him again." The Shakespearian stress upon this "well" is a product of style; the sentence stays in the mind. But the art of his poetry has been usually slighted also, and is much greater. Crane, so far as I am aware, is singular in this regard. Crane's poetry is characteristically and recognizably by the author of his prose; it shows the style of a master—as the soldier "raging at his breast," the horse a "Blowing, staggering, bloody thing"—and this is almost his prose-style. But it shows *less* style, less of devoted *art*. The prose looks often crafty, the poetry scarcely ever. We shall come back to this.

Crane I daresay is one of the great stylists of the language. These words "master" and "great" will trouble some readers, as they trouble me. But they seem unavoidable. The trouble we feel arises from several causes, which are worth examination. Crane's works that matter are all short. We don't see how works so little can be with any decency called great. Greatness of prose-style, however, does not require length for display. We hear Dryden in his *Essay of Dramatic Poesy*, Johnson in the letter to Chesterfield, fully. Another trouble is that Crane was writing greatly, if he ever did, in his early twenties. We are told that prose-writers mature slowly; scarcely anyone writes prose worth reading under thirty. There are exceptions. Congreve is a large one, Miss Austen is, there are others; and Crane anyway, as I have been trying and shall try more exactly to show, is in several respects a case unique. We wish if we can to avoid preconceptions. A third trouble is just that he is comparatively recent; this matters less. Then there are the words themselves, grandiose. We have no objection to calling the boy Keats a master, Rimbaud a master, but the word "great" sticks a little. It looks like a catchword. Our major troubles, though, I think are two, both of them proceeding from the nature of his work and of its historical situation. There is first the relation of his style to prose style in English and American before him, and second the relation of his general art-form, the story, to Western fiction before him. (The term West-

ern is unsatisfactory because it must include Russian fiction, but no
other seems better.) Though these troubles are closely related, we
must take them separately.

Nothing very like Crane's prose style is to be found earlier; so
much will probably be granted at once by an experienced reader.
Here I must observe that Crane wrote several styles. He had even
an epistolary style—extended, slow, uninflected, during most of his
life, curter and jotty towards the end—but we are interested in his
narrative styles. He began with the somber-jocular, sable, fantastic prose of the *Sullivan County Sketches* and the jagged, colored,
awkward, brilliant *Maggie*. *Maggie* he probably revised much bar-
barousness out of before anyone except brothers and friends saw it,
and he abandoned deliberately the method of the sketches—though
fantasy, and fantasy in the quality of the prose, remained intermit-
tently an element in his work to the end. A movement towards fluidity increases in *The Red Badge* and the "Baby Sketches" he was
writing at the same time and produces a Crane norm: flexible, swift,
abrupt, and nervous—swift, but with an unexampled capacity for
stasis also. Color is high, but we observe the blank absence of the
orotund, the moulded, which is Crane's most powerful response to
the prose tradition he declined to inherit. In the fusion of the impassive and the intense peculiar to this author, he kept on drawing
the rein. "Horses—One Dash" and "The Five White Mice" lead to
the supple majesty of "The Open Boat," a second norm. *The Monster*, much more closed, circumstantial, "normal" in feeling and
syntax, is a third. Then he opened his style again back towards the
second norm in the great Western stories, "The Bride Comes to Yellow Sky" and "The Blue Hotel," and thereafter (for his two years)
he used the second and the third styles at will, sometimes in combination, and the third usually relaxed as his health failed but
peculiarly tense and astonishing in "The Kicking Twelfth." In certain late work also, notably in "The Clan of No-Name," a development toward complexity of structure is evident, which death broke
off. Nevertheless we may speak of "Crane's style" so long as we
have these variations in mind, and my point is that it differs *radi-
cally* both from the tradition of English prose and from its modifications in American prose. Shakespeare, Dryden, Defoe, Johnson,
Dickens, Arnold, Kipling, as these develop into Edwards, Jefferson,
Hawthorne, Melville, James—Crane writes on the whole, a definite
and absolute *stylist*, as if none of these people had ever existed. His
animation is not Kipling's, his deadpan flatness is not Mark Twain's.

He is more like Tacitus, or Stendhal in his autobiography, say, than like any of the few writers of narrative English who actually affected his development. He was a rhetorician who refused to be one. In Crane for the first time the resources of American spareness, exaggeration, volcanic impatience, American humor, came into the hands of a narrative author serious and thoughtful as an artist as Hawthorne or James, and *more* serious than any others of the New England-New York hegemony. Thus he made possible—whether by way of particular influence or as a symbolic feat in the development of the language—one whole side of twentieth century prose. It is hard to decide that a boy, that anyone, did this, and so we feel uncomfortable about the word that characterizes the achievement with great justice.

The second difficulty with "great" is the newness of his form. I am not referring to the immense burst of talented story-writing in England and America during the nineties, though this is relevant; the short story had scarcely any status in English earlier, and we are less eager, naturally, to concede greatness to its artist than to crown a novelist. Poe is an exception, absolutely genuine, very seldom good, more limited than Crane, superbly overvalued. Any sort of standard has hardly been in force for a generation. As late as 1923, in a survey not exceptionally stupid (Pattee's *Development of the American Short Story*), Crane existed merely at the head of thirteen nonentities (all save O. Henry and Harold Frederic) of whom Jack London was the one perhaps "most sure of literary permanence." The intensive literary criticism of the last twenty years has devoted itself largely to poetry and literary criticism, less to the novel, less still to the short story and the nearly extinct drama. If we are in a more enlightened state than Pattee was, we still owe it mostly to Mencken's generation. But I was referring to an operation that Crane performed. As he stripped down and galvanized prose, so he gutted the story of practically everything that had made it a story. "One fact is certain," Hardy decided in 1888: "in fiction there can be no intrinsically new thing at this stage of the world's history." This was one of the major blunders of all time, as James was then demonstrating, Crane would in a moment, and Joyce would presently. Hardy's novels can now be seen as really traditional and conservative when they are compared with something revolutionary, when *Tess* for instance is compared with *The Ambassadors*. Kipling, a story-writer neglected just now except by several of the best critics on both sides of the Atlantic, is less conservative and profounder than Hardy. But both Englishmen keep to the range. By setting a sentence characteristic of Crane against the sentence by Hardy quoted some pages ago, one learns. It is the two Americans who make formal war. James warred in the direction: elaboration of sensibility, consistency of point of view, qualification of style. The campaign cost him, progressively in his work, narrative in the old sense, even though he goes to every *length*. But his stories are still recognizably stories. Idiosyncratic and extended though they are, they are essentially far more like Kipling's than the stories of either are like Stephen Crane's.

Crane's stories are as unlike earlier stories as his poems are unlike poems. He threw away, thoughtfully, plot; outlawed juggling and arrangement of material (Poe, Bierce, O. Henry); excluded the whole usual mechanism of society; banished equally sex (Maupassant) and romantic love (Chekhov—unknown to him) ; decided not to develop his characters; decided not to have any conflicts between them as characters; resolved not to have any characters at all in the usual sense; simplified everything that remained, and, watching intently, tenderly, and hopelessly, blew Fate through it—saying with inconceivable rapidity and an air of immense deliberation what he saw. What he saw, "apparently." The result is a series of extremely formidable, *new*, compact, finished, and distressing works of art. Mencken dated modern American literature from *The Red Badge of Courage*. The new *Literary History of the United States*, coming to hand as I write, dates it from the reissue of *Maggie* in 1896. It must come from about there, apparently.

Of course Crane did nothing such as I have just described. He was interested, only, in certain things, and kept the rest out. It is the ability to keep the rest out that is astounding. But the character of the deliberate in his prose too is conspicuous. We saw that this was absent from his poetry, and it is time to come to the difference. The difference is that between presentation (in the poetry) and apparent presentation (in the prose); in the figure of the savage's dream that we were employing, between *rehearsal* and *investigation*. The poem can simply say what the dream (nightmare) was; at once it gets rid of the dream, and is solaced in hearing it said. An effect of style is undesirable. To *study* the dream, to embody it, as in a story—this is another matter. One needs a suit, a style, of chain armor to protect the subject from everything that would like to get into the story with it: the other impressions of life, one's private prejudices, a florid and hypocritical society, existing literature. The style of the prose aims at the same thing as the unstyle of the poetry, namely, naked presentment, but its method is ironic. Other authors are saying what things "are," with supreme falsity. Crane therefore will only say what they *seem* to be. "The youth turned, with sudden, livid rage, toward the battlefield. He shook his fist. He seemed about to deliver a philippic."

"Hell—"
The red sun was pasted in the sky like a wafer.

Half of Crane's celebrated "coldness" is an effect of this *refusal to guarantee.* "He seemed about to deliver a philippic." It sounds as if he weren't going to; but he is; but he isn't; but—one does not know exactly where one is. The style is merely honest, but it disturbs one, it is even menacing. If this extremely intelligent writer will not go further than that insistent "seemed," says the reader nervously to himself, should *I?* The style has the effect of obliterating with silent contempt half of what one thinks one knows. And then: a policeman begins "frenziedly to seize bridles and beat the soft noses of the responsible horses." In the next sentence the noses are forgotten. But to tell us about the horses if the author is not going to commiserate with them seems brutal. It makes the reader do the feeling if he wants to; Crane, who cared more for horses than any reader, is on his way. Again the reader is as it were rebuked, for of course he *doesn't* feel very strongly about horses—he would never have put in that "soft" himself, much less clubbed it in with "responsible." Or: "A saloon stood with a voracious air on a corner." This is either funny, a little, or an affront: it might be after the reader. One is not enough guided. Just: there it is, hungry, very hungry.

This is supposed, by the way, to be Realism or Naturalism. Frank Norris, who was a romantic moralist, with a style like a great wet dog, and Stephen Crane, an impressionist and a superlative stylist, are Naturalists. These terms are very boring, but let us agree at least to mean by them *method* (as Howells did) rather than *material* (as Norris, who called his serious works "Romance," did). "Tell your yarn and let your style go to the devil," Norris wrote to somebody. The Naturalists, if there are any, all *accumulate,* laborious, insistent, endless; Dreiser might be one. Crane selected and was gone. "He knew when to shut up," as Norris put it. "He is *the only* impressionist," said Conrad in italics to Garnett, "and *only* an impressionist." This is not quite right either: Crane's method shows realistic and also fantastic elements. But it would be better, as a label for what has after all got to be understood anyway in itself, than the categorical whim established now in the literary histories. Crane was an impressionist.

His color tells us so at once. This famous color of his plays a part in his work that has been exaggerated, but it is important. Gifted plainly with a powerful and probably very odd sense of color, fortified then by Goethe, he did not refuse to use it; sometimes he abused it, and he increasingly abandoned it. Most authors use color. "The sun emerges from behind the gray clouds that covered the sky and suddenly lights up with its bright red glow the purple clouds, the greenish sea . . . the white buildings." So Tolstoy at the end of *Sevastopol,* and it bears no relation whatever to Crane's use of color. "At this time Hollanden wore an unmistakable air of having a desire to turn up his coat collar." This is more like one of Crane's colors than Tolstoy's actual colors are. Color is imposed, from an angle, like this apparently physical and actually psychological detail. Crane was interested in what Goethe called the "moral-sensual effect of color." He owes nothing whatever, apparently, to painting.[1] The blue hotel "screaming and howling"—"some red years"—"fell with a yellow crash." The color is primitive. So with adverbs, metaphors. A man leans on a bar listening to others "terribly discuss a question that was not plain." "There was a general movement in the compact column. The long animal-like thing moved slightly. Its four hundred eyes were turned upon the figure of Collins." Here there is none of Crane's frequent, vivid condensation; and yet the eyes are not human eyes. It is primitive, an impression. A psychologist lately called red the most panicky and explosive of colors, the most primitive, as well as the most ambivalent, related equally to rage and love, battle and fire, joy and destruction. Everywhere then, in style, a mind at stretch.

We may reach toward the subject of all this remorseless animation through his characters. They are very odd. To call them types is a major critical error, long exposed, ever-recurrent. The new *Literary History* describes the hero of *The Red Badge* as "impersonal and

---

[1] This is an opinion. Wells disagreed, relying on very late passages like this in "War Memories": "I bring this to you merely as . . . something done in thought similar to that which the French impressionists do in color. . . ." But all such allusions are metaphorical in Crane, who does not use color in the least like a painter. He knew, by the way, few real painters—Linson, Jerome Myers, later Ryder; mostly illustrators.

typical," for which read: intensely personal and individual. George Wyndham (and Wells after him) fifty years ago showed the boy an idealist and dreamer brought to the test. Pete in *Maggie* is not a bartender, but Pete. Billie Higgins in "The Open Boat" is not an oiler, but the oiler. Crane scarcely made a type in all his work. At the same time, he scarcely made any characters. His people, *in* their stories, stay in your mind; but they have no existence outside. No life is strongly imaginable for them save what he lets you see. This seems to me to be singular, to want explanation. I think he is interested in them individually, but only as a crisis reaches them. The "shaky and quick-eyed" Swede of "The Blue Hotel" is certainly an *individual* mad with fear, one of Crane's most memorable people, but it is as an individual *mad with fear* that he grimly matters. "Stanley pawed gently at the moss, and then thrust his head forward to see what the ants did under the circumstance." When this delightful thing happens, a love-scene is taking place two feet away, one of the most inhibited and perfunctory ever written. It is only or chiefly in animals that Crane can be interested when a *fate* is not in question. Once it is, he is acutely and utterly present with the sufferer, attending however to the fate.

"Apparently" the state of the soul in crisis: this is his subject. The society against the person will do; he uses the term "environment" in regard to *Maggie*, and this is more generally dramatized in *The Monster*, more particularly dramatized in "The Bride Comes to Yellow Sky." But one has less feeling in these works, and in a number of others like them, that the men are themselves against each other, than that they have been set simply facing each other— not by Crane—by a fate. War is the social situation that does this most naturally and continually, so he possesses himself of it; in imagination first, again and again, and then in fact. "The Open Boat" is his most perfect story partly because here for once the fate is in the open: one is *fully justified* in being afraid, one can feel with confidence that one is absolutely tested. The antagonist will not fail one, as another man might, as even society might. The extraordinary mind that *had* to feel this we shall look at in the next chapter [of *Stephen Crane*]; here we are concerned with the art. Now these states of crisis, by their nature, cannot persist; so Crane succeeded only in short work. *The Red Badge of Courage,* as most critics have noticed, is not really a novel at all, but a story, and it is a little too long, as Crane thought it was. His imagination was resolute in presenting him with conditions for fear; so that he works with equal brilliance from invention and from fact. To take "The Open Boat," however, as a *report* is to misunderstand the nature of his work: it is an action of his art upon the remembered possibility of death. The death is so close that the story is warm. A coldness of which I was speaking earlier in Crane is absent here. Half of this I attributed to the stylistic refusal to guarantee. The other half is an effect from far in the mind that made the art, where there was a passion for life half-strangled by a need for death and made cold. Life thaws under the need when the death nears. In the eggshell boat, the correspondent knew even at the time, under dreadful hardship, that this was "the best experience of his life"—the comradeship, he says this is, but it was really something else: "There was a terrible grace in the move of the waves, and they came in silence, save for the snarling of the crests. . . ."

The immense power of the tacit, felt in Crane's accounts of Maggie's brother's nihilism, her mother's self-pity, Henry Fleming's self-pride, George's dreams, gives his work kinship rather with Chekhov and Maupassant than Poe. "I like my art"—said Crane—"straight"; and he misquoted Emerson, "There should be a long logic beneath the story, but it should be carefully kept out of sight." How far Crane's effect of inevitability depends upon this *silence* it would be hard to say. Nowhere in "The Open Boat" is it mentioned that the situation of the men is symbolic, clear and awful though it is that this story opens into the universe. Poe in several great stories opens man's soul downwards, but his work has no relation with the natural and American world at all. If Crane's has, and is irreplaceable on this score, it is for an ironic inward and tragic vision outward that we value it most, when we can bear it. At the end of the story a word occurs that will do for Crane. "When it came night, the white waves paced to and fro in the moonlight, and the wind brought the sound of the great sea's voice to the men on the shore, and they felt that they could then be interpreters." Crane does really stand between us and something that we could not otherwise understand. It is not human; it is not either the waves and mountains who are among his major characters, but it acts in them, it acts in children and sometimes even in men, upon animals, upon boys above all, and men. Crane does not understand it fully. But he has been driven and has dragged himself nearer by much to it than we have, and he interprets for us.

For this reason, as well as for his technical revolution, he is indispensable. By a margin he is probably the greatest American story-writer, he stands as an artist not far below Hawthorne and James, he is one of our few poets, and one of the few manifest geniuses the country has produced. For a large sane art we will not go to Crane of course, nor to any other American so far. We do not go to Dostoevski either. For a *normal* art you have to go to artists much greater still: Shakespeare, Mozart, Tolstoy; and not alone to their greatest works, where the range of experience dealt with is utterly beyond any range yet dealt with by an American, but to their small works also, like "Master and Man." Whether Tolstoy's is a *better* story than Crane's fantastic "The Blue Hotel" it is less easy to decide. *The Red Badge of Courage* is much better than *Sevastopol*.

Crane and Hemingway

by Philip Young

It is a bit too much to say that "all American writing" comes from Twain's [*Adventures of Huckleberry Finn*], but not too much to say that Hemingway has accurately identified the progenitor of his own prose. Still, there is a generation missing in this heredity; Clemens was born early enough to be Hemingway's grandfather. Too, there is a quality of flat intensity in Hemingway that is usually absent in Twain. But we have a writer who offers a general atmosphere of played-down tension, and effectively links the two men—Stephen Crane. Twain is one of the few novelists Crane is known to have read while he was struggling to compose a style of his own, and Hemingway has correctly named him as the steppingstone that makes the gap between himself and the author of Huck's adventures negotiable.

The parallels which exist between Hemingway and Crane as human beings are so numerous and exact that they will go a long way toward explaining why the two men so resemble each other as prose stylists, and even on occasion as poets. Both Hemingway and Crane began very young their careers as reporters, and quickly became foreign correspondents. They traveled widely, and to the same places: Key West, the American West and Cuba; Europe, a Greco-Turkish War, and so on. Mainly they journeyed to wars, when they were able. Both had very religious mothers, neither ever quite got over the death of his father, and both rebelled in various ways against their families. Each childhood was marred by the painful experience of violence; and it was eventually in warfare, sought out and embraced, that each man found a fascinating formalization

"Crane and Hemingway." From *Ernest Hemingway* (New York: Holt, Rinehart & Winston, Inc., 1952); this passage appears also in Mr. Young's *Ernest Hemingway: A Reconsideration* (University Park, Pa.: Pennsylvania State University Press, 1966). © 1952, 1966 by Philip Young. Reprinted by permission of the author.

of violence, and his essential metaphor for life. Both made an art of their preoccupations, and sought above all things the varied meanings of war. Chiefly they were compelled to learn what it had to teach them about themselves, and to test themselves against it, to make of danger a kind of mystic ceremony, or rite, or crucible. The results were identical. Each man found violence, pitted himself against it in terror, sought courage for its own sake, and was cited for its uneasy attainment. They worried at great length the problems of the relation of fear to bravery, and in the end they acted with a similarity that is startling. The pictures of Hemingway's behavior under fire in the Second World War are identical with those of Crane in Cuba, where the earlier reporter took suicidal risks in what appear to be truly desperate attempts to get hit.

Often dedicated in their attitudes and their work to the annihilation of romantic idealisms and lies, both men seem themselves romantic individualists. Both stubbornly self-reliant, they disdained those who would not strike out for themselves, and as a result both held unpopular attitudes toward people who condoned or awaited a social reliance. Both opposed and insulted respectability, violated in dress, language, frankness and behavior the genteel traditions of their periods, and developed defiant affections for people in disrepute. Partly as a result, both men became the victims of gossip and found their characters the subjects of hot debate. They livened our literary scene with their color, and—lonely, handsome to women, and a bit heroic—watched legends grow from their personalities and adventures. Crane had no devotion to bullfighting, but he was an amateur athlete of note; he also loved to shoot and was good at it. He ended his career in the midst of friends, fame, wealth, partial expatriation and small animals at Brede Place—the perfect precedent for Finca Vigia [Hemingway's home in Cuba]. Crane's whole dark view of existence, of man damaged and alone in a hostile, violent world, of life as one long war which we seek out and challenge in fear and controlled panic—it is all an amazing forecast of Hemingway.

The work which Stephen Crane tore out of his sickness was rescued from the obscurity into which it had fallen after his death in 1900 at a moment which could not have been more perfectly timed for Hemingway than it was. Damaged himself, and in every imaginable way prepared to find in Crane what would have most meaning for him, Hemingway was in 1921 learning how to write the things Crane had written. This was the year in which Vincent Starrett selected among Crane's nearly forgotten stories and brought out a volume called *Men, Women and Boats*. A friend of Hemingway's, Ford Madox Ford, called these the "best short stories in English," and the young writer could not possibly have missed them.

At any rate it does not look as though he missed them. In Crane he could find his own strict sense of personal integrity and honesty, exercised in a rigorous effort to look for himself directly and immediately at things, so that he might see them as if they had not been seen before. Here was a writer who must have worked on the theory that a complete honesty of vision would mean a new originality, so false are our clichés and our commonplace attitudes, and the notion was validated by the results on paper. Here, as he would hope for himself, the effort had resulted in a concentrated, exclusive and brilliant prose style, simple, bare and tense. Here were vivid, clear impressions and perceptions, fresh pictures of the sensuous surface of life, and a precision and originality in language. Here too a sense of tight design, a startling immediacy in description and even (in *The Red Badge of Courage*) a fascinated, glaring picture of a battlefield corpse, compulsive and intense. In Crane he could see also an attempt to make dialogue a true imitation of colloquial American speech (though it often failed) and could always feel sharply the country in the background—"the places and how the weather was." Here there were even the laconic, understated endings to stories that people complained were "pointless."

In *The Green Hills* Hemingway chose two stories for special praise—"The Open Boat" and "The Blue Hotel." The first of these is often called Crane's masterpiece; at times it sounds enough like Hemingway to have been written by him. There are several such places, but take one in which Crane's ear did not fail him:

. . . the cook and the correspondent argued as to the difference between a life-saving station and a house of refuge. The cook had said: "There's a house of refuge just north of the Mosquito Inlet Light, and as soon as they see us they'll come off in their boat and pick us up."

"As soon as who see us?" said the correspondent.

"The crew," said the cook.

"Houses of refuge don't have crews," said the correspondent. "As I understand them, they are only places where clothes and grub are stored for the benefit of shipwrecked people. They don't carry crews."

"Oh, yes, they do," said the cook.

"No, they don't," said the correspondent.

"Well, we're not there yet, anyhow," said the oiler, in the stern.

"Well," said the cook, "perhaps it's not a house of refuge that I'm thinking of as being near Mosquito Inlet Light; perhaps it's a life-saving station."

"We're not there yet," said the oiler in the stern.

Here is all the flatness, and yet all the cadence, too, of Hemingway's famous conversation. Here is the realistic yet mannered effect, the same terse and unliterary tone, the same repetitions of words, phrases and statements, and the same muted tension.

"The Blue Hotel" has as many resemblances, particularly to "The Killers," and has in addition a dead Swede propped up in front of a cash register—a device Hemingway used in "An Alpine Idyll" and reused in *The Fifth Column*. But it is a story that Hemingway failed to mention which most clearly establishes his great debt to Crane. This is "An Episode of War," and it is enlightening to compare it with a story of Hemingway's like "A Clean Well-Lighted Place," which has all the "monotony," the regularly rising and falling cadence, the depressed tone and the razor-edged impressions and perceptions for which Hemingway is famous.

"A Clean Well-Lighted Place" is a fairly "typical" Hemingway story. An old man has tried to commit suicide, and has failed even in this. He sits alone in a café until late at night an unsympathetic waiter sends him along, and closes the place. Another waiter is the central figure in the story, and he feels quite differently from his colleague about those who need a clean, well-lighted café to sit up late in. There is little else in life to help support it. "Hail nothing full of nothing, nothing is with thee," he thinks, . . . as he heads homeward in the realization that there is nothing else he can do but go to his room and to bed. The story ends with a characteristic understatement:

> Now, without thinking further, he would go home to his room. He would lie in the bed and finally, with daylight, he would go to sleep. After all, he said to himself, it is probably only insomnia. Many must have it.

Crane's story is of a lieutenant who, while distributing a ration of coffee, is suddenly shot in the arm. The wound is not serious, but in the confusion of battle it is not properly cared for, and the arm is amputated. With the same flat, reserved, depressed understatement and absolute lack of comment for which Hemingway is well known, Crane ends "An Episode of War":

And this is the story of how the lieutenant lost his arm. When he reached home, his sisters, his mother, his wife, sobbed for a long time at the sight of the flat sleeve. "Oh, well," he said, standing shame-faced amid these tears, "I don't suppose it matters so much as all that."

"After all, he said to himself, it is probably only insomnia. Many must have it."

Crane and Poetic Tradition

by Daniel Hoffman

I

In tracing the evolution of Crane's craft let us begin with a simple allegory. Here character and action are explicit embodiments of moral qualities. Perhaps the most striking of Crane's allegorical poems is this one:

> The wayfarer,
> Perceiving the pathway to truth,
> Was struck with astonishment.
> It was thickly grown with weeds.
> "Ha," he said,
> "I see that none has passed here
> In a long time."
> Later he saw that each weed
> Was a singular knife.
> "Well," he mumbled at last,
> "Doubtless there are other roads."
>
> *(War Is Kind* **XIII)**

This allegorical cameo might well have been modeled on a medieval morality play. As in the best of Crane's poems in this vein, the language is direct and, but for the phrase "a singular knife," uncomplicated by nuance. This is a diction without association or metaphor.

At one remove from such directness are poems in which we find, instead of allegorical personages, actions whose import is in direct correspondence to a state of feeling the poet wishes to evoke. Here the language may be more ornate—in the fifteen lines following

there are nine qualifying adjectives, adverbs, and phrases—yet the
narrative is still relatively straightforward.

> A youth in apparel that glittered
> Went to walk in a grim forest.
> There he met an assassin
> Attired all in garb of old days;
> He, scowling through the thickets,
> And dagger poised quivering,
> Rushed upon the youth.
> "Sir," said this latter,
> "I am enchanted, believe me,
> To die, thus,
> In this mediæval fashion,
> According to the best legends;
> Ah, what joy!"
> Then took he the wound, smiling,
> And died, content.
>
> (*Black Riders* XXVII)

Mr. Stallman considers this poem "a miniature copy of *The Red
Badge of Courage*," the conflict in both being that "between *illusion and reality*." Some of Henry's illusions, it is true, are dreams of
medieval glory (he thought of war as a time of "heavy crowns and
high castles") but there is surely a difference between the panic and
courage of the novel and the satisfied nihilism of the poem. Stylis-
tically the poem is elaborate, dressed as it were in antique brocade.
The youth's glittering apparel is not only his clothing; his mind too
is dressed "In this mediæval fashion." "Apparel that glittered" of
course suggests armor, the function of which is to fend off poised
daggers. But this youth longs for death "According to the best
legends" and is purposely as defenseless as though he were naked.
Although the narrative in this poem is complete in itself, the language is richer in associations than that in the simple allegories.

As Crane moves from a poetry of direct correspondences toward
a less discursive, more allusive idiom, his language may take on
metaphoric functions simply because the referents of the narrative
are undefined, e.g.,

> On the horizon the peaks assembled;
> And as I looked,
> The march of the mountains began.

> As they marched, they sang,
> "Ay, we come! we come!"

(Black Riders XXXVII)

Although much plainer in style than "A youth in apparel that glittered," this is more complex in effect. Crane leaves it to us to infer
that the mountains, normally massive and immobile, represent
the immitigable force in the natural universe. He does not state that
their march is *toward him*, the insignificant human observer, yet
we feel this to be so. Although all that is said—and that is precious
little—is said in a diction sparse and plain, the tone is hugely ominous. Crane does not say, but we know, that the human protagonist stands awe-stricken, dumb and still as stone while the horizon of
peaks chants as it closes in upon him—as would the growling peaked
waves in the later poem, "A man adrift on a slim spar."

That poem may be taken to represent the fourth stage in the complexity of Crane's poetic idiom. There . . . the discursive narrative element is still further suppressed; by indirect suggestion the
purposeful ambiguities and interlocking associations of the metaphoric diction reinforce the development of theme which the infer-
ential narrative supplies.

Thus it is evident that Crane develops distinctive methods of
poetic structure, as well as . . . several styles of diction. . . . This
I take to be a refutation of John Berryman's assertion that "There
is no evidence in the poetry or outside it that he ever experimented
in verse." Indeed, it is because Crane was what later generations
would call an experimental writer that the sum of his work seems as
discontinuous as we have found it to be. This is true to a degree of
his prose also—many readers have noted the fantasy and impressionism of *Sullivan County Sketches*, the naturalistic determinism
of *Maggie* and *George's Mother*, the irony and dreamlike association
of incident and metaphor in *The Red Badge*, the naturalism again
in "The Open Boat" but now in combination with a superbly controlled symbolistic style, the frontier humor of "The Bride Comes
to Yellow Sky," the sustained combination of tension and suppleness
in "The Blue Hotel," the irony undercutting the baroque prose of
The Monster, and the style "flexible, swift, abrupt, nervous . . .
with an unexampled capacity for stasis also" which Berryman remarks as the norm for Crane's prose. Although Crane's experimen-
talism led him to absorb many technical influences that came his
way, the unifying quality which makes these stories all unmistak-

ably his own is the sensibility they express. The authority of his style, highly individual despite all these modifications, is the guarantee of the uniqueness of that sensibility.

In verse, too, we find several varieties of excellence, unified despite variation by the authority of the style. The four stages of increasing complexity we have just noted actually merge into one another, but on the whole we can distinguish between two generic types of Crane poems, the allegories and the non-discursive symbolistic poems. The former category includes such unadorned allegorical narratives as "The wayfarer / Perceiving the pathway to truth," "There was one I met upon the road," "A man saw a ball of gold in the sky," "In heaven / Some little blades of grass," and "The trees in the garden rained flowers." There are also the parables of simple paradox—"A man said to the universe," "I saw a man pursuing the horizon," " 'It was wrong to do this,' said the angel," "A man feared that he might find an assassin," and "Forth went the candid man."

Subtler than these are the metaphorical parables capable of symbolistic extension, such as "A youth in apparel that glittered," "The patent of a lord," "On the horizon the peaks assembled," and the fable of the heart-eater in the desert.

The symbolistic poems which, by virtue of their more complex organization, the larger commitments they express, and the subtlety and resorcefulness of their language, I take to be Crane's most substantial verse, include "A man adrift on a slim spar," "Do not weep, maiden, for war is kind," and "The Blue Battalions"—these I think his three best; and also "Bottles and bottles and bottles," "The Battle Hymn," "Black riders came from the sea," "Fast rode the knight," "I explain the silvered passing of a ship at night," and the opening lines of "There exists the eternal fact of conflict." But this schematization does not accommodate such other poems worthy of mention as the impressionistic "Each small gleam was a voice," the imagistic "To the maiden / The sea was a blue meadow," or the discursive "A newspaper is a collection of half-injustices."

If we compare the intentions of Crane's most complex verse to those of the French Symbolists we can at once identify the characteristics which isolate Crane from them and which link him to the greater writers of the American Renaissance. Mr. Tindall has conveniently summarized Mallarmé's aesthetic, and it is instructive to juxtapose this to Crane's:

> Without intended reference to external reality, his worlds or poems are "inclosed." Fictions or virtual realities, they exist as a piece of

music does, by symmetry, interaction of parts, and what he called
"reciprocal reflections" . . . as far as possible from discourse. . . .
[Mallarmé] said that symbolism consisted in evoking an object little
by little in order to reveal a state of mind, or, inversely, choosing an
object and from it disengaging a state of mind. . . . This state, far
from being a reminder of anything we have known, is a fresh creation; and this creation is the effect of analogy, not from nature's store
but made by the poet. What it is an analogy for must be guessed by
the reader as the poem creates his state of mind.[1]

It is evident, if the readings I have proposed of his best poems
have any merit, that the means by which Crane's verse creates its
intended effects resemble those of Mallarmé. But it is equally clear
that despite these similarities in technique there is a basic difference
in intention. Crane's poems, autonomous though they are, are never
"without intended reference to external reality." When his verse
moves "as far as possible from discourse" it is not, as is the case with
Mallarmé, to construct an automonous private universe as an alternative to the world of nature. "The nearer a writer gets to life the
greater he becomes as an artist"—this is a constant tenet in Crane's
artistic practice. The world of his poems is made with the allego-
rist's prerogative of providing an imaginary construct to represent
the real world, not, as the Symbolist would, to substitute for it.

Crane abandons discursiveness when the truths of life which he
seeks to discover and reveal cannot be reached by means so direct.
In order to express the complexity inherent to a faithful representation of his own sensibility, Crane felt in his early poems that he must
break with the conventions of the genteel verse of his time. Hence
the iconoclasm, the repudiation of traditional structure and orna-
ment:

> "Think as I think," said a man,
> "Or you are abominably wicked;
> You are a toad."
>
> And after I had thought of it,
> I said, "I will, then, be a toad."
>
> *(Black Riders* XLVII)

Thus in 1893. But two or three years later Crane writes a poem in
six regular stanzas, alternating questions with replies: "What says
the sea, little shell?" (*War Is Kind* II) first appeared in the *Philistine*

[1] William York Tindall, *The Literary Symbol* (New York, 1955), pp. 48-49.

in February, 1896. The next month the *Chap-book* printed "In
the night," whose three stanzas . . . presented a definite time
scheme in consistent metrical form. By April "The Blue Battalions"
had been written . . . with still more complicated regular stanzas
incorporating internal refrains. "Do not weep, maiden, for war is
kind" is perhaps Crane's most complexly organized poem, but this
had been written by August, 1895. From that time on Crane was no
longer in willful rebellion against such conventional techniques as
stanzas and refrains, although he never did adopt rhyme or iambic
meter. His best longer poems combine firm stanzaic structure with
the allusiveness of controlled metaphor. This parallels the conjunction in his prose, remarked above, of metaphoric richness with the
skilled organization of incident.

In these more complexly organized poems, Crane, like the French
Symbolists, does demand that we guess at the significance of the
states of mind or feeling which his poems little by little reveal. But
whereas "a symbolist work," Mr. Tindall concludes, "has no certain
meaning," this we do not feel to be the case with Crane. The meaning, complex and ambiguous though it may be, is certain nonethe-
less. His symbols are not metaphors "detached from their subjects"
but metaphors whose relation to their subjects must be inferred.
They are metaphors of fixed reference, yet their use takes advantage
of the ambiguous and symbolic nature of language itself. Crane re-
tains the certainty of the ethical significance of experience, the assurance of the spiritual significance of natural facts, which made
allegory the natural expression of his early work.

II

In so far as Crane's symbols have assigned though unstated meanings they are much closer to the objective correlative described by
T. S. Eliot than they are to either the symbols of Symbolism or the
images of Imagism. The image, as Ezra Pound defined it, "is that
which presents an intellectual complex in an instant of time. . . .
It is the presentation of such a 'complex' instantaneously which
gives that sense of sudden liberation; that sense of freedom from
time limits and space limits; that sense of sudden growth, which we
experience in the presence of the greatest works of art."[2] Crane

[2] *The Literary Essays of Ezra Pound* (New York, 1954), p. 4.

seems to resemble the Imagist poets because, like them, in many of his poems he uses direct treatment, economical diction, and organic rhythm. Yet he actually conforms to the aesthetic Pound describes in only his simplest verse. The Imagist aims at a static representation of a caught moment of experience; this, by virtue of its associations, elicits in us intellectual and emotional awareness of things outside itself. But almost all of Crane's simple "imagistic" poems are themselves in motion. They have plots as allegories have plots. Granting their governing metaphors, they force attention inward upon themselves, not outward to extrinsic associations. There are no such associations; there are only the poems.

In his more complex verse, however, Crane is more ambitious than the Imagist aesthetic allows. In so far as his verse resembles the work of that movement, it is in his impressionistic pieces; Imagism, after all, attempted merely to expand by association the significance of the impression. While Crane appealed to Pound, Sandburg, Edith Wyatt, and others as a forebear of the then contemporary movement, he had long since gone beyond the limitations of the Imagist aesthetic. This was a journey almost all the Imagists themselves were to make—Eliot moving toward soliloquy and drama, Stevens toward the most Symbolist symbolism in English verse, Fletcher reverting to the lush romanticism of Lanier, Marianne Moore developing a unique combination of moral sensibility and parable derived from Whitman and La Fontaine, Sandburg losing completely the economical control Imagism had imposed on his language as he literally appropriates the idiom of everyday speech for poetry. Of the original Imagists, H. D., William Carlos Williams, and Pound remained most influenced by their own programme of the Little Renaissance. H. D. continues with admirable integrity to chisel verbal cameos, and fails to deal successfully with themes rather than with impressions. Pound and Williams have more omnivorous ambitions, the one Ovidian, the other Whitmanesque, but in the organization of both *The Cantos* and *Paterson* we see the limiting effectiveness of Imagist images connected chiefly by mood. Of the two attempted epics, *Paterson* is the more cohesive, but its flaw is another Imagist limitation: the philosophical naïveté of "no ideas but in things."

Since Crane was heralded as a forebear of the movement in which these important poets participated, why, one wonders, has his actual influence on twentieth-century verse been so slight? One reason . . . is the relative unavailability of his verse during the period when its influence might have been most felt. Neither of his books was reprinted nor, except for E. C. Stedman's collection in 1900, did any anthology contain Crane's verse until after his *Work* appeared in 1926. By then Imagism had had its heyday. But a more fundamental reason for Crane's seeming lack of influence is that despite his anticipation of some techniques later to be widely adopted, he held a conception of poetry which later poets and critics could not share.

The first tenet of Crane's view of poetry was his notion of the brevity of poetic form. This may at first seem not incongruous with Imagist compression; indeed, until quite recently twentieth-century poetry has been almost without exception based upon compact lyric techniques, whether of symbolist, imagist, or metaphysical origin. Yet at the same time modern poets have attempted to move beyond the brevity of lyric form to vehicles more ambitious: the cycles of interconnected lyrics of Yeats's Crazy Jane poems; the attempted epics of *The Waste Land, The Bridge, The Cantos, Paterson, The People, Yes*; the baroque mock-epic of *The Comedian as the Letter C*; the extended soliloquys of Senlin and the *Four Quartets*; the verse drama of Yeats, Eliot, MacLeish, Eberhart, and their younger emulators. But Crane was intransigently committed to envisaging the proper dimension of all art as brief. *War and Peace, Anna Karenina, Nana*, the books of Mark Twain, all seemed to him too long for the work they set out to do. His own best fiction is either novella or the short story. And in poetry we have seen him ruthlessly reduce to their minimal essences the works that influenced him and attempt to keep his best original compositions tightly knit and nondiscursive as possible.

This is because Crane seeks the ultimate concentration of experience in art. His valuing of brevity may have derived from Poe's aesthetic theory, yet Crane's observance of this precept does not resemble Poe's. Crane seeks the moments of highest intensity not, like Poe, for the sake of the sensation, but because life experienced at that pitch will reveal to him the meanings which are otherwise diffused and rendered indecipherable. That intensity is the result of the collision of forces which operate upon experience, and the work, to be true to the life it represents, must contain the forces, the experience, and the intensity all together. This it can do either by presenting a dialectic or in terms of a plot. Crane's best poems use both methods; they present the bare outlines of a narrative situation in which there is a tension between two opposed forces. The tension may be expressed in terms of antithetical statements, dialogue, description, or the effect upon the observer of an action he witnesses. Crane's mind is always attuned to narrative, to the dynamic representation of man in conflict. But in his poems he seeks the most universal statements possible of the themes which possess his imagination. Hence he must eliminate from the presentation all the particularities of the conflicts which might restrict his statements only to the described events. By making his human figures faceless and nameless, by pitting them against elemental forces, by describing their ambitions and their plights in simple yet overwhelming metaphors, Crane created for his poetry a symbolical form which represented a great advance in subtlety and flexibility over its allegorical beginnings.

But these considerations lead us to the second tenet of Crane's poetic credo which later writers could not share. Twentieth-century verse has recoiled not only from allegory but from narrative itself, concentrating instead upon lyric and dramatic expression. Even the attempted epics named above have been made in terms of lyric, rather than narrative or allegorical strategy (except for Stevens' *Comedian*, which in no respect resembles Crane). Crane, however, went his own way and made his own styles to do the work to which he had to put them. His diction is intrinsic to the structure of his poems; the one cannot be imitated without the other. And since the combination Crane made of allegory (explicit or implied), assigned symbols, dialectic, direct treatment, brevity, and narrative situation remains his own, his verse remains singular after almost half a century of post-Imagist emphasis on directness and economy. A style such as Crane's is the product both of his extraordinary sensibility and of his cultural situation, which was much more impoverished than that of any twentieth-century American poet of distinction.

*   *   *

Although Crane's poems are restricted in range, they have the unexampled authority which the work of an original artist who explores the furthest reaches of the human spirit, in whatever direction, rightfully commands.

Only Poe and Hemingway have neared Crane's lonely outpost from which in his verse he views, and makes us feel, the reality of a universe where force is law, where love is doom, where God is cold, where man's lot is fated misery, where hope is narrowed to the possibility of courage, and the reward of courage is self-sacrifice. None has surpassed him in the imaginative expression of this sensibility of isolation. Emerson, with his openness to life, could scarcely have had such an artist in mind when he defined "The Poet," yet we do no violence to either man in applying to Crane these words:

> He is isolated among his contemporaries by truth and by his art, but with this consolation in his pursuits, that they will draw all men sooner or later. For all men live by truth and stand in need of expression. In love, in art . . . we study to utter our painful secret. The man is only half himself, the other half is his expression.

What Crane's poems express is partly his private doom. But the sensibility of isolation is a bitter gift which Stephen Crane did not hold alone. In lesser degree than was true of him, it is also a characteristic of his country and his culture. Crane takes his authority to be an interpreter from the very extremity of his commitment so widely shared. In these poems which explore the menaced condition of man in isolation, Crane developed new techniques and made available to poetic expression a further reach of imaginative experience than had any American writer before him. His best poems impose aesthetic form on the stark vision that haunted his imagination. They free us to participate in that vision and to contemplate with deepened understanding a part of ourselves.

Stephen Crane's Metaphor of Decorum

by George W. Johnson

To the girl who wanted a "man of fashion" Stephen Crane proclaimed himself "a savage," "docile . . . only under great social pressure," "by inclination a wild shaggy barbarian." At the same time, however, this rebel against middle class conventionality strove to remain a gentleman, gallant if only to streetwalkers, chivalric to the déclassé, ministerial to reckless youth, and grandly hospitable at Brede Place to friend and stranger alike. While his friends might grumble that he "had no sense of propriety," Crane, self-conscious and self-deprecatory, tried to be both the isolated Bohemian and "Baron Brede." Able to breathe only "in the slums or among aristocrats," as a contemporary remembered him, he seems to have struggled all his life between the appeal of the "wild free son of nature" and the need to find a place in society and tradition. Like his Henry Fleming, he struggled to gain the respect of his fraternity without surrendering his life or his individuality to the "moving box" of tradition; he tried, like his Swede, to make a place for himself as a gentleman without impaling himself on his purchase. This apparent temperamental need for a role both docile and savage was transmuted into the impersonalities of his fiction, in which the fate of the hero—soldier, honeymooner, outcast, or outlander—is the measure of his ability to establish the grounds for proper conduct. In that transmutation Crane defined himself as an artist; and to pursue a metaphor of decorum through his best stories is to discover anew his view of life and the courage of his response to it.

The patrician-plebeian stance which Crane adopted was in the script of his age, a period in which highbrow litterateurs worried lest literature become overcivilized and in which the most success-

"Stephen Crane's Metaphor of Decorum." From *PMLA*, LXXVIII (June 1963), 250-256. Reprinted by permission of the Modern Language Association of America.

ful political aspirant was a product of both a Harvard curriculum and Dakota ranch-life. For by 1890 the hitherto glossed-over conflict between the inner life of anarchial passion and instinct and the outer subservience to genteel norms had been brought into the open. It was, as Frank Norris called it, a period of "instability and changeableness," in which the latent contradictions of American experience were all too manifest. The conflict between the claims of idealism and realism, of a cultural elite and democracy in life and art, or of a vigorous West and a civilized but effete East, found literary columnists and social utopians groping for programs of harmonization. In the meantime American subculture was busy supplying reconciling images. Masculine sport came into its first prominence. National and democratic—football was "All America" by 1889—the Game glorified ferocity and élan within clearly defined rules of gentlemanly decorum: it was a ritualization of a central American conflict. It was apparently satisfying enough to redeem the absurdities of literary creations like Richard Harding Davis' Van Bibber, that patrician sportsman who strolled the slums and knocked thugs into quivering heaps, or Frank Norris' Buldy Jones, that wealthy football-baseball hero who painted miniatures when not fighting duels with baseballs—and who, after all, was not so unlike the powerful Frederic Remington who played football with Camp at Yale, painted Indians in the West, and rode with T. R. in Cuba. Indeed, the metaphor of sport perhaps prepared the way for the Rough Riders, that fraternity of Ivy League gentlemen and Western toughs. And it provided a role for those young men impatient with the irrationality of their experience. For Crane was not alone in wanting to get nearer to "life," "nature and truth."

But while, like other young barbarians under social pressure, Crane immersed himself in games, celebrated the West, and pursued war, he did not tell himself, as Norris did, that the players all moved to the strains of some meaningful "Master Note." Often vain and attitudinizing, Crane in the conduct of his life was to remain childlike to the end, inveighing against society's distancing ceremonies yet vulnerable to social pressure, most at home with children yet panting to go to war. In the conduct of his fiction, however, he was very early a very old child, who if not amenable to rules was susceptible to nightmare. For before he had ever gone to war in the flesh and before he was ever to buy the Texas ranch he longed for, he was to test the neo-Romantic role in his fiction. And unlike

Norris, who went on and on seeking some ultimate harmonization which would transcend his difficulties of temperament, thought, and language, Crane stopped to confront the irreconcilable. His talk, his dreams, his itinerary might go on following the rough rider, still yearning to touch reality and remain a gentleman, but after *The Red Badge of Courage* his imagination hardly moved at all. For there he had already discovered that the game of the strenuous life had no goal, that men were nothing without rules but that the rules killed them. The mastery of only one game remained significant: Crane was perhaps not simply posturing when he said he wished to write verse as well as he could play poker. Only the mind of the artist could participate with the soldier like a "savage religion mad" and remain as detached as an "old fellow upon the cracker-barrel." Only the artist could accept a discipline which did not render him helpless. As a naturalist, an impressionist, an ironist, Crane found his decorum.

Thomas Beer reports that when Stephen Crane was twelve he was discovered disinterring from the sand a young comrade who, he said, had been improvidently buried with a canteen of whiskey still on him. Veterans, of course, could not be so careless. A Miss Brett promptly spanked him for his outrage of propriety. If the incident did not actually take place, it should have, for it dramatizes a theme which runs through most of Crane's war stories. The decorum of veterans, unlike the pretensions of normative society's ceremonies of behavior, was created in response to reality, searing and annealing. The "nonsense" of civilization's traditional rituals and the "furniture" of conventional dress Crane could not abide; the display of flags by a signaller who stood up amid the bullets he adored. On the well-publicized exploits of Teddy Roosevelt he was silent; but he rhapsodized T. R.'s devotion to the welfare of his troop in Cuba and bestowed upon him the ultimate Crane accolade: "He was a gentleman, down there." He did not need the experience of Cuba, however, to understand that the discipline and fraternal sense which marked a man a veteran also rendered him helpless. For "the interesting thing" about war—the "mental attitude of the men"—he already knew. Indeed, it is even possible to speculate that what literally drove Crane to Cuba was the ironic realization that the decorum of the veteran was no more meaningful than the rituals of tea. For the movement of his war fiction is

from the ostensible integration of savagery and docility toward a
final metaphor of man's plight: of his untenable position between
an unknowable world and incongruous ceremonies.

That movement begins, of course, with *The Red Badge of Courage*, in which Henry Fleming supposedly learns to abide incon-
gruity and find the world meaningful. Having assumed that "secular and religious education" have banished savagery and heroic op-
portunities, Henry feels he must nevertheless make the most of his
chance to behave like a man. As a recruit he enjoy's society's caress
and looks forward to the mark he will make as a returning veteran.
He is provided with a set of rules, first by his mother, then by the
"moving box" of law and tradition. Reacting badly to battle, however, he is swept into the forest, an individual, alone. Fortuitously
he survives, loses the "sore badge of his dishonor," and regains mem-
bership in good standing. Now apparently both savage and docile
in an integration on which the sun shines, Henry finds "the world
was a world for him." Despite the dramatic falseness of this implicitly optimistic close, the book is magnificent. But it may not be
exactly war. That enlisted veterans liked it while generals sputtered
over it is not, we might remember, testimony that the GI is always
the closer to reality. One might instead argue that the book's appeal,
like its genesis, is rooted in the vulgar. For, while redeemed by
Crane's imagination, the book grew out of rather cheap stuff. Crane
seems to have been quite right in guessing that he imagined it on
the basis of the emotions of a football game, and certainly Henry's
satisfaction on being initiated into the "mysterious fraternity" seems
very nearly that of a successful pledge to Delta Upsilon. Moreover,
Henry, having rejoined his company, is able to view a skirmish as
remarkably like "a matched game," and in charging onto the field
with a stained rag around his head he looks suspiciously like an
1890 halfback wearing his sweatband. One can suggest, at least, that
a college sensibility dictated the supposed success of the youth's
decorum.

In writing it, however, Crane seems to have grown immeasurably
older. In the summer prior to Fleming's appearance between covers,
Crane was writing "A Mystery of Heroism," and in this story of a
soldier he found little ground for optimism. In the account of a foolhardy dash across a battlefield, the experience of Fred Collins, a veteran, picks up where Henry's left off, and the irony of acceptance
and docility, rather than their achievement, is now the focus of
composition. The experience is framed in the opening conventions

of josh and dare and the concluding horseplay of two lieutenants
—within, that is, the conventions of the fraternity. Superintended
by a "pious" officer, the "mystery" of Collins' exploit lies in his acceptance of a meaningless code. At the outset he thinks it "super-
naturally strange" that he has let the dare pressure him into danger,
but by the time he checks his wild career to safety in order to succor
a dying officer he is not thinking at all, and, untroubled by problems
of loyalty, acts without mercy or meaning. The captain to whom he
reports sends the water to the men in the best of Crane's gentlemanly
tradition, and Collins obeys orders. His docility having been established, Collins then drops out of the account. After one has become a veteran, after one has touched the "composite monster"
(*The Red Badge*), one apparently abides by conventions and maintains decorum. "In their fashion," however, the two lieutenants
spill the water, and the conventions, like the bucket, are with
terrible finality quite empty at the close.

The necessity of conventions despite their fatality becomes the
central metaphor of two war stories Crane wrote in 1899, after his
experience in Cuba and less than a year before his death. The one,
"An Episode of War," deals with the temporary detachment of a
nameless lieutenant, wounded during the small ceremony of al-
lotting the coffee ration, set adrift from his unit and the battle, returned at last to a schoolyard and instruction in how to be "properly
wounded." During his detachment the lieutenant glimpses the "wonder" of man's life: soldiers struggling astride "maniacal horses" to
"preserve their respectful interval"; a dying man serenely smoking
his corncob pipe in the shadow of the schoolhouse, whose essential
function is now symbolically revealed in its use as a surgery. The
lieutenant wishes to cry out; he resists the social pressure exerted
by the genially scornful surgeon; he sees the door of the schoolhouse
as "sinister." But he is recaptured and rendered docile. A veteran,
he can say at the end, "I don't suppose it matters so much as all that."

The other story, "The Upturned Face," completes the development of an imaginative polarity which began with the interment
of Miss Brett's nephew. The men of a burial squad enter no-man's
land to dig a grave for a comrade. There they must complete the
ceremony, maintaining a respectful interval, despite the terrors of
battle. They must obey the rules of the fraternity—"you can't, you
know, leave your intimate friends rotting on the field." They must
strive for some notion of ultimate propriety—they cannot bear to
cover their comrade's eyes, and, stammering, they try in the ritual

of the service to phrase a metaphor of man's relationship to the cosmos. But this is no-man's land and nothing signifies. The tension
between the need for meaning and the need to carry out "this business" is carried through the story in the antiphonies of the adjutant's hysteria and Timothy Lean's "Tumble him in"; the adjutant's epithet of "beasts" and the "brisk," "measured volleys" of the
disciplined sharpshooters. The men struggle to follow Lean's in-
structions, delivered with an "academic expression," in the proper
timing of the service; Lean and the adjutant struggle to maintain
the decorum of prayer despite the tigerish impulse to hurry the dirt
in, to maintain military subordination and still get the job done.
They succeed. And the dirt, making a "pendulum curve," concludes
the antiphony: "plop."

These stories lack the ostensible value of communal forms which
supplied the humanistic veneer of *The Red Badge*. Here, humanism
must operate in a void. In the face of the amorphous unknowable,
one must become docile lest one lose one's "direction of safety."
For to leave the "moving box" of tradition, as Fleming learns, is
to be alone with one's thoughts, constructing "rules for the guidance
of the doomed" which every new moment repeals. Events are either
portentous or prosaic: war is either a cataclysm or a game, soldiers
are gods or muddiggers, one is a hero or a coward. But outside the
regiment one cannot tell which. Having allowed "his mind to ma-
noeuvre his body" into no-man's land, Collins cannot tell whether
he is a hero or merely "an intruder," he finds the cool well become
"a furnace," and he flees before an "angel of death" but runs like
a dairy farmer chased by a bull. Struck by something from out of
the "mystic green face of a wood," the wounded lieutenant can no
longer rely on his "right arm" and finds his sword become a "strange
thing"—"a trident, a sceptre, or a spade." Within the forms of the
regiment the docile veteran finds safety from neither physical nor
mental trauma, but he can function. As a member of the fraternity
Henry becomes "a carpenter . . . making still another box." The
man of the adjutant's burial party suffers between his need to see
"whence the bullets" come and to cover the face that looks "keenly
out of the grave," but he completes the job like a "tired labourer."
Despite its lack of ultimate meaning, decorum thus allows the veteran to accept incongruities which would otherwise overwhelm his
imagination. It is a sanctuary from conceptual warfare. It is, perhaps, the most "interesting thing" about war.

The fraternity of veterans thus becomes a metaphor for society or civilization, a group defining itself by the incongruities it is capable of accepting. An imagined battlefield was for Crane the natural scene in which to isolate the conventional in response to the monstrous. He was frustrated, however, in his attempts to confirm in experience what he knew in imagination, unable in the winter and spring of 1897 to reach Cuba or to "see" in Greece. Meanwhile he had endured the forces of propriety, maligned by name-droppers, hounded by New York police, and rendered vulnerable to slurs in his relationship with Cora Taylor. Even during his escape to the West in 1895 he had discovered the rigors of decorum, having "offended a local custom" in Lincoln, Nebraska, by intervening in what appeared to his "Eastern scruples" to be an unfair fight. The brawl met the terms of Nebraskan rules, however, and for his pains Crane was taken to a judge and chided, the incident "very saddening." Social pressure was everywhere. But by the fall of 1897, settled in England, Crane was ready to deal with it. In a burst of creativity he wrote three great stories—*The Monster*, "The Bride Comes to Yellow Sky," and "The Blue Hotel"—and then broke for Cuba and war. The first takes place in a settled Eastern town. Here a faceless Negro, erupting from the "black mass" of a burned house, evokes concentric rings of ceremony as society attempts to reestablish equilibrium. The other two stories occur in a raw, new West. There, at the center of a shimmering yellow of sky and sand or a swirling whiteness of snow, conventions converge relentlessly until the constrictive pressure is released in a hiss of sardonic laughter or an explosion of physical and psychic violence.

The contracting and expanding spirals which comprise the structure of *The Monster* reflect in themselves society's attempt to right itself. The first four chapters move outward, from Jim and his father, to Jim and Henry, to Henry and the townspeople, to the townspeople assembled: a stable and decorous society. At the "revolutionary outbreak" of the fire those circles contract—"all roads" leading to Trescott's house—and then expand again through the ceremonies of fire-watching and the obsequies for a supposedly dead hero to the judge's final retreat to the "cold manner of the bench" and the pronouncement: "It is hard for a man to know what to do." The problem confronting the townspeople, an "old problem," is that which confronted Henry Fleming: how, having touched the monster, can one regain decorum? To do so, the doctor, the housewife, the lawyer, the official, and the child must each finally abide by the rules of his fraternity. It is all child's play, but it is all there is. Obeying his

private feelings and rejecting "public institutions," Trescott fulfills
one human obligation, but he also learns that he cannot "beat the
game." And while the wind whines outside and the snow beats on
the windows, the repose of the parlor is dominated by the fifteen
teacups, however empty.

Whilomville accepts what it can put a good face on, and the question posed in Reifsnyder's emporium of faces is what to do with
the faceless black mass. When Henry Johnson first passes the bar-
bershop, making a "front" on his way to the "tremendous civilities"
of the Farraguts' porch, the lawyer cries "Wow!" to the "parliament,"
but the reply is, "Why, that's only Henry Johnson." A parody of
white decorum, Henry's incongruities of dress and manner are first
accepted as comic, as part of the game. It is on his second trip to
the Farraguts', "a monster making a low and sweeping bow," that
the parody becomes horrific, decorum now revealed not only as the
restraint on blackness but as its agent.

What the Negro is to *The Monster*, the reference by which we see
both the necessity and duplicity of decorum, the West is to "The
Bride Comes to Yellow Sky" and "The Blue Hotel." The dress of
Scratchy Wilson and the language of Scully are incongruous mix-
tures accepted matter-of-factly by members of the fraternity. The
marshal's job evokes a "Wow!" from the Eastern drummer but is
thoroughly conventionalized in Yellow Sky. The etiquette of card-
quarreling in its "fabulous dignity" evokes laughter from the Swede
but "discreet silence" from Romperites. Westerners do not see disturbing incongruities—this ain't "*out West*," they chorus—and
they assume that their life is as decorous as life anywhere. It is. What
we see more clearly in the West than elsewhere is that while insulat-
ing life from the chaos without—lest man stand before "profligate
fury" like "a gatepost" "with a blanched face"—conventions also
carry man in a moving box toward "hideous rites" and final impro-
prieties.

"The Bride Comes to Yellow Sky" sets forth the comic aspects of
the "transaction" which occurs between two different conventions,
two different humors. Two roles confront each other: the one in
the Eastern, feminized (hence, in the rhetoric of the nineties, civilized) script of the honeymoon; the other in the Western, masculine (hence, savage) ceremonies of the gunfight. The one is prompted
by the porter, a "fatherly pilot," who "chuckles fatuously" and reads
in the bride and groom's discomfiture only the conventions of the
honeymoon. The other is superintended by the bartender, who in-

structs the Eastern salesman in the norms of Western life. When in the streets of Yellow Sky the two roles converge before the house which squats like a "stone god" of domesticity, the stage is set for climactic violence. But it fails to occur. Before the "hideous rites" of Yellow Sky, the Bride "goes yellow as old cloth"; allowed a glimpse of another world, Scratchy Wilson asks feebly whether Potter has "been to Sunday school"; and the scene runs out in sand and Scratchy's "funnel-shaped" tracks. That nothing more occurs is perhaps the latent horror of this gaily comic tale. On "the plains of Texas"—which in the opening lines of the story are seen "pouring eastward . . . sweeping over the horizon, a precipice"—two roles have been momentarily juxtaposed before going over the edge. For what the confrontation shows us is that there is no ultimate meaning to either role, and that under a yellow sky men and their traditions make but passing indentations in the sands of time.

This latent horror of what might be called the precipitation of roles is made manifest in "The Blue Hotel." A self-conscious decorum pervades this story, epitomized in the conduct of Scully and the gambler, each of whom in his own way aspires to the status of an "honored and respicted gintleman." Scully identifies himself vociferously as a hotel-keeper and devotes himself to the honor of his calling, preserving the "sacred privileges" of his guests. The gambler, on the other hand, preys wolfishly on the stupidity of his clients, but is "delicate in manner," "judicious," a "thoroughbred," meticulous in observing social gradations and devoted to preserving his own honor. And it is as "Gentlemen" that the Swede addresses them in his stilted and desperately decorous way, seeking his role, self-conscious, "accusing them dramatically," winking significantly, making his entrances "theatric." "Gentlemen," he cries in the hotel, "I suppose I am going to be killed before I can leave this house." "I'm a gentleman," he announces to the bar, "and I want people to drink with me."

Uncertain of his role, shaking fearfully in the absence of conventions he can count on, the Swede, a tailor looking for the reality that hides behind appearances, is inducted into the rites of Romper. While the wind howls outside, he is taken into the "proper temple" of the hotel and gradually reassured by a priestly Scully that he is safe, that a promise of trolley cars, a love of daughters, a deference to gentility, and an offer of a drink operate here as anywhere. Once convinced that he is secure, that the social forms of Romper serve rather than threaten him, the Swede, "this citadel of virtue, wisdom,

power," is ready for the final convention of the gambler's knife. All
confidence, he leaves the sanctuary of the hotel and "sails" to the
radiant bar. The shrine of pride, its "indomitable red light" trans-
forming the snow to "blood-colour," the bar is the scene of a celebration of man's vitality. Here the Swede tries to "impart a deep
significance" to his comment on the weather; here the businessmen
feel "a kind of pride" that the "wolf" would never "dare think of
attacking their wisdom and courage"; here the gambler adopts a
tone of "heroic patronage" to the burly intruder. Here each has his
own sense of what is proper. But proprieties collide, control disintegrates, murder is done. Rather than the result of a significant
struggle between an individual and the world, the Swede's death
is the ritual sacrifice of an unwitting victim to the gods of decorum.
In the hotel, men draw together in the game of cards and the ceremonies of basin and board. From the bar they spill out into the
night, the bartender "dinning through the storm for help and, moreover, companionship."

The Swede, having lost the shakiness of his solitary imaginings,
dies when he feels at home. And in a sense he dies because the men
of Fort Romper feel at home and obey the typology of their fraternity. For each of the figures appearing in the story is a stereotype:
the Hotelkeeper, the "tall bronzed" Cowboy, the Card-player, the
Easterner, the Bartender, the Gambler. As his calling requires,
Scully seduces a traveler; in his simple aggression the cowboy creates
tension; in a pattern which can be expected in a "western," Johnnie,
by cheating at cards, provokes the second card quarrel of the story;
"silent" in his Eastern reticence, Mr. Blanc fails to set matters
straight; making the "pretension of blindness . . . of his class,"
the bartender refuses to warn the Swede of his folly; and like his
colleagues in almost a century of pulp and film, the gambler silently
draws his knife. Together they create the "social pressure" which
renders the Swede docile in death.

Only the Easterner is aware of the collective responsibility, which,
as he says, is bared starkly in the world of Romper, a society in its
infancy with a decor of screaming contrasts. But his indictment creates only a "fog of mysterious theory" to the Cowboy, the man of
action. And justly so, for the Easterner, the bearer of letters, remains
bound by his typology. *The* Easterner, Mr. Blanc, continues to assume that men control their forms, their thought, and their language: if he had *spoken,* he insists, the gambler would not have be-

come merely an "adverb." Yet his very faith in thought and language
has confined him to his habitual role of the spectator, unable to act.
In his own way he is as blind as the Cowboy, who sees only the pri-
macy of act: "if the bartender had been any good," the latter says,
"he would have cracked that there Dutchman on the head . . . in
the beginning of it and stopped all this murderin'." "What did I
do?" he asks. The two speeches together close the drama of irresolu-
tion, which in concluding at the antipodes of Whilomville, on the
empty expanse of Dakota plains, nevertheless reveals again the impossibility of man's control and understanding.

"The conceit" for which man must be "conceded a glamour of
wonder" is his foredoomed effort to create order despite the monstrous. His collective forms exist, however, like the blue hotel, as an
"island of the sea." Set off from life, so much smaller and narrower
than the world they cannot hope to comprehend, they become the
self-created determinants of his fate. The individual imagination
requires the inhibition of social pressure lest, as Trescott learns, the
monster be "purely your own creation." Yet by remaining docile
within the moving box of tradition, we find our experience meaningless or we confront ourselves as murderers.

In the stories which frame the ironies of this cruel dilemma, Crane
made what H. G. Wells was to characterize as his "enormous repudiations." Inheriting the Transcendentalist contention that communal forms constitute man's self-created Atropos (to use Tho-
reau's figure), Crane could find no salvation in self-reliance or essential thinking. Emerson's living eyeball was now glazed: the ants
crawl horrifically toward the eyes of the corpse from which Fleming
flees; the Swede looks blindly at the register of his fate; the eyes of
Lean's dead comrade stare at the sky. Knowing that without moral
absolutes man might stand like Hawthorne's Dimmesdale, "in great
horror of mind," forced to extend "his egoism over the whole expanse of nature," Crane nevertheless found God dead in heaven.
Recoiling from the brush of the monster, like Ishmael he reached for
the handclasp of his buddy in the fraternity, only to have even that
solidarity splinter under his irony. Caught in no-man's land between
the absolute rest of death and the inscrutable dynamism of the
world, the Crane hero seems doomed to halter himself in society or
wander through the wilderness without hope of validating his experience. He totters, in short, on the precipice of Romantic solip-

sism, and fraternity is a precarious emotional ledge, precious at the price of a harness.

Thus Thomas Beer's often repeated diagnosis that Crane paid the price for having "made his body a testing ground for all sensations of living" might be amended, for it was Crane's mind, his imagination, which seems to have endured the greatest stress of testing. Like other neo-Romantics he sought to confront reality and be a true man, to harmonize the Cowboy's straightforward life of action and the Easterner's hold on certain certainties. But willing was not imagining, and "hope," he found, was "the most vacuous emotion of mankind."

His last real attempt to conceive of harmony was fought out in *The Red Badge*, a work whose hero constantly "conceives" of himself in relation to a meaningful world and suffers continual derangement. Crane tries to suggest that Fleming can gain salvation in losing his egocentricity in the "delirium" which is the "temporary but sublime absence of selfishness," and which apparently allows Henry to assume "unconsciously" the decorum of the color-bearer. While his great moments seem principally a result of a dulling of consciousness, we are nevertheless told discursively that in battle Henry remains "deeply absorbed as a spectator." Crane, that is, would like to imagine that the youth has achieved both commitment and detachment, both participation and withdrawal. But although we are told that Henry's mind has been "undergoing a subtle change," he is at the last again conceiving of himself self-consciously and the tension between rules and terror would seem unrelieved.

With "A Mystery of Heroism," however, Crane both accepts the impossibility of the integration Henry has ostensibly achieved and discovers a new heroic role. "Almost . . . a part of the clay bank," Collins can find no wholeness short of it, and amid the "clamour of death" only the guns retain "demeanours of stolidity and courage," "typical of something infinitely self-possessed." Fragmented men, fragmented action are tied together only by meaningless rules, and Collins, his "dulled mind groping after the form and colour of this incident," is unable to gain imaginative stability. His is the experience of the typical Crane protagonist, the internal struggle of a solitary man caught between incongruous conceptual modes: the metaphor of his fate is that of the metaphor hopelessly mixed. But if one's experience is bounded by the conventions, roles, and metaphors which constitute one's fraternity, bravery consists in abiding the contradictions which result. And the artist becomes *the* hero. The artist who committed himself to writing his stories as a single passionate and irrevocable act, who told a friend that the cry "I cared so much" was the beginning of wisdom, was a "savage religion mad." Yet, in arguing that one "can never do anything with anything that's any good except aesthetically" and counseling young men to consider the world's "artists in alligator growing and the promulgation of mixed vegetables," he was also a "carpenter." Barbaric and decorous, an individual yet a member of his fraternity, he officiates over what he calls "A Mystery": he becomes the master of ceremonies, the arbiter of conceptual modes, the completer of metaphor, whole and self-possessed in his demeanor of stolidity and courage. Thus the paradoxes of a Bohemian seeking order, a quiet gentle boy yearning for the boisterous West, a minister's son chasing war, a savage seeking propriety, are all subsumed in the experience of the artist. And the decorum of the artist becomes the measure of a man.

Naturalism and Impressionism
in Stephen Crane's Fiction

by Sergio Perosa

One of the most interesting aspects of Stephen Crane's fiction lies in its characteristic combination of naturalistic and impressionistic elements. The composite nature of his work has given rise to many one-sided interpretations; but the novelty, significance, and representative quality of his fiction is to be found in its combination and, as it were, symbiosis, of some freely-accepted naturalistic premises with an impressionistic method of presentation, at first instinctively, then consciously applied to his work.

The interrelationship of the two terms is further complicated by the fact that in Crane the practice of writing often precedes theoretical formulations and critical statements. He expounds theories at the very moment of contradicting them in his work; he puts forth literary principles that his artistic performance has already superseded. Moreover, influences and borrowings which would seem unquestionable at first glance are in fact, more often than not, known and appreciated *post factum*—*after* the composition of those works they should presumably influence.

The critic wanders in a labyrinth of possibilities, which every new turn taken by Crane's fiction seems to explode or deny. But neither this, nor the dialectic relation between Naturalism and Impressionism in his work, ought to surprise. These two artistic trends, far from being mutually exclusive, developed almost simultaneously at the end of the nineteenth century, and the particular nature of

"Naturalism and Impressionism in Stephen Crane's Fiction." From "Stephen Crane fra naturalismo e impressionismo" in *Annali di Ca' Foscari*, III (1964), 119-142, reprinted with minor changes in *Le vie della narrativa americana* (Milano: Mursia, 1965). Reprinted by permission of Ugo Mursia Editore and of the author, who has prepared an abridged and slightly revised version of his original essay especially for this volume. The translation is the author's.

their relation is in fact of the greatest importance for a proper understanding of *fin de siècle* and early twentieth-century fiction on both sides of the Atlantic.

In the 1890s, Walter Pater's and Oscar Wilde's aestheticism developed side by side with William Archer's and George Bernard Shaw's battle for the acceptance of Ibsen's "naturalistic" theatre; the experimental and impressionistic formulations of Henry James and Joseph Conrad coincided with the renewed naturalistic *engagement* of George Gissing, George Moore, and Thomas Hardy himself. The decade was an incredible crucible, bristling with contradictions. The Celtic Revival, with its fairies and romantic yearning, was contemporary with the ironic and *blasé* explosion of the Yellow Book; Arthur Symons discovered the French Symbolists while Emile Zola and the Goncourt brothers excited interest and enthusiasm. Never was *l'art pour l'art* so much talked about, and yet social documents and denunciations multiplied, while writers like Shaw, H. G. Wells, and Rudyard Kipling still showed a belief in the relevance of a moral, social, or political message.

Impressionistic painting began as a reaction against illustrative realism—the very method of Naturalism. Yet, although they were later to follow different routes, one can safely maintain that they were born out of the same nineteenth-century matrix: the pretence, or the illusion, of developing new artistic methods in accordance with the premises and the practice of science.

As is well known, in *Le roman experimental* (1880) Zola offered the experimental scientist as a model for the novelist. To reproduce reality, he maintained, one should first gather the data and the documentation; one dissects the human animal and analyzes his behavior in order to trace the course of the great scientific laws that regulate life—physiological heredity, environment and social determinism, etc.—and that confirm the writer's diagnosis. (In the far background looms large the theory of evolution, which fascinated and at the same time frightened the second half of the century.)

On the other side, impressionistic painting was originally an attempt to apply to traditional painting the new optic discoveries on the nature of colors and on the decomposition and recomposition of light on the retina to produce them. Here we are in a different context, but still under the spell of science. Impressionistic painters and writers ended up, of course, by breaking up the nineteenth-century ideal of photographic realism, which Naturalists pursued to its extreme consequences; but suffice it here to note that their starting point was similar and that it accounts, at least partially, for the historical concurrence of the two phenomena.

This concurrence is in fact perfectly recognizable in Stephen Crane's fiction. His first literary attempts (the *Sullivan County Sketches*, completed in 1892) betray the stylistic influence of early Kipling. But in that same year, Crane realized that he had to renounce "the clever school in literature" in order to develop the "little creed of art" which he was soon to find "identical" with that of William Dean Howells and Hamlin Garland. In a letter to Lily Brandon Munroe in March, 1894 he was to write:

> You know, when I left you [August, 1892], I renounced the clever school in literature. It seemed to me that there must be something more in life than to sit and cudgel one's brains for clever and witty expedients. So I developed all alone a little creed of art which I thought was a good one. Later I discovered that my creed was identical with the one of Howells and Garland and in this way I became involved in the beautiful war between those who say that art is man's substitute for nature and we are the most successful in art when we approach the nearest to nature and truth, and those who say—well, I don't know what they say. They don't, they can't say much but they fight villainously and keep Garland and I out of the big magazines. Howells, of course, is too powerful for them.
>
> If I had kept to my clever, Rudyard-Kipling style, the road might have been shorter but, ah, it wouldn't be the true road.

Howells had recently expounded his concept of genteel realism in *Criticism and Fiction* (1891), where he upheld the principles of truth and faithfulness to nature, within the framework of the "highest morality," as the test of good writing:

> I confess that I do not care to judge any work of the imagination without first of all applying this test to it. We must ask ourselves before we ask anything else, Is it true? . . . This truth, which necessarily includes the highest morality and the highest artistry—this truth given, the book cannot be wicked and cannot be weak. . . . In the whole range of fiction I know of no true picture of life—that is, of human nature—which is not also a masterpiece of literature, full of divine and natural beauty. . . .
>
> If I were authorized to address any word directly to our novelists I should say, Do not trouble yourselves about standards or ideals; but try to be faithful and natural.

"To discover principles, not to establish them; to report, not to create," was Howells' precept. But his realism was in fact a theory of

the average and the commonplace, the expression of a domestic—
not even bourgeois—ideal.

It was easy for Hamlin Garland to maintain that Howells' realism,
with its insistence on decorum, decency, and humor, was not "that
of the French." Zola, it is true, had gone "to the opposite extreme";
but Garland himself was mildly to follow in that direction. Three
years later, in *Crumbling Idols* (1894), he expounded the principles
of what, for want of a better term, he called "Veritism." Garland accepted to a far greater extent than Howells the naturalistic principles of physiological heredity and social determinism, together
with the concept of a scientific, photographic, and documentary reproduction of life, even at its lowest, to serve the purposes of social
denunciation: principles which had inspired to a remarkable extent
his first book, *Main-Travelled Roads* (1891).

In 1892, Crane might have known this book, and it is likely that
he knew *Criticism and Fiction*: in his dedication of a copy of *Maggie*
to Howells, he was to attribute to his influence the "readjustment
of point of view" of which he speaks in the letter already quoted.
At this stage he repeated Howells almost verbatim in his insistence
on truth and faithfulness to life as requisites for the writer, convincing himself (as appears from a letter of November, 1895 to an editor of *Leslie's Weekly*) that "the nearer a writer gets to life, the
greater he becomes as an artist." All his fiction, he maintained in
the same letter, aimed at the ambitious goal of realism: Tolstoy was
the writer he most admired.

In the same letter, however, Crane wanted to make it clear that
he had always been "an independent writer," writing on any subject
that might occasionally interest him. No matter how sincere and
spontaneous, therefore, his acceptance of Naturalism, equally instinctive and deep appears to be his early misunderstanding and
betrayal of it: and here is the crux of the critical question.

For that matter, an example of "selective" realism, which might
have opened the way and provided an early model for impressionistic writing, could already be found in writers like Maupassant and
Gautier, whom young Crane had greatly admired. Zola himself,
an early admirer and supporter of impressionistic painting, had
specified, although in a different context, that the new "experimental novel" was to be *"une expérience 'pour voir.'"* Garland
too, in *Crumbling Idols*, had devoted an essay to impressionistic
painting and had stressed the necessary *subjectivity* of the artist,
writing that his task lay in "facing certain facts and telling his indi-

vidual relations to them"; in a letter to Eldon C. Hill, moreover, explaining the meaning of the word "Veritism" he had invented, Garland would have declared himself an impressionist: "In truth I was an impressionist in that I presented life and landscape as I personally perceived them, but since I sought a deeper significance in the use of the word, I added a word which subtended verification. I sought to verify my impression by comparing impressions separated by an interval of time."

Now, at his official début with *Maggie: A Girl of the Streets* (1893), Crane was hailed as a "pure naturalist" by both Howells and Garland, and he was encouraged and indeed urged by them to proceed in that direction. He gladly accepted the recognition and his inclusion among the writers of "narrative radicalism," justifying, as we have seen, their trust and expectation by numerous repetitions of their favorite tenets concerning the role of the artist. In obeisance to their views, he would try to get a more direct and documentary experience of life in New York, by which to profit in his work.

The first draft of *Maggie*, however, had already been written in 1891, before he came to New York City and had any experience of slum life. Although the short novel was rewritten in the winter of 1892-93, it dealt originally with an "imagined reality" only later to be subjected to "experimentation." Crane insisted on its naturalistic inspiration, in his well-known statement to the effect that he was trying to show that environment is a tremendous thing and often shapes our lives regardless: but this is only one side of the question.

In fact, the naturalistic principle of physiological heredity plays an important part in the girl's degeneration (her mother is an alcoholic) ; social determinism is clearly indicated (the oppressive presence of the factory); only at a later stage were the characters given names, the main purpose being at first strictly documentary. The insistence on squalid details is typical of social denunciations; the use of slang itself answers a documentary and photographic need, rather than an expressive purpose.

Crane was soon to realize, however, as he states in a letter to John N. Hilliard, that preaching would be fatal to literature; although he offered the reader "a slice of life," he would leave him free to draw the moral lesson. In the case of *Maggie*, we can easily draw the moral lesson: but we realize, too, that the "slice of life" is not given in a documentary and photographic manner, but according to an instinctive principle of impressionistic rendering.

The short novel is built on a sequence of short and intense dramatic scenes. The use of foreshortening emphasizes only the crucial episodes; the setting is rendered through vivid and precise notations of visual details; and most of the incidents are presented through the limited point of view of the single characters: Pete (in section XVI), Jimmie, and Maggie herself, dazzled by the lights of the theatre, dismayed by the insensibility of her family, filled with consternation by the hostile city. The method of presentation is on the whole indirect; for example, in the crucial scene of Maggie's seduction, the episodes are filtered through the eyes— if not yet the conscience—of the characters.

The plot is reduced to a minimum and the 19 sections are juxtaposed, as it were, in a cinematographic way—cut, selected, and pieced together by a kind of rapid and essential montage, which is more evocative and suggestive than descriptive; it is desultory and a bit disconnected, as in the case of silent films. A neglect of plot was not uncommon in naturalistic fiction: but the careful montage of dramatic and suggestive scenes was already a feature of impressionistic fiction—in Conrad as well as in Chekhov, in Katherine Mansfield as well as in the Joyce of *Dubliners*. The sharpness and precision of diction in *Maggie* remind us of this work; the girl's disconsolate melancholy foreshadows Katherine Mansfield's existential suffering; the pervasive pathos of the story, especially at the end, seems to prefigure Georges Bernanos' *Nouvelle histoire de Mouchette*.

In tracing the course of Maggie's pathetic initiation into life and sin, that is, Crane has instinctively discovered and applied the basic canons of impressionistic writing: the apprehension of life through the play of perceptions, the significant montage of sense impressions, the reproduction of chromatic touches by colorful and precise notations, the reduction of elaborate syntax to the correlation of sentences, which leads to a sketchy, and at the same time evocative, kind of writing. A quotation from Section II is sufficient to illustrate this:

> Eventually they entered a dark region where, from a careening building, a dozen gruesome doorways gave up loads of babies to the street and the gutter. A wind of early autumn raised yellow dust from cobbles and swirled it against a hundred windows. Long streamers of garments fluttered from fire-escapes. In all unhandy places there were buckets, brooms, rags, and bottles. In the street infants played or fought with other infants or sat stupidly in the way of vehicles. Formidable women, with uncombed hair and disordered dress, gos-

sipped while leaning on railings, or screamed in frantic quarrels. Withered persons, in curious postures of submission to something, sat smoking pipes in obscure corners. A thousand odours of cooking food came forth to the street. The building quivered and creaked from the weight of humanity stamping about in its bowels.

The conclusion of Section VI would offer an equally convincing example. The first intention, therefore, may aim at a naturalistic denunciation; but the artistic rendering gives us an impressionistic vision of that sordid reality. Crane himself was to realize that his short novel was "a succession of sharply outlined pictures, which pass before the reader like a panorama, leaving each its definite impression." Van Wyck Brooks saw the work as "consisting of verbal impressions mainly," while Charles C. Walcutt, so much interested in Crane's naturalism, was to stress the naturalistic quality of what he called, after all, Crane's "impressionism."

The same can be said of the other "Bowery Tales," in which disconnected sense impressions—for the most part visual and auditory impressions—and chromatic vignettes serve to evoke (not to describe) a colorful reality and a direct "impression of life." A thoroughly objective attitude is enlivened by the intensity of a personal —and therefore *subjective*—vision.

For "An Experiment in Misery" and "The Men in the Storm" (probably written in 1894) Crane had gathered a direct experience of life, living among the underdogs of the Bowery at Garland's instigation; but his documentary purpose resolves itself into a wealth of visual details and an impressionistic vividness of social notations. Everything is made colorful, visible, immediately evident; the impression of life that is conveyed is always filtered through the writer's subjectivity. Any discursive or purely narrative possibility is sacrificed to immediacy: the descriptive beginning of "An Experiment in Misery" was discarded before book publication. The vividness of details leads thus to sudden "epiphanies" of reality: Edward Garnett was right in stressing the "nervous audacity of phrasing, . . . the quality of chiaroscuro of a master's etching" to be found in this tale. Crane was experimenting with new forms of writing and finding confirmation in his impressionistic vocation.

He said he was aiming at the real thing ("But to get at the real thing!"), using Henry James's own metaphor; and like James, he was soon to realize that the artist's greatness lies in imagining and recreating reality, not in transcribing it. This was his youthful advice to his friend Arthur Oliver, who has kept record of it:

Treat your notions like that—he said, scooping up a handful of sand and tossing it to the brisk sea-breeze—Forget what you think about it and tell how you feel about it.—And then years later, when this same inquiring writer queried Crane whether he would now revise the advice he had given him that day on the beach, Crane said emphatically—No. You've got to feel the things you write if you want to make an impact on the world.

It was a plea not only for the artist's personal involvement, but also for the necessary subjectivity of his vision. In his war tales Crane was to rely more and more on the principles of impressionistic rendering—writing as he was of a war he did not know but only imagined and recreated on the page.

Written in 1893, shortly after the "naturalistic" *Maggie, The Red Badge of Courage* shares with the earlier novel the theme of a young person's initiation into life, or indeed the wider theme of the individual's relation to a hostile world, over which, in this case, the protagonist triumphs. "It was an effort born of pain—despair, almost; and I believe that this made it a better piece of literature than it otherwise would have been. It seems a pity that art should be a child of pain, and yet I think it is," Crane was to write in his letter to the editor of *Leslie's Weekly*. He considered *The Red Badge* as the amplification of a mere episode; elsewhere he was to call it a psychological portrait of fear. All these definitions are fairly accurate and useful: the novel can be seen as an amplification of a mere episode—a crucial episode that marks the transition from the illusions of adolescence to an acceptance of responsibility in life. It is a psychological portrait of fear: but it is artistically valid exactly because it is "realized" in a context of vivid and concrete sense impressions, of physical references to the field of battle. The "mere episode" achieves all the conspicuousness and the resonance bestowed upon it by an impressionistic rendering of the details within the scenes, and of the scenes within the general framework.

Although Crane had no personal experience of war, he had probably read Tolstoy and Ambrose Bierce on the subject, and had listened to his brother William recounting episodes of the Civil War. But he was more than ever dealing with "imagined reality," and this was bound to lead him to a kind of evocative, rather than descriptive, writing. The novel belongs to the tradition of the *Lehrjahre* and the *Bildungsroman*; but the story of Henry Fleming's victory over himself achieves a perfect thematic *and* formal unity thanks to the impressionistic quality of its texture. According to Agostino Lombardo (in his introduction to the Italian edition of the *Tales*), this kind of impressionism is an instrument for the representation of the moral and psychological inner life of the protagonist. But the contrary is also true: the inexhaustible ferment of Henry Fleming's moral and psychological inner life achieves its own peculiar kind of "epiphany" by being rendered in concrete and physical terms—in terms of light and shadow, sounds and colors, images and sense impressions.

The Red Badge of Courage is indeed a triumph of impressionistic vision and impressionistic technique. Only a few episodes are described from the outside; Fleming's mind is seldom analyzed in an objective, omniscient way; very few incidents are extensively *told*. Practically every scene is filtered through Fleming's point of view and seen through his eyes. Everything is related to his *vision*, to his *sense*-perception of incidents and details, to his *sense*-reactions rather than to his psychological impulses, to his confused sensations and individual impressions. Reality exists and can be artistically recreated in that it affects his eyes, his ears, his touch—his sensory, rather than mental, imagination. The battlefield is to Henry Fleming colorful and exciting, new and phantasmagoric, mysterious and unforeseen; it stimulates beyond measure, it exasperates his sensations. Thus stimulated, his impressions—above all his visual and auditory impressions—give *substance*, not only vividness, to the picture. Even his meditations on the psychological dilemma of fear are rendered as a staccato sequence of mental *impressions*, typical of a young mind dismayed by the spectacle of war.

It is basically a question of sight. Henry Fleming's is, first of all, a point of *view*: he is a source and a receptacle of impressions, and it is in their disconnected sequence that the phantom, and the meaning, of life is gradually brought to light. A simple statistical analysis on the linguistic level is quite revealing in this respect. One is struck at first glance by the recurrence of terms indicating visual perceptions. Verbs like *to see, perceive, look, observe, gaze, witness, watch, stare, peer, cast eyes, discover,* etc. appear on practically every page, indeed, no less than 350 times in this fairly short novel. Expressions like *to seem, appear, look like, exhibit, glare, gleam, shine, flash, glimmer, display, loom, show, reveal,* etc. occur no less than 200 times. Less numerous, but still quite frequent, are verbs of auditory perception (like *to hear,* etc.) or those expressing inner feeling (*to feel,* etc.), especially when Henry Fleming is wounded or regaining consciousness. Examples like the following are quite common and, indeed, quite revealing (italics added) :

> The youth *turned quick eyes* upon the field. He *discerned* forms begin to swell in masses out of a distant wood. He again *saw* the tilted flag speeding forward.

> He *saw* that the ground in the deep shadows was cluttered with men, sprawling in every conceivable posture. *Glancing* narrowly into the more distant darkness, he *caught* occasional *glimpses* of visages that *loomed* pallid and ghostly, *lit* with a phosphorescent glow.

> The youth's *eyes* had instantly turned in the direction indicated by the awakened and agitated lieutenant, and he *had seen* the haze of treachery *disclosing* a body of soldiers of the enemy. They were so near that he could *see* their features. There was a *recognition* as he *looked at* the types of faces. Also he *perceived* with dim amazement that their uniforms were rather gay in effect, being light gray, accented with a brilliant-hued facing. Too, the clothes *seemed* new.

> He stood, erect and tranquil, *watching* the attack begin against a part of the line that made a blue curve along the side of an adjacent hill. His *vision* being unmolested by smoke from the rifles of his companions, he had opportunities to *see* parts of the hard fight. It was a relief to *perceive* at last from whence came some of these noises which had been roared into his ears.

The rhythm of perception is ceaseless and pressing, continual and almost obsessive. We get the impression of life displaying itself to the apprehension of human conscience. Henry Fleming's "mind took a mechanical but firm impression, so that afterward everything was pictured and explained to him." The impression can be mechanical, but it is firm and allows us to form the picture; once the picture has been formed, everything can be explained. It sounds almost like a definition of Crane's own method, if it is true that he identifies himself with Fleming's point of view and consciousness. By faithfully recording *his* sensations, Crane gives substance and shape to the dramatic scene or the evoked picture, and the gradual unfolding of the meaning coincides with the slow process of perception. The total picture is the sum of the infinite touches and sense impressions, and must be focused anew at each step or turn of the process: it is the characteristic manner of impressionistic rendering.

Crane sticks to this method also in those parts which are not seen through Fleming's limited point of view and in which only the *sense* of his *possible* perceptions is given. And such a method, of course, as appears from the previous quotations, deeply affects the stylistic texture. It forces language to an unprecedented terseness of diction and conciseness of statement, breaking it down into very short sentences, whose *progression d'effet* is cadenced and leads in each case to an intense revelation of reality:

> He lay down on a wide bunk that stretched across the end of the room. In the other end, cracker boxes were made to serve as furniture. They were grouped about the fireplace. A picture from an illustrated weekly was upon the log walls, and three rifles were paralleled on pegs. . . . A folded tent was serving as a roof. The sunlight, without, beating upon it, made it glow a light yellow shade.

> The fire crackled musically. From it swelled light smoke. Overhead the foliage moved softly. The leaves, with their faces turned toward the blaze, were colored shifting hues of silver, often edged with red.

> When another night came the columns, changed to purple streaks, filed across two pontoon bridges. A glaring fire wine-tinted the waters of the river. Its rays, shining upon the moving masses of troops, brought forth here and there sudden gleams of silver or gold. Upon the other shore a dark and mysterious range of hills was curved against the sky. The insect voices of the night sang solemnly.

Crane himself had written to John N. Hilliard: "My chiefest desire was to write plainly. I endeavoured to express myself in the simplest and most concise way." The fleeting image of life is here captured and recreated in a phantasmagoric "panorama" of lines, colors, forms, and tones. The paragraphs break down into mere sentences, and the sentences are reduced to the simplest statements, according to a stylistic principle that was to influence, among others, Ernest Hemingway, and is the counterpart of the touch of pure color directly applied to the canvas by the impressionist painter.

This fragmentation of syntax, in fact, aims at the precision and terseness of the visual impression and leads to a "pictorial" achievement—to an airy "picture of life" which is the sum of the single impressionistic details: a lively and colorful picture of life apprehended, as it were, in action, in its displaying itself to Henry Fleming's, the writer's, and the reader's, perception.

What matters, of course, behind and beyond the inner vibration of Crane's impressionistic rendering, is the quality and the significance of the total achievement. But it is important here to stress the nature of the technical method that makes it possible and gives a particular flavor to the underlying theme of the novel. In this respect, it is clear that Fleming's basic experience can be identified with the gradual process of his perception and recognition of reality —a process which becomes all the more meaningful and significant in that it is impressionistically presented *as such*. His ordeal is the ordeal of fear; his dilemma is whether to face or to escape reality: but the moral victory he achieves over himself is strictly related to the gradual disclosing of his perception over the spectacle, and the meaning, of life.

A few naturalistic remnants are still to be found in the novel: Crane's avowed intention of making Fleming as "representative" as possible; his resorting to types, rather than full characters, for the secondary roles; the use of descriptive, rather than proper, names (the "tall soldier" etc.) ; the use of slang for documentary purposes; and the attempt to present the common soldiers as "underdogs" in a careless and ruthless world (the officers call them "mule drivers" or "mud diggers") and therefore trampled on and irresponsibly sent to a useless death.

But the cultural and historical context in which the novel was written and the inspiration sustaining it remain basically impressionistic: and this explains why, when in 1897 Crane moved to England, he was hailed by English writers and critics as "the chief impressionist of the age" (Edward Garnett), as "the impressionist par excellence" (Joseph Conrad). They referred of course to the fiction-writer, but it is also to be remembered that Crane's recent collection of poems (*The Black Riders and Other Lines*, 1895, which he seemed to value more than *The Red Badge of Courage*) gave further proof of his mastery of the short, impressionistic notation and of the sharp formulation of thoughts and images. It was clearly influenced by Emily Dickinson's taste for the short lyric; but it also paved the way for the Imagist poets, leaving no doubt as to Crane's double role as an innovator.

His fiction seemed indeed to conform to the new principles of impressionistic writing which were being developed at the time in England by Conrad, Garnett, and Ford Madox Hueffer (Ford). The best definition of its aims and methods is to be found in Conrad's well-known preface to *The Nigger of the "Narcissus"* (1897). Fiction, Conrad wrote, if it at all aspires to be art—appeals to temperament. . . . Such an appeal to be effective must be an impression conveyed through the senses. . . . All art, therefore, appeals primarily to the senses, and the artistic aim when expressing itself in written words must also make its appeal through the senses. . . . It must strenuously aspire to the plasticity of sculpture, to the colour of painting, and to the magic suggestiveness of music—which is the art of arts.

The writer's task is to render and convey to the reader the sense impression in all its terseness and conspicuity, to capture the fleeting image of life in order to reveal its underlying secret:

> My task which I am trying to achieve is, by the power of the written word to make you hear, to make you feel—it is, before all, to make you *see*. . . .
>
> To snatch in a moment of courage, from the remorseless rush of time, a passing phase of life, is only the beginning of the task. The task approached in tenderness and faith is to hold up unquestioningly, without choice and without fear, the rescued fragment before all eyes in the light of a sincere mood. It is to show its vibration, its colour, its form; and through its movement, its form and its colour, reveal the substance of its truth—disclose its inspiring secret: the stress and passion within the core of each convincing moment. . . .
>
> And when it is accomplished—behold!—all the truth of life is there: a moment of vision, a sigh, a smile. . . .

Ford Madox Ford was later to repeat incessantly the same concepts and to provide the epistemological grounds of the new technique ("We saw that Life did not narrate, but made impressions on our brains. We in turn, if we wished to produce on you an effect of life, must not narrate but render . . . impressions"). They both aimed at conciliating objective reality with subjective vision; in both cases, the final meaning and the total effect was to be achieved by reproducing the process of perception and discovery; each "moment of vision" led to the revelation of the whole truth.

The Red Badge of Courage appeared right in the middle of this tranquil literary revolution, embodying all the features of the new impressionistic novel. Crane was taken for a follower and a disciple: he was in fact a forerunner, instinctively applying to his work all the new principles that were being formulated in England. His novel can be read in the light of Conrad's poetics, which seems to account perfectly well for its method and its achievement.

It is based, as we have seen, on an impressionistic rendering of sense perceptions (its appeal is "made through the senses") ; it tries strenuously to make us hear, to make us feel, to make us, before all, *see*; by showing the vibration, the color, the form of the rescued fragment, it gradually reveals the substance of its truth, its inspiring secret—"the stress and passion within the core of each convincing moment." In Crane, too, the truth of life is revealed in the "moment of vision" incessantly repeated. If art, as Conrad maintained, could be defined as "a single-minded attempt to render the highest kind of justice to the visible universe," this was indeed Crane's achievement; Crane too was trying to bring to light the truth underlying its aspects, its forms, its colors, its lights and shadows—as Conrad had required of the artist in the same preface. Through his impressionistic rendering he aimed at discovering what is "fundamental, lasting and essential" in the fleeting aspects of life; and if he succeeded in capturing it, then the final picture is a composite, and at the same time unified, revelation of life—an interpretation, almost, of its secret, as it is given in terms of human suffering and moral conscience.

The fact is that the technical method is not only perfectly suited to express the theme of the novel: it actually merges and *coincides* with it. Henry Fleming has to undergo his initiation into life and achieve a moral victory over himself: but the *leitmotiv* of his adventure lies first of all in his gradual discovery of reality. He has to discover what is "fundamental, lasting and essential" in the rescued fragments of life which are offered to his perception: this is what he does, and what the writer himself does, through the gradual unfolding of Henry Fleming's process of perception. Capturing the phantom of life in its many-colored and mysterious aspects is for Fleming an initiation into life; the sum of his impressions leads him to a recognition of the world and to an acceptance of his own role in it. This is the meaning of his experience, but also a description of Crane's rendering of the theme. Theme and process coincide.

This is why Crane's impressionistic rendering is perfectly in keeping with the theme of the novel and embodies it in the best possible way. Henry Fleming's initiation into life coincides and is one with his perception of it; by assuming Fleming's point of view and sticking to *his* process of perception, Crane can succeed in unfolding the meaning of his experience and in conveying its ultimate sense to the reader. In this way *The Red Badge of Courage* can be regarded as a triumph of impressionistic rendering: it is not merely a question of technical devices and expressive vehicles, but of a perfect coincidence of aims and means, of formal intention and thematic substance. A formal method strictly consistent with the theme enhances and enlivens in an original way an artistic vision which is, by its very nature, an experience of life.

The dialectic of Naturalism and Impressionism does not stop here, but runs through the rest of Crane's fiction. A detailed analysis would show that while *George's Mother* (completed in 1894, the year following *The Red Badge*) represents a backward step in its fundamental adherence to naturalistic principles, war tales like "A Mystery of Heroism," "The Upturned Face," and "An Episode of War" are further examples of an impressionistic rendering of "imagined reality." "The Open Boat," with its rigorous application of the point of view and its balanced structure, with its dramatic compression and impressionistic foreshortening, transfigures an actual occurrence into existential drama, and confers universal meaning and poetic value on the simple retelling of man's struggle for survival.

The final turn of Crane's fictional parable is again twofold: the quiet realism of his Western tales (like "The Bride Comes to Yellow Sky") and child stories ("The Knife," "His New Mittens") contrasts markedly with the grotesque, almost expressionistic violence of tales like "The Blue Hotel," "An Illusion in Red and White," and *The Monster*. This later development, which would of course deserve a fuller treatment, is perfectly in keeping with Crane's early achievement and with the historical trend of the time: Expressionism grew out of, as much as it reacted to, Impressionism, and such a transition is distinctly recognizable in Crane's later fiction, especially in *The Monster*.

Judging now of his achievement in the context of his time and in the light of an analysis that is fully aware of its composite nature, we can then see how Crane—willingly or unwillingly, consciously or unconsciously—succeeded in a personal and original reconciliation of two of the most significant literary trends of the period. Such a reconciliation was admirably achieved in at least two of his major works and characterizes his most interesting attempts. If, however, the dialectic relation of Naturalism and Impressionism is the peculiar feature of Crane's fiction, it is also typical of his period. In its intrinsic value lies also its representative quality; Stephen Crane's unmistakable sign is also the revealing sign of his age.

Stephen Crane's Magic Mountain

by James B. Colvert

The weaknesses of Stephen Crane's *The Red Badge of Courage* are important clues to the real issue raised in the novel—indeed, to the fundamental issue raised in all of Crane's important work. These weaknesses all stem, actually, from one weakness: Crane's inability to control the metaphor which is not only central to his novel but is also the master symbol of his characteristic attitudes, ideas, and feelings about man, God, and the universe. I refer to the constantly recurring image in his work—both poetry and fiction—of the little man in conflict with the hostile mountain. The meaning of the figure is complex, and I shall deal with it directly later on. But I should like first to approach it indirectly by examining the consequences of Crane's imperfect mastery of it in *The Red Badge of Courage*.

Although the novel might appear to be a straightforward account of how a self-centered young man acquires, as a result of his war experiences, a measure of redeeming wisdom, the problems raised in the story are not clearly defined or resolved. As a consequence the ending is confused and unconvincing. We are told that Henry Fleming is a changed man, but we are not told how he is supposed to have met the conditions implicitly required of him in the first sixteen chapters. In the first part of the story Henry is the target of the narrator's relentless ironic criticism, scored for his delusions of grandeur, his assumption that he somehow merits a special place in the regard of the universe. And though Crane labors in the final chapter to convince us that his hero has rid himself of these delusions, the deterioration in the quality of the writing—the appearance of a tendency toward incoherence—shows that the task is too much for him. The tone shifts inappropriately, the irony is erratic and often misdirected, and the hero is permitted certain assumptions

"Stephen Crane's Magic Mountain." This essay was written especially for this volume by Professor Colvert. © 1967 by James B. Colvert.

inconsistent with his previous characterization and Crane's established attitudes toward him.

Here is an example of Crane's treatment of Henry early in the novel, when the hero is under the spell of his sentimental image of himself as a conquering hero:

> In visions he had seen himself in many struggles. He had imagined peoples secure in the shadow of his eagle-eyed prowess. . . . He had burned several times to enlist. Tales of great movements shook the land. They might not be distinctly Homeric, but there seemed to be much glory in them. He had read of marches, sieges, conflicts, and he had longed to see it all. His busy mind had drawn for him large pictures extravagant in color, lurid with breathless deeds.

It is just such sentimental hallucinations, Crane makes clear, that render Henry unfit by upsetting his moral balance. This being the case, the reader of course expects to be shown a corrected state of mind proper to the redemption claimed for him at the end of the book. But Crane disappoints us. Consider, for example, Henry's state of mind as he leads the regiment in a magnificent charge against the enemy:

> Within him, as he hurled himself forward, was born a despairing fondness for this flag which was near him. It was a creation of beauty and invulnerability. It was a goddess, radiant, that bended its form with an imperious gesture to him. It was a woman, red and white, hating and loving, that called him with the voice of his hopes. Because no harm could come to it he endowed it with power. He kept near, as if it could be a saver of lives.

Now there may be irony in Crane's treatment of Henry in this, but if so it is a different kind of irony. Crane approves the deed, and so we must assume that he approves the attitudes which motivate it. But the emotions here are not very much different from those Henry experiences in his self-glorifying daydreams. They do not seem appropriate. They are, one suspects, not the hero's feelings but Crane's; and if so, the passage suggests that the author's own heroic ideal is hardly more viable than that he mocks in his naïve hero. Even at best, the sense of the passage is ambiguous.

This tendency in Crane's treatment of Henry is not always obvious, but it represents fairly enough, I think, the insecurity of the author's control over his point of view. The tendency is also revealed in another, perhaps more significant, way. We recall that Crane's irony is directed not only against Henry's heroic reveries, but also against his egotistical assumptions about his relation to Nature. When things go badly, Henry believes unquestioningly that Nature is against him; when things go well, he believes just as deeply that Nature is friendly and sympathetic. Humiliated when he proves a coward in his first battle, he turns to Nature for solace and comfort. Wending his way in a forest, he is gratified by his reflection that Nature is "a woman with a deep aversion to tragedy"; he believes that She has provided in the high, arching boughs of the trees a little chapel for the refreshment of his spirit. Entering the chapel-like bower he is suddenly transfixed with horror and loathing. Sitting on the gentle brown carpet in the religious half-light, is a rotting corpse. When he tries to flee, it seems to him that nature has suddenly turned against him all its malice and fury, that the branches of the bower are now trying to throw him over on the unspeakable corpse.

Now at the end of the book when we are told that Henry's eyes are "at last opened to some new ways," that he "could look back upon the brass and bombast of his earlier gospels and see them truly," we must expect to be shown that he has cast off the crippling burden of this senseless subjectivism. Surely, we think, the lesson in the forest has been so well driven home that he would no longer find it strange to see a pure blue sky over the carnage of battle, no longer be astonished that Nature goes "tranquilly on with her golden process in the midst of so much devilment." Yet in the very last paragraphs of the novel we find him still on personal terms with Nature, turning "with a lover's thirst to images of tranquil skies, fresh meadows, cool brooks—an existence of soft and eternal peace." The last sentence is notoriously sentimental: "Over the river a golden ray of sun came through the hosts of leaden rain clouds." Thus Crane approves in Henry once again what he criticizes relentlessly up to the very turning point of the novel; and when Crane throws away in this manner the issue of his hero's conflict with Nature, he throws away also the richest theme in the story—and the basic theme of all his work.

Perhaps Crane suspected how inappropriate this resolution was to the true theme of the book, for as the manuscript shows, he edited the last pages heavily, deleting from Henry's final thoughts all references to his experience with Nature. In effect, Crane was attempting to eliminate the emphasis on Henry's struggle against a hostile Nature and the issue of the hero's sentimental misreading of Nature's meaning. One omitted sentence reads: "Echoes of his terrible combat with the arrayed forces of the universe came to his ears. . . ." Henry's thought that Nature might be capable of moral judgment—that "he had been wrong not to kiss the knife and bow to the cudgel"—is also edited out. References to the possible indifference of Nature are omitted, and a mocking observation that Henry, whose mood grows self-congratulatory at one point, "was . . . fraternizing again with nature" is likewise pencilled out. In short, the moral issue which Crane raises in his treatment of Nature in the novel is abandoned—or rather Crane attempts to abandon it. We should think that Henry's reflection that he could "no more stand upon places high and false, and denounce the distant planets" would be one of the essential earned insights, but Crane, trying to avoid the whole issue, struck the passage out, as if he himself had little faith in what he was really in effect claiming for his hero. Crane surely could not have accepted Henry's sentimental faith in a benign and sympathetic universe; yet this is the faith Crane gives him: "Over the river a golden ray of sun came through the hosts of leaden rain clouds."

The failure of the book then is a failure in tone and theme, and although the two weaknesses are related, they must be explained in different ways. The failure in tone is relatively easy. Crane's biography makes it clear that for all his cool skepticism and irony he was an imperfectly suppressed sentimentalist laboring under the spell of a naïve heroic ideal. A member of his family described him once as one of those "terribly romantic young men who would think it delightful to be shot at dawn and all that sort of thing." He was addicted to a certain romantic attitudinizing; he followed wars compulsively all his life, and his despatches from the battlefield often reflect the kind of sentimental chauvinism we sense in the "flag" passage quoted above. Still, Crane distrusted this in himself, and if we may judge from his letters, ironic self-criticism was habitual with him. Addicted himself to sentimentality, his ironic mockery of Henry is in effect self-censorship. So long as Crane's secret sympathies are exposed to the correction of his irony, the critical sense of his writing is clear enough. But how was Crane really to portray Henry as a genuine hero when his own conception of the heroic was undermined by a naïve and spurious sentimentalism? This is Crane's problem at the end of *The Red Badge*, and he has no real solution for it: he is forced to fall back upon the only conception of the heroic available to him, and stripped of its correcting irony it turns out after all to be not too much different from Henry Fleming's.

The uncertainty in the treatment of the Nature theme is harder to account for, but it is also more interesting because it leads directly to the most important issue in the study of Crane's work, throwing light not only on the flawed novel but on all of his important fiction and poetry.

A starting place is a passage in Chapter XVII of *The Red Badge* the description of Henry's first reactions on discovering that he is suddenly a hero:

> He had been a tremendous figure, no doubt. By this struggle he had overcome obstacles which he had admitted to be mountains. They had fallen like paper peaks, and he was now what he called a hero. And he had not been aware of the process. He had slept and, awakening, found himself a knight.

The passage is interesting for several reasons. It contains the main elements of the novel: the vainglorious hero, the image of Nature as antagonist, the critical irony of the narrator. It summarizes the situation up to this point and marks the turning point in the narrative. But the most interesting point is that Henry, at this crucial moment, should think of himself as securing a victory, not over the enemy or his fear of them, but over Nature. It is almost as if, in his imagination, he sees it as a revengeful victory over the traitorous forest which refused him the solace of its cathedral-like bower.

We are reminded, reading this passage, that Nature from the very beginning has been the real source of Henry's terror. Mountains, fields, streams, the night, the sun, appear in his disordered fancy in the guises of living creatures, monstrous and terrible. He sees the "red eyelike gleam of hostile campfires set in the low brows of distant hills," the "black columns [of enemy troops] disappearing on the brow of a hill like two serpents crawling from the cavern of night." Crossing a little stream he fancies that the black water looks back at him with "white bubble eyes," and that "fierce-eyed hosts" lurk in the shadow of the woods. When he deserts in his first battle he flees, not the attack of enemy troops, but the "onslaught of redoubtable dragons," the approach of the "red and green monsters."

Images of a hostile Nature may take a variety of metaphorical forms—monsters, dragons, ogres, demigods, and other such grotesqueries—but the most characteristic is the figure of the sinister mountain. It occurs several times in *The Red Badge*: "A dark and mysterious range of hills . . . curved against the sky," "the low brows of distant hills," huge careening boulders, "a cliff over which one tumbles at midnight." In one variation or another the mountain turns up somewhere in almost all of Crane's writings, always as an inimical force or spirit. The horizon in "The Open Boat" is "jagged with waves that seemed thrust up in points like rocks." Life's problems confront the hero of *George's Mother* like "granite giants" and he is "no longer erect to meet them." George shrinks from "chasms with inclined approaches" and "peaks" that "leaned toward him." The buildings in the sketches of slum life appear to the little people at their feet in "pitiless hues sternly high, forcing regal heads into the clouds, throwing no downward glances." But once the hero of *George's Mother,* like Henry Fleming, had a vision in which he saw himself as a conqueror, "a stern general pointing a sword at the nervous and abashed horizon."

Most of the stories in Crane's earliest work, *Sullivan County Sketches,* two years earlier in composition than *The Red Badge,* show its hero in conflict with various natural presences—black caves, bears, ghostly forests—but the most interesting is "The Mesmeric Mountain." The unnamed hero is "the little man." Hiking through the wild countryside he becomes lost and climbs a tree to get his bearings. In the distance he sees a mountain, glowering so angrily that he falls out of the tree in a fit of terror. After a time he approaches cautiously and sits under a tree to watch. The mountain looks harmless enough, and the little man returns, watchful and wary. The mountain attacks again, and again the hero is overwhelmed with terror—and this time, rage.

> As he felt the heel of the mountain about to crush his head, he sprang again to his feet. He grasped a handful of small stones and hurled them. "Damn you!" he shrieked loudly. The pebbles rang against the face of the mountain.

> The little man then made an attack. He climbed with hands and feet wildly. Brambles forced him back and stones slid from beneath his feet. The peak swayed and tottered, and was ever about to smite with a granite arm. The summit was a blaze of red wrath.

But the little man gains the summit, at last, and when he does, he experiences the wild emotions of a conqueror of the world. He struts grandly across the peak, strikes a heroic pose, and surveys the universe. He is no longer lost. "There," he says grandly, "is Boyd's house." The last sentence of the story reads: "But the mountain under his feet was motionless."

The relation of the fable to *The Red Badge* is obvious. It is at once a summary of the plot of the novel and an expansion of the

metaphor by which Henry interprets his victory. There are the familiar elements—the terror and rage of the hero, the hallucinatory imagery, the antagonism of Nature, the delusive victory, the
heroics, the narrator's ironic commentary. By the time Crane
started writing *The Red Badge* in 1893 he had repudiated the Sullivan County stories as immature and unworthy; but he was never
to repudiate the basic elements of these tales, for they are expressive of his deepest sense of the meaning of life. When we trace the
metaphor of the mountain through his poems, especially those in
The Black Riders, we get further indication of its meaning.

The Black Riders was Crane's favorite of all his books. He once
described it as "an ambitious effort" in which it was his "aim to comprehend [his] thoughts about life in general." Almost all of the
nearly 70 poems are on religious themes—the inscrutability of God,
man's futile quest for God, God's wrath, the terrors of a Godless
universe, human pride, and human impotence. One poem, oddly,
is a mockery of romantic idealism, the hero being a medieval young
man who dreams of his noble death in full armor, sword in hand,
in a forest fight with a black assassin. Several give versions of the
fable of the little man and the angry mountain:

> On the horizon the peaks assembled;
> And as I looked,
> The march of the mountains began.
> As they marched, they sang,
> "Ay! we come! we come!"

The opening lines of another read:

> Once I saw mountains angry,
> And ranged in battle-front.
> Against them stood a little man;
> Ay, he was no bigger than my finger.

Another poem implies that the mountain is the cruel way to an
unattainable heaven:

> The hard hills tore my flesh;
> The ways bit my feet.
> At last I looked again.
> No radiance in the far sky,
> Ineffable, divine;
> No vision painted upon a pall;
> And always my eyes ached for the light.

In a manuscript version of still another poem where the image appears in a variation as housetops, the hero flings a challenge at the sun and God appears leading an army:

> Once a man clambering to the housetops
> Appealed to the empty heavens.
> With strong voice he called to the imperturbable stars;
> A warrior's shout he raised to the higher suns.
> Lo, at last, there was an indication, a dot,
> Then—finally—God—the sky was filled with armies.

And still again the central image of a poem is mountains in lofty communion with God, indifferent to man:

> In the night
> Grey heavy clouds muffled the valleys,
> And the peaks looked toward God alone.

The poem goes on to contrast the imperturbable vigil of the mountains with the daytime scurry of humanity in their "little black cities"; at the end it is night again. Man is shrouded in darkness once more and the silent peaks still "look toward God alone."

Finally, the image appears in a more hopeful poem on the resurrection theme:

> When a people reach the top of a hill,
> Then does God lean toward them,
> Shortens tongues and lengthens arms.
> A vision of their dead comes to the weak.

The single-minded earnestness with which Crane pursues his disturbing visions is remarkable. Clearly, these poems express a state of profound spiritual unrest. Is God dead in heaven, the questioning runs, and man alone in a heedless universe? Or is He terribly alive, breathing malice and hatred on helpless little men? Or is He perhaps a kindly God, screened from the view of man? What hope has man, burdened with sin and guilt, pride and self-love, to enter His Kingdom, if it does exist? Worrying these questions, Crane is torn between blasphemy and piety. "I hate Thee, unrighteous picture," he rages against the God of Wrath. But to the man who says the roaring thunder is the voice of God, he says, "Fool. Not so. The voice of God whispers in the heart." Crane's skepticism, nevertheless, seems to tip the balance: the idea of a personal God, either wrathful or kindly, he cannot accept; his reluctant conclusion is that God, whoever He might be, is simply unknowable to man. The bitter irony he turns on the blind little men of earth who strut and rage and cry out for Him is at once the mockery of their outrageous presumption and his own painful disbelief.

Considering the facts of Crane's biography, we find nothing surprising in this. His father was the Reverend Jonathan T. Crane, a gentle-hearted minister of the Methodist faith who bolted the Presbyterian Church as a young man because he refused to believe that God punished unconfirmed infants in the fires of hell. He wrote books inveighing against the evils of card-playing and dancing, and arguing, with the self-sufficient logic of the theologian, the existence of a benign, though inscrutable, God. "God could," he wrote in his book *Holiness the Birthright of All God's Children,* "if he deemed it best, so reveal himself that unbelief would be impossible. He might write his laws upon the azure skies. . . . He could smite every sinner at the very moment of his transgression with so stern and visible a hand that obedience would have little moral value. . . . That moral liberty may not be destroyed, God withdrew himself from human vision." Mrs. Crane's religion was not so gentle. Descended of a long line of fire-breathing Methodist preachers of the "old ambling-nag, saddle-bag, exhorting kind" (as Crane described her), she was herself a writer of religious tracts. Her views, apparently, were represented in a book by her uncle, Bishop Peck, titled *What Must I Do to be Saved?* "Your sins are remembered," Bishop Peck warned. "Every one charges upon your soul its infinite wrong, and demands the wrath of your offended Sovereign without mixture of mercy forever. . . . The Savior himself has condescended to inform you of the fearful doom which awaits you. You shrink from it with indescribable terror."

But we see Crane as a boy refusing the faith. "I used to like church and prayer meetings when I was a kid but that cooled off and when I was thirteen or about that, my brother Will told me not to believe in Hell after my uncle had been boring me about the lake of fire and the rest of the sideshows." We see him as a young man, Puritan turned Bohemian, in the old Art Students League Building in New York, living with a crowd of painters— "irresponsibles," a contemporary called them. We see him suffering because of his reputation for vicious living, hunted by the scandal of his common-law marriage to the madam of a Jacksonville bordello. We see him writing his brother Will of his "unworthiness," confessing from England that he had "managed his success like a

fool," reporting only three years before he died that he felt that he
was "slowly becoming a man." His biography reminds us of his
characteristic way of turning his irony against his own egotism and
pride. "I saw," he wrote in reference to his growing fame, "the
majestic forces which are arrayed against man's true success—not
the world—the world is silly, changeable, any of its decisions can
be reversed—but man's own colossal impulses more strong than
chains and I perceived that the fight was not going to be with the
world but with myself."

It is to all this—the spiritual unrest, the sense of guilt, the Christian abhorrence of pride, the fear of the thrusting ego—that the
metaphor of the little man and the mountain refers. The angry
mountain is an egotistical projection of the little man's demand
upon the notice of God, his bid for a place in God's personal affection and sympathy. And God, thus peremptorily summoned, sends
him green dragons and armies in the sky and rotting corpses in the
nave of Nature. The ironic narrator, taking a cue from the Reverend
Crane on the inscrutability of God, prompts the little man to note
the pure, blue unconscious sky, and heaps upon him his uneasy
scorn.

The meaning of the fable is amplified elsewhere in Crane's fiction. The Swede in "The Blue Hotel," his mind swarming with terror at the threat of an unknown menace is, we discover, really at
war with himself and an angry Nature. "We picture the world,"
Crane writes in his description of the Swede battling his way through
a storm,

> as thick with conquering and elate humanity, but here, with the
> bugles of the tempest pealing, it was hard to imagine a peopled earth.
> One viewed the existence of man then as a marvel, and conceded a
> glamor of wonder to these lice which were caused to cling to a whirl-
> ing, fire-smitten, ice-locked, disease-stricken, space-lost bulb. The con-
> ceit of man was explained by this storm to be the very engine of life.

"This weather," the Swede boasts later to the bartender, "I like it.
It suits me." The little man on the mountain. A few minutes later,
the Swede is dead, his open eyes fastened melodramatically on the
words on the saloon cash register: "This registers the amount of
your purchase."

And again we find the symbols of the fable in "The Open Boat,"
the story of the correspondent's anguished speculation about the
meaning of an ambivalent Nature. Is Nature the sign of God's mal-

ice, as the angry waves, the sinister gulls, the deadly shark suggest? Or is it the sign of God's benevolence, as the gentle swells, the beauty of the sea-birds sweeping across the sky suggest? Or is it merely impersonal and indifferent as the high cold star says? The correspondent is the only one of Crane's heroes who is allowed to see beyond the curtain of his conceit. And yet how little comfort in what he sees. "When it occurs to a man," he poignantly reflects,

> that Nature does not regard him as important . . . he at first wishes to throw bricks at the temple, and he hates deeply the fact that there are no bricks and no temples. Any visible expression of nature would surely be pelleted with his jeers. Then, if there be no tangible thing to hoot, he feels, perhaps, the desire to confront a personification and indulge in pleas, bowed to one knee, and with hands supplicant, saying, "Yes, but I love myself."

But the hero of *The Red Badge* conjures up tangible things to assault—the baleful sun at which he shakes his fist, the green dragons he charges at the head of his regiment, the angry mountain. As he stands victorious over the fallen peaks, he perceives, like the nameless hero of "The Mesmeric Mountain," that he is the conqueror of the world. But—to return at long last to the failure in the resolution of the novel—the idea is unthinkable. It violates the meaning of Crane's master symbol—the metaphor of the little man before the mountain. There are, after all, only victories in secular wars, inspired by flags; but there are no victories in wars against heaven. The contradiction, arising out of the rich implications of Crane's metaphor, brilliantly developed throughout the first sixteen chapters, is impossible to resolve. If Henry must be a victor, there is nothing to do but to revise him downward to an earthly hero, credit him with insights he has not earned, place on his shoulder the comforting arm of a tender mother Nature, and march him, serene and confident, out of the novel.

III

Discussions of Individual Works

Outstripping the Event:
Crane's *Maggie*

by Larzer Ziff

By January 1896 Crane, though not yet twenty-five years old, was famous enough to be assured of employment by Pulitzer or Hearst as a star reporter. Then he began reaping the crop of malice he had confidently expected when, as an unknown youngster, he had sown the seeds of naughty behavior. If his life with the art students on East Twenty-Third Street now gave rise to fallacious stories of his alcoholism and dope addiction, he was not surprised; indeed, he may have felt some gratification. A neophyte reporter caught up with him one night in New York, where Crane had stopped off after the shipwreck of his filibustering expedition, en route to the Greek War, and where he seemed to be lurking about the perimeter of night life. The cub tried to draw out his idol about his literary career with no success. But when he mentioned that he too was a minister's son, Crane immediately came to life and greeted him as a brother in a very special fraternity. "Have you ever observed," asked Crane, "how the envious laity exult when we are overtaken by misfortune?" And then, the cigarette in his lips marking time to the words, he added, "This is the point of view: The

"Outstripping the Event: Crane's *Maggie*." From *The American 1890's: Life and Times of a Lost Generation* (New York: Viking Press, 1966). © 1966 by Larzer Ziff. Reprinted by permission of The Viking Press, Inc.

bartender's boy falls from the Waldorf roof. The minister's son falls from a park bench. They both hit the earth with the same velocity, mutilated beyond recognition."

Crane was so convinced of this that his life had been led in anticipation of extreme reactions; he was determined to make good his belief if he had to climb to the roof of the Waldorf to be seen falling off the park bench. When he made enemies of the New York police by defending Dora Clark from their harrying, even though she was a known prostitute, he was acting on his sense of the way society would behave, a sense which he had projected into *Maggie* three years earlier without benefit of queanly associates. When rumor seized upon his gallant efforts on Dora Clark's behalf and concocted legends about his sexual life, he walked unerringly into an actual though less publicized liaison with the madam of a house of assignation, Cora Taylor. He would outstrip the event.

In the copy of *Maggie* which he had presented to Garland in 1893, Crane wrote:

> It is inevitable that you be greatly shocked by this book but continue, please, with all possible courage to the end. For it tries to show that environment is a tremendous thing in the world and frequently shapes lives regardless. If one proves that theory one makes room in Heaven for all sorts of souls (notably an occasional street girl) who are not confidently expected to be there by many excellent people.
>
> It is probable that the reader of this small thing may consider the Author to be a bad man, but, obviously, this is of small consequence to
>
> The Author

Before Garland read the book, the twenty-one-year-old author had been telling him what his reaction should be—"shock"—and how this might lead him to feel that the author was a bad man. The inscription reveals that in *Maggie* Crane was attempting to impose his personality on imagined material rather than to organize documentary material into a fiction. For the young author burning to be recognized, *Maggie* had less of an objective existence apart from himself than is ordinarily seen in the relation between novelists and their works. The objective content laid claim to in the inscription, that "environment is a tremendous thing," is qualified by the subjective expectation that "many excellent people" will have their confident beliefs overturned by it. Crane was, in *Maggie*, calling attention to himself, to a reality projected by his will rather than to one observed and ordered.

The shock received by the few early readers of the work, however, was probably no different from the one received today by those
unfamiliar with the work of Stephen Crane, and it did not stem
from fancying any wickedness in the author. It came, rather, from
encountering an imagination so powerful that it could sweep cus-
tomary fictional devices aside, replacing them with a series of com-
pressed scenes set forth in a style that was somewhat mannered, to
be sure, but was nevertheless amazingly effective in its reliance on
the simple sentence, vividly put, to carry its meaning.

Here was no recruit to Howells' realism. The world projected by
Crane has no topographical or temporal existence. To be sure, the
tale opens in Rum Alley and never strays far from it, and Rum Alley
is in the slums of New York. But the sense of Rum Alley's being a
specific—even if symbolic—piece of a total social structure, like,
say, Dickens' Tom-All-Alone's, is missing. Instead we are plunged
into selected details of urban squalor and human viciousness, unrelieved by specific addresses, commonplace activities, or basic com-
municative speech. Crane's characters, gabbling on in a lingo which
is, like their setting, chosen only for being extreme, communicate
not at all when they talk to one another. There is no literal level of
social reality. With regard to the setting, for instance, the reader
realizes that there simply isn't enough furniture and crockery
available in a habitation like that of the Johnsons to yield the supply necessary for the crunching destruction which is as fixed a feature of that place as the breaking waves are of a beach scene. While
Maggie is not an allegory, it is a vision of what typically happens
rather than a report of what actually happens. . . .

To some extent, the extremes of this world are the inevitable result of the fact that the writer is making it all up. What Hesketh
Pearson says of Oscar Wilde's *Lord Arthur Savile's Crime* may easily be applied to Crane's *Maggie*: "His picture of low life . . . has
the unreal melodramatic quality one might expect from a youth
who is making the most of his first contact with things beyond his
normal experience." But the work is the beneficiary as well as the
victim of the youth's imagination, and Crane's was powerful. The
grotesque setting, though it achieves only uneasy coherence with
the social theme, is of a piece with the rest of *Maggie* viewed as a
subjective projection that finds its center in the psyches of the characters, chiefly Maggie and Jimmie. The longings of these dumb creatures are represented as images rather than as ideas. Jimmie stood
at street corners "dreaming blood-red dreams"; he "menaced mankind at the intersections of streets." Maggie's "dim thoughts were

often searching for far away lands where the little hills sing together in the morning." Not only does Crane emphasize in this way
the irrational, non-verbal sources of their behavior, but he gains
his impression through using particular kinds of images. In the
brief quotations, for instance, Jimmie in his furious outlook is not
dangerous because he overleaps the mark; instead of threatening
anybody in particular, his mute wrath is drained off into a gen-
eralized menacing of "mankind." Maggie's wistfulness, similarly,
does not carry any specific pathos, since it is directed past things
presumably within her ken toward a biblical image of joy, ideal and
unattainable.

These images are typical of the ruthless irony dealt out by the
young Crane. He has, as it were, no middle distance. On one hand,
his inarticulate characters exist in a vortex of maiming incidents.
On the other hand, they are not measured in terms of what they
could be under realistically improved conditions, that is, what they
could be if they had more money or if they lived in Scarsdale
rather than Rum Alley. Instead, their condition is contrasted with
hints of romantic, chivalric, or biblical ideals which never had a real
embodiment. What Maggie is is the result not of the action of her
environment on a plastic personality, but rather of the reaction
of that environment to the proposals made to it by her pretensions
and her longings. She, not the environment, is the first mover. Jimmie and the other characters also have pretensions and fears
which underlie their behavior and which are imperfectly realized
in it rather than being significantly shaped by it. In this kind of
world the flaws in the setting that result from the author's lack of
experience are not damaging, because the setting is an appropriate symbolic extension of inner chaos; it is of a piece with the
characters who inhabit it.

Maggie, however, cannot be read as a consistently subjective performance, although its strengths lie in this area. The youthful
Crane was also drawn to the objective view that society has crushing
effects on the individual, and the result is that *Maggie,* brief as it is,
is an uneven performance. Its undeniable power, though, comes
from his not hesitating to brush aside social reality in favor of his
vision of what is really happening and from his freeing himself from
any concern with the actual or with conscious reflection and relying upon his inner consciousness as the source of his creation. Crane
was mining himself, as his inscription to Garland showed when he
calls attention to that self and its fancied relation to society far more
than he does to a detached work of fiction.

Stephen Crane's *Maggie*
and American Naturalism

by Donald Pizer

Stephen Crane's *Maggie: A Girl of the Streets* has often served as an example of naturalistic fiction in America. Crane's novel about a young girl's fall and death in the New York slums has many of the distinctive elements of naturalistic fiction, particularly a slum setting and the theme of the overpowering effect of environment. Crane himself appeared to supply a naturalistic gloss to the novel when he wrote to friends that *Maggie* was about the effect of environment on human lives. Yet the novel has characteristics which clash with its neat categorization as naturalistic fiction. For one thing, Crane's technique of irony is foreign to the naturalistic vision; for another, Maggie herself, though she becomes a prostitute, is strangely untouched by her physical environment. She functions as an almost expressionistic symbol of inner purity uncorrupted by external foulness. There is nothing, of course, to prevent a naturalist from using irony and expressionistic symbolism, just as there is nothing to prevent him from introducing a deterministic theme into a Jamesian setting. But in practice the naturalist is usually direct. He is concerned with revealing the blunt edge of the powerful forces which condition our lives, and his fictional technique is usually correspondingly blunt and massive. When Zola in *L'Assommoir* and *Nana* wished to show the fall into prostitution of a child of the slums, his theme emerged clearly and ponderously from his full description of the inner as well as outer corruption of Nana and from his "realistic" symbolism. Crane's method, on the other hand, is that of obliqueness and indirection. Irony and expressionistic symbolism ask the reader to look beyond literal meaning, to seek beyond the immediately discernible for

"Stephen Crane's *Maggie* and American Naturalism." From *Criticism*, VII (Spring 1965), 168-175. © 1965 by Wayne State University Press. Reprinted by permission of the Wayne State University Press.

the underlying reality. Both are striking techniques which by their compelling tone and their distortion of the expected attempt to shock us into recognition that a conventional belief or an obvious "truth" may be false and harmful. Perhaps, then, *Maggie* can best be discussed by assuming from the first that Crane's fictional techniques imply that the theme of the novel is somewhat more complex than the truism that young girls in the slums are more apt to go bad than young girls elsewhere.[1]

The opening sentence of *Maggie* is "A very little boy stood upon a heap of gravel for the honor of Rum Alley." The sentence introduces both Crane's theme and his ironic technique. By juxtaposing the value of honor and the reality of a very little boy, a heap of gravel, and Rum Alley, Crane suggests that the idea of honor is inappropriate to the reality, that it serves to disguise from the participants in the fight that they are engaged in a vicious and petty scuffle. Crane's irony emerges out of the difference between a value which one imposes on experience and the nature of experience itself. His ironic method is to project into the scene the values of its participants in order to underline the difference between their values and reality. So the scene has a basic chivalric cast. The very little boy is a knight fighting on his citadel of gravel for the honor of his chivalrous pledge to Rum Alley. Crane's opening sentence sets the theme for *Maggie* because the novel is essentially about man's use of conventional but inapplicable abstract values (such as justice, honor, duty, love, and respectability) as weapons or disguises. The novel is not so much about the slums as a physical reality as about what people believe in the slums and how their beliefs are both false to their experience and yet function as operative forces in their lives.

Let me explore this idea by examining first the lives of the novel's principal characters and then the moral values which control their thinking about their lives. Crane uses two basic images to depict

[1] The interpretation of *Maggie* which follows has been evolving in criticism of the novel for some years, though it has not been pursued as fully or pointedly as I do here. Both R. W. Stallman, in "Crane's *Maggie*: A Reassessment," *Modern Fiction Studies*, V (Autumn 1959), 251–59, and Charles C. Walcutt, in *American Literary Naturalism, A Divided Stream* (Minneapolis, 1956), pp. 67–72, touch briefly on the theme of *Maggie* somewhat as I do. I have also been aided by Edwin H. Cady, *Stephen Crane* (New York, 1962), pp. 102–111; Joseph X. Brennan, "Ironic and Symbolic Structure in Crane's *Maggie*," *Nineteenth-Century Fiction*, XVI (March 1962), 303–315; and Janet Overmyer, "The Structure of Crane's *Maggie*," *University of Kansas City Review*, XXIX (Autumn 1962), 71–2.

the Bowery. It is a battlefield and it is a prison. These images appear clearly in the novel's first three chapters, which describe an evening and night in the life of the Johnson family during Maggie's childhood. The life of the family is that of fierce battle with those around them and among themselves. The novel opens with Jimmie fighting the children of Devil's Row. He then fights one of his own gang. His father separates them with a blow. Maggie mistreats the babe Tommie; Jimmie strikes Maggie; Mrs. Johnson beats Jimmie for fighting. Mr. and Mrs. Johnson quarrel. Mrs. Johnson beats Maggie for breaking a plate; Mr. Johnson strikes Jimmie with an empty beer pail. Mr. Johnson comes home drunk and he and Mrs. Johnson fight—all this in three rather short chapters. Crane's fundamental point in these chapters is that the home is not a sanctuary from the struggle and turmoil of the world but is rather where warfare is even more intense and where the animal qualities encouraged by a life of battle—strength, fear, and cunning—predominate. The slum and the home are not only battlefields, however, but are also enclosed arenas. Maggie's tenement is in a "dark region," and her apartment, "up dark stairways and along cold, gloomy halls," is like a cave. Crane's description of the Johnson children eating combines both the warfare and cave images into one central metaphor of primitive competition for food.

> The babe sat with his feet dangling high from a precarious infant's chair and gorged his small stomach. Jimmie forced, with feverish rapidity, the grease-enveloped pieces between his wounded lips. Maggie, with side glances of fear of interruption, ate like a small pursued tigress.

By means of this double pattern of imagery, Crane suggests that the Johnsons' world is one of fear, fury, and darkness, that it is a world in which no moral laws are applicable, since the Johnsons' fundamental guide to conduct is an instinctive amorality, a need to feed and to protect themselves.

Once introduced, this image of the Bowery as an amoral, animal world is maintained throughout *Maggie*. Mr. Johnson dies, Jimmie assumes his position, and the Johnsons' family warfare continues as before. Maggie and Jimmie go to work, and each finds that struggle and enclosure mark his adult world. Jimmie becomes a belligerent truck driver, imprisoned by his ignorance and his distrust. He respects only strength in the form of the red fire engine which has the power to crush his wagon. Maggie works in a prison-like sweat shop where she is chided into resentment by her grasping employer. Theirs are lives of animal struggle and of spiritual bleakness in which they only faintly realize their own deprivation.

Maggie sits with the other girls in her factory workroom in a vague state of "yellow discontent," and Jimmie, the brawling teamster, "nevertheless . . . , on a certain star-lit evening, said wonderingly and quite reverently, 'Deh moon looks like hell, don't it?' "

The moral values held by the Johnsons are drawn almost entirely from a middle-class ethic which stresses the home as the center of virtue, and respectability as the primary moral goal. It is a value system oriented toward approval by others, toward an audience. In the opening chapter of the novel, Jimmie hits Maggie as Mr. Johnson is taking them home. Mr. Johnson cries, "Leave yer sister alone *on the street*" (my italics). The Johnsons' moral vision is dominated by moral roles which they believe are expected of them. The roles bring social approbation, and they are also satisfying because the playing of them before an audience encourages a gratifying emotionalism or self-justification. The reaction to Maggie's fall is basically of this nature. She is cast out by her mother and brother for desecrating the Home, and her seducer, Pete, rejects her plea for aid because she threatens the respectability of the rough-and-tumble bar in which he works. The moral poses adopted by the Johnsons and by Pete have no relation to reality, however, since the home and the bar are parallel settings of warfare rather than of virtue.

The key to the morality of the Bowery is therefore its self-deceiving theatricality. Those expressing moral sentiments do so as though playing a role before a real or implied audience. Crane makes the dramatic nature of Bowery morality explicit in scenes set in dance halls and theatres. In a dance hall, an audience of Maggies, Jimmies, and Petes listens enraptured to a song "whose lines told of a mother's love, and a sweetheart who waited, and a young man who was lost at sea under harrowing circumstances." Later, Maggie and Pete see plays

> in which the dazzling heroine was rescued from the palatial home of her treacherous guardian by the hero with the beautiful sentiments. . . . Maggie lost herself in sympathy with the wanderers swooning in snowstorms beneath happy-hued church windows, while a choir within sang "Joy to the World." To Maggie and the rest of the audience this was transcendental realism. Joy always within, and they, like the actor, inevitably without. Viewing it, they hugged themselves in ecstatic pity of their imagined or real condition.

The audience identifies itself with maligned and innocent virtue despite the inapplicability of these roles to their own lives. "Shady persons in the audience revolted from the pictured villainy of the drama. With untiring zeal they hissed vice and applauded virtue.

Unmistakably bad men evinced an apparently sincere admiration for virtue."

This same ability to project oneself into a virtuous role is present in most of the novel's characters. Each crisis in the Johnson family is viewed by neighbors who comprise an audience which encourages the Johnsons to adopt moral poses. In the scene in which Maggie is cast out, both Jimmie and Mrs. Johnson are aware of their need to play the roles of outraged virtue in response to the expectations of their audience. Mrs. Johnson addresses the neighbors "like a glib showman," and with a "dramatic finger" points out to them her errant daughter. The novel's final scene is a parody of Bowery melodrama. Mrs. Johnson mourns over the dead Maggie's baby shoes while the neighbors cry in sympathy and the "woman in black" urges her to forgive Maggie. In the midst of her exhortations, "The woman in black raised her face and paused. The inevitable sunlight came streaming in at the window." Crane in this scene connects the sentimental morality of melodrama and the sanctimoniousness of Bowery religion. Both the theatre and the mission purvey moral attitudes which have no relation to life but which rather satisfy emotional needs or social approval. The heroes and heroines of melodrama cannot be confronted with reality, but the church is occasionally challenged. When it is, as when the mission preacher is asked why he never says "we" instead of "you," or when Maggie seeks aid from the stout clergyman, its reaction is either non-identification with reality ("What?" asks the preacher) or withdrawal from it (the clergyman sidesteps Maggie). It is as though the church, too, were a sentimental theatre which encouraged moral poses but which ignored the essential nature of itself and of its audience.

Both of these central characteristics of the Bowery—its core of animality and its shell of moral poses—come together strikingly in Mrs. Johnson. There is a bitter Swiftian irony in Crane's portrait of her. Her drunken rages symbolize the animal fury of a slum home, and her quickness to judge, condemn, and cast out Maggie symbolizes the self-righteousness of Bowery morality. In a sense she symbolizes the entire Bowery world, both its primitive amorality and its sentimental morality. It is appropriate, then, that it is she who literally drives Maggie into prostitution and eventual death. Secure in her moral role, she refuses to allow Maggie to return home after her seduction by Pete, driving her into remaining with Pete and then into prostitution. Maggie is thus destroyed not so much by the physical reality of slum life as by a middle-class morality imposed on the slums by the missions and the melodrama, a morality which allows its users both to judge and to divorce themselves from responsibility from those they judge.

Crane's characterization of Maggie can now be examined. His description of her as having "blossomed in a mud-puddle" with "none of the dirt of Rum Alley . . . in her veins" is not "realistic," since it is difficult to accept that the slums would have no effect on her character. Zola's portrait of Nana dying of a disfiguring disease which symbolizes her spiritual as well as physical corruption is more convincing. Crane's desire, however, was to stress that the vicious deterministic force in the slums was its morality, not its poor housing or inadequate diet, and it is this emphasis which controls his characterization of Maggie. His point is that Maggie comes through the mud-puddle of her physical environment untouched. It is only when her environment becomes a moral force that she is destroyed. Maggie as an expressionistic symbol of purity in a mud-puddle is Crane's means of enforcing his large irony that purity is destroyed not by concrete evils but by the very moral codes established to safeguard it.

But Maggie is a more complex figure than the above analysis suggests. For though her world does not affect her moral nature, it does contribute to her downfall by blurring her vision. Her primary drive in life is to escape her mud-puddle prison, and she is drawn to Pete because his strength and elegance offer a means of overcoming the brutality and ugliness of her home and work. Her mistaken conception of Pete results from her enclosed world, a world which has given her romantic illusions just as it has supplied others with moral poses. Her mistake warrants compassion, however, rather than damnation and destruction. She is never really immoral. Throughout her fall, from her seduction by Pete to her plunge into the East River, Crane never dispels the impression that her purity and innocence remain. Her weakness is compounded out of the facts that her amoral environment has failed to arm her with moral strength (she "would have been more firmly good had she better known how"), while at the same time it has blinded her with self-destructive romantic illusions ("she wondered if the culture and refinement she had seen imitated . . . by the heroine on the stage, could be acquired by a girl who lived in a tenement house and worked in a shirt factory").

There is considerable irony that in choosing Pete Maggie flees into the same world she wished to escape. Like Mrs. Johnson, Pete desires to maintain the respectability of his "home," the bar in which he works. Like her, he theatrically purifies himself of guilt and responsibility for Maggie's fall as he drunkenly sobs "I'm good f'ler, girls" to an audience of prostitutes. And like Maggie herself, he is eventually a victim of sexual warfare. He is used and discarded by the "woman of brilliance and audacity" just as he had used and discarded Maggie. In short, Maggie can escape the immediate prison of her home and factory, but she cannot escape being enclosed by the combination of amoral warfare (now sexual) and moral poses which is the pervasive force in her world.

In his famous inscription to *Maggie,* Crane wrote that the novel "tries to show that environment is a tremendous thing in the world and frequently shapes lives regardless." But he went on to write that "if one proves that theory one makes room in Heaven for all sorts of souls (notably an occasional street girl) who are not confidently expected to be there by many excellent people." The second part of the inscription contains an attack on the "many excellent people" who, like Maggie's mother, immediately equate a fallen girl with evil and hell. Crane is here not so much expressing a belief in heaven as using the idea of salvation and damnation as a rhetorical device to attack smug, self-righteous moralism. The entire novel bears this critical intent. Crane's focus in *Maggie* is less on the inherent evil of slum life than on the harm done by a false moral environment imposed on that life. His irony involving Mrs. Johnson, for example, centers on the religious and moral climate which has persuaded her to adopt the moral poses of outraged Motherhood and despoiled Home.

Maggie is thus a novel primarily about the falsity and destructiveness of certain moral codes. To be sure, these codes and their analogous romantic visions of experience are present in Maggie's environment, and are in part what Crane means when he wrote that environment shapes lives regardless. But Crane's ironic technique suggests that his primary goal was not to show the effects of environment but to distinguish between moral appearance and reality, to attack the sanctimonious self-deception and sentimental emotional gratification of moral poses. He was less concerned with dramatizing a deterministic philosophy than in assailing those who apply a middle-class morality to victims of amoral, uncontrollable forces in man and society. *Maggie* is therefore very much like such early Dreiser novels as *Sister Carrie* and *Jennie Gerhardt,* though Dreiser depends less on irony and more on an explicit documentation and discussion of the discrepancy between an event and man's moral evaluation of an event. *Maggie* is also like *The Red Badge of Courage,* for the later novel seeks to demonstrate the falsity of a moral or romantic vision of the amorality which is war.

Crane, then, is a naturalistic writer in the sense that he believes that environment molds lives. But he is much more than this, for his primary concern is not a dispassionate, pessimistic tracing of inevitable forces but a satiric assault on weaknesses in social morality. He seems to be saying that though we may not control our destinies, we can at least destroy those systems of value which uncritically assume we can. If we do this, a Maggie (or a Jennie Gerhardt) will at least be saved from condemnation and destruction by an unjust code.

Writers who seek greater justice, who demand that men evaluate their experience with greater clarity and honesty, are not men who despair at the nature of things. They are rather critical realists. Like William Dean Howells, Crane wishes us to understand the inadequacies of our lives so that we may improve them. Although Crane stresses weaknesses in our moral vision rather than particular social abuses, there is more continuity between Howells' critical realism and Crane's naturalism than one might suspect. This continuity is not that of subject matter or even of conception of man and society. It is rather that of a belief in the social function of the novel in delineating the evils of social life. If one sees such a writer as Crane in this light, the often crude and outdated determinism of early American naturalism lessens in importance. One begins to realize that American naturalism, like most vital literary movements, comprised a body of convention and assumption about the function and nature of literature which unprescriptively allowed the writer to mold this shared belief into a personally expressive work of art. Crane's fiction is therefore permanently absorbing and historically significant not because he was a determinist or fatalist writing about the slums or about the chaos of war. His fiction still excites because his ironic technique successfully involves us in the difference between moral appearance and reality in society. His fiction is historically important because his expression of this theme within the conventions of naturalistic fiction reveals the relationship between critical realism and naturalism. But his fiction is perhaps even more significant historically because he revealed the possibility of a uniquely personal style and vision within naturalistic conventions. Our writers have responded to the critical spirit and the fictional sensationalism and freedom of naturalism without a sense of being burdened by doctrinaire precepts and forms. And it is no doubt this invigorating freedom within continuity which has been one of the principal reasons for the strength and influence of the naturalistic movement in America, from Crane and Dreiser to our own times.

The Design of Stephen Crane's Bowery "Experiment"

by Maurice Bassan

In *Stephen Crane: An Omnibus* (New York, 1952, p. 11), Robert W. Stallman argues that Crane has not "patterned the imagery" of his Bowery story, "An Experiment in Misery," or "made it consistently metaphorical," and that "details that might have been converted to evoke symbolic overtones are wastefully misspent." These statements may be misleading to students of Crane's art. The somber tone of this powerful story, which has been admired by such writers as Edward Garnett, Ludwig Lewisohn, Vernon Parrington, and John Berryman, is achieved through a masterful and complex fusion of imagery and structure, both of which are designed to discharge strong emotions and to express the author's carefully concealed point of view. As William Van O'Connor declares, "The maturity with which a moral or political view emerges from the aesthetic form is dependent in part on how well, how impressively, and how vividly the view has been investigated and refracted through the aesthetic medium." Crane's mastery of his medium in this story to express a deeply felt moral and political view is no less than we might expect from the author who had already written *Maggie* and *The Red Badge of Courage*. Crane framed the "Experiment" as a mere report of conditions, in accordance with his deliberate intention "not to let any theories or pet ideas" of his own creep into his work:

> Preaching is fatal to art in literature. I try to give to readers a slice out of life; and if there is any moral or lesson in it, I do not try to point it out. I let the reader find it for himself.

"The Design of Stephen Crane's Bowery 'Experiment.'" From *Studies in Short Fiction*, I (Winter 1964), 129-132. This version is slightly revised. Reprinted by permission of *Studies in Short Fiction*.

It is the reader's task, then, through his understanding of the fusion of structure and metaphor, to penetrate to the core of Crane's indictment of social evil, and his sympathy with the predicament of what was widely labeled in his time "the lowest order of society." And further: for unerringly Stephen Crane reaches beyond social statement to a metaphor of the human condition itself.

The design of Crane's "Experiment" is geographically circular. The tale begins with the youth's wandering in the park, moves to the voracious saloon which briefly swallows him up, and then pictures his tormented night in a seven-cent lodging-house; the circle continues through a visit to a restaurant in the morning, and to the final scene again set in City Hall Park. The circularity of movement reinforces the rhythm of monotony, of hopeless repetition which characterizes the life of these depraved tramps, with whom the inexperienced youth has "aligned himself." This rhythm is repeated in the fragments of autobiography related by the youth's bizarre comrade, a clownish Virgil who guides him through the Bowery nether world. This "assassin's" life has been marked by parental rejection and a course of meaningless wandering from place to place; and he is finally reduced to that most contemptible of states, sponging from the tramps themselves.

The rhythm of circularity is broken in only one, very significant, way. The story as originally printed in the New York *Press* contained an opening and closing "frame," which must be read as part of the tale despite some repetition of the language of the opening sequence in the first paragraph of the story proper. "An Experiment in Misery" begins with two observers, a youth, and an older man who speaks "with an air of authoritative wisdom." The former is speculating about the feelings of the tramp they are observing, and is answered, "You can tell nothing of it unless you are in that condition yourself. It is idle to speculate about it from this distance." The youth takes up the implied challenge, and declares, "I think I'll try it. Rags and tatters, you know, a couple of dimes, and hungry, too, if possible. Perhaps I could discover his point of view or something near it." And thus, Crane writes, begins this "veracious narrative of an experiment in misery." At the end of the story, after the youth confesses himself "an outcast," having entered profoundly into the spiritual condition of the homeless, he again confronts his friend:

> "Well," said the friend, "did you discover his point of view?"
> "I don't know that I did," replied the young man; "but at any rate I think mine own has undergone a considerable alteration."

There are qualifications in the youth's lines, but the "considerable
alteration" measures his moral growth, his expansion of pity, his
understanding of the nature of the environmental and class struggle
waged in the slums. The broken rhythm of the frame thus supplies
the only qualifiedly optimistic note in this gloomy narrative.

In the night-scene at the flophouse occurs the story's central
image, around which most of the rest cluster. This image generates
precisely that aura of pathos that arises from the tale's circular
structure. The youth, lying on his cot, hears long wails which, to
him, "were an utterance of the meaning of the room and its oc-
cupants. It was to him the protest of the wretch who feels the touch
of the imperturbable granite wheels, and who then cries with an
impersonal eloquence, with a strength not from him, giving voice
to the wail of a whole section, a class, a people." The wheels suggest
the impersonal, unconcerned grinding processes of a mill, or the
action of a juggernaut; perhaps Crane was thinking of Hamlin
Garland's play *Under the Wheel* (1890), whose title was taken from
a deathbed utterance of Bazarov in Turgenev's *Fathers and Sons*.
The individual beneath, suffering; the society above, hostile or un-
caring: this is the central, unifying metaphor of man's fate in "An
Experiment in Misery." Metaphor and structure thus join, not only
to define clearly Crane's emotional attitude toward his subject, but
to commit the reader himself to an act of identification and sympathy.

Most of the details and images of the first part of the story in-
tensify this pattern of pressure and malignancy. The experimental
tramp's old velvet collar presses against his neck as the night storms
down around him, and he is "plastered with yells of 'bum' and
'hobo.'" He watches the cable cars move by, "with formidable
power, calm and irresistible, dangerful and gloomy," and sees the
moving throngs whose shoes leave "scar-like" impressions on the
muddy pavement. The station of the elevated railroad, "upon its
leg-like pillars seemed to resemble some monstrous kind of crab
squatting over the street." Then, in the cheap lodging-house, the
youth is assailed by unspeakable odors, "like malignant diseases
with wings." Shadows, "like mighty black fingers," curl around the
naked bodies. The men snore with tremendous effort, "like stabbed
fish"; the youth watches a man who is "like a body stretched out
expectant of the surgeon's knife"; the wailer is a "vision-pierced
man." The images of stabbing and piercing are reinforced by the
descriptions of the sun's rays: "a long lance-point of gray light,"

"bright spears of the sun"; while the companion of the youth has "long fingernails that rasped like files."

Finally, at the end of the tale, the youth again contemplates the moving throngs of humanity "upon important missions." He sees them as "black figures changing yet frieze-like," very much like the "squads" of well-dressed people he had observed the night before. He feels intensely his separation from, his infinite distance *beneath*, those things he had valued; and the buildings reaching into the sky in the background are to him "emblematic of a nation forcing its regal head into the clouds, throwing no downward glances; in the sublimity of its aspirations ignoring the wretches who may flounder at its feet." While the unifying metaphor is clear enough, there has occurred an important shift in emphasis. Crane allows himself to hold (or, perhaps, could not decide between) two related positions: the first, that society literally grinds, stabs, tortures; the second, that it is so far above the floundering wretches that it does not care what is happening to them. Translated, as it were, into metaphysical terms, these may be the activities of Nature itself, and here Crane closely resembles Melville, who, in *Moby Dick*, leaves perplexingly ambiguous the vexing question of the malevolence or mere indifference of Nature.

Thematically related to this central metaphor are the images of a Poe-like living death, of an "unholy," un-Christian atmosphere, and of money. In the dormitory, approached through a gloom-shrouded corridor, the youth sees the men lying in "death-like silence," in a "stillness as of death," "statuesque, carven, dead." The chill of his leather-covered cot, as cold as melting snow and "like a slab," gives him peace. Near his cot stands a locker for clothes "with the ominous air of a tombstone"; these lockers give "a strange effect of a graveyard where bodies were merely flung." Crane's portrait is of a graveyard of human hopes, of men either ground down by society and left to die, or so far removed from the things in life they value that Death-in-Life becomes their pathetic fate. In the saloon the men are greeted at the free soup line by a man "presiding like a priest behind an altar." In the park the next morning, the wanderers sit "in the little circle of benches sanctified by traditions of their class." Crane's ironic insistence upon the conjunction of religious symbols and terminology with the blasted hopes of unredeemed men further documents his passionate vision of a betrayal by a whole society. The youth's irreverent companion takes oath, appropriately, by "strange gods." The motive force of this hard, ruthlessly competitive society is made perfectly clear by the persistent allusions to coppers, pennies, and coins, as in the youth's final knowledge that "The roar of the city in his ear was . . . the clink of coin, the voice of the city's hopes, which were to him no hopes." It is at this point that the youth "confessed himself an outcast," the logical outcome of his deliberately assuming, though at first only through curiosity, the mask of Ishmael.

One brief paragraph may serve to indicate, finally, how almost every detail in the story functions to expand this painful vision of man's destiny. The youth observes the men in the flophouse in the morning:

> A few were parading in unconcerned nakedness. Here and there were men of brawn, whose skins shone clear and ruddy. They took splendid poses, standing massively like chiefs. When they had dressed in their ungainly garments there was an extraordinary change. They then showed bumps and deficiencies of all kinds.

These are not Mr. Peachum's rogues. The passage is unobtrusively symbolic of the tragic division between man made by God and man made by society. Divinity is not at home in a flophouse.

The imagery of "An Experiment in Misery" is, in short, patterned, and tightly welded to the structure. The grim narrative initiates the reader, like the latter-day Goodman Brown who is its hero, into the reality of evil, and into what Crane was to call, in "The Open Boat," the "pathos" of man's condition. William Dean Howells' words about one of J. M. Barrie's novels are perfectly applicable here: "The pathos is in the situation, the inevitable sadness of human life limited and at disadvantage, and not in the sentimentality of the observer. To put himself in this attitude towards his material requires the finest literary art."

His War Book

by Joseph Conrad

One of the most enduring memories of my literary life is the sensation produced by the appearance in 1895 of Crane's *Red Badge of Courage* in a small volume belonging to Mr. Heinemann's "Pioneer Series of Modern Fiction"—very modern fiction of that time, and upon the whole not devoid of merit. I have an idea the series was meant to give us shocks, and as far as my recollection goes there were, to use a term made familiar to all by another war, no "duds" in that small and lively bombardment. But Crane's work detonated on the mild din of that attack on our literary sensibilities with the impact and force of a twelve-inch shell charged with a very high explosive. Unexpected it fell amongst us; and its fall was followed by a great outcry.

Not of consternation, however. The energy of that projectile hurt nothing and no one (such was its good fortune), and delighted a good many. It delighted soldiers, men of letters, men in the street; it was welcomed by all lovers of personal expression as a genuine revelation, satisfying the curiosity of a world in which war and love have been subjects of song and story ever since the beginning of articulate speech.

Here we had an artist, a man not of experience but a man inspired, a seer with a gift for rendering the significant on the surface of things and with an incomparable insight into primitive emotions, who, in order to give us the image of war, had looked profoundly into his own breast. We welcomed him. As if the whole vocabulary of praise had been blown up sky-high by this missile from across the Atlantic, a rain of words descended on our heads, words well or ill chosen, chunks of pedantic praise and warm appreciation, clever words, and words of real understanding, platitudes, and fe-

"His War Book." From *Last Essays* (New York: Doubleday, Page, 1926). Reprinted by permission of J. M. Dent & Sons, Ltd. and the Executors of the Joseph Conrad Estate.

licities of criticism, but all as sincere in their response as the striking piece of work which set so many critical pens scurrying over the paper.

One of the most interesting, if not the most valuable, of printed criticisms was perhaps that of Mr. George Wyndham, soldier, man of the world, and in a sense a man of letters. He went into the whole question of war literature, at any rate during the nineteenth century, evoking comparisons with the *Memoires* of General Marbot and the famous *Diary of a Cavalry Officer* as records of a personal experience. He rendered justice to the interest of what soldiers themselves could tell us, but confessed that to gratify the curiosity of the potential combatant who lurks in most men as to the picturesque aspects and emotional reactions of a battle we must go to the artist with his heaven-given faculty of words at the service of his divination as to what the truth of things is and must be. He comes to the conclusion that: "Mr. Crane has contrived a masterpiece."

"Contrived"—that word of disparaging sound is the last word I would have used in connection with any piece of work by Stephen Crane, who in his art (as indeed in his private life) was the least "contriving" of men. But as to "masterpiece," there is no doubt that *The Red Badge of Courage* is that, if only because of the marvellous accord of the vivid impressionistic description of action on that woodland battlefield, and the imagined style of the analysis of the emotions in the inward moral struggle going on in the breast of one individual—the Young Soldier of the book, the protagonist of the monodrama presented to us in an effortless succession of graphic and coloured phrases.

Stephen Crane places his Young Soldier in an untried regiment. And this is well contrived—if any contrivance there be in a spontaneous piece of work which seems to spurt and flow like a tapped stream from the depths of the writer's being. In order that the revelation should be complete, the Young Soldier has to be deprived of the moral support which he would have found in a tried body of men matured in achievement to the consciousness of its worth. His regiment had been tried by nothing but days of waiting for the order to move; so many days that it and the Youth within it have come to think of themselves as merely "a part of a vast blue demonstration." The army had been lying camped near a river, idle and fretting, till the moment when Stephen Crane lays hold of it at dawn with masterly simplicity: "The cold passed reluctantly from the earth. . . ." These are the first words of the war book which was to give him his crumb of fame.

The whole of that opening paragraph is wonderful in the homely dignity of the indicated lines of the landscape, and the shivering awakening of the army at the break of the day before the battle. In the next, with a most effective change to racy colloquialism of narrative, the action which motivates, sustains and feeds the inner drama forming the subject of the book, begins with the Tall Soldier going down to the river to wash his shirt. He returns waving his garment above his head. He had heard at fifth-hand from somebody that the army is going to move tomorrow. The only immediate effect of this piece of news is that a Negro teamster, who had been dancing a jig on a wooden box in a ring of laughing soldiers, finds himself suddenly deserted. He sits down mournfully. For the rest, the Tall Soldier's excitement is met by blank disbelief, profane grumbling, an invincible incredulity. But the regiment is somehow sobered. One feels it, though no symptoms can be noticed. It does not know what a battle is; neither does the Young Soldier. He retires from the babbling throng into what seems a rather comfortable dug-out and lies down with his hands over his eyes to think. Thus the drama begins.

He perceives suddenly that he had looked upon wars as historical phenomenons of the past. He had never believed in war in his own country. It had been a sort of play affair. He had been drilled, inspected, marched for months, till he had despaired "of ever seeing a Greek-like struggle. Such were no more. Men were better or more timid. Secular and religious education had effaced the throat-grappling instinct, or else firm finance held in check the passions."

Very modern this touch. We can remember thoughts like these round about the year 1914. That Young Soldier is representative of mankind in more ways than one, and first of all in his ignorance. His regiment had listened to the tales of veterans, "tales of grey bewhiskered hordes chewing tobacco with unspeakable valour and sweeping along like the Huns." Still, he cannot put his faith in veterans' tales. Recruits were their prey. They talked of blood, fire, and sudden death, but much of it might have been lies. They were in nowise to be trusted. And the question arises before him whether he will or will not "run from a battle"? He does not know. He cannot know. A little panic fear enters his mind. He jumps up and asks himself aloud, "Good Lord! What's the matter with me?" This is the first time his words are quoted, on this day before the battle. He dreads not danger, but fear itself. He stands before the unknown. He would like to prove to himself by some reasoning process that he will not "run from the battle." And in his unblooded regiment he can find no help. He is alone with the problem of courage.

In this he stands for the symbol of all untried men.

Some critics have estimated him a morbid case. I cannot agree to that. The abnormal cases are of the extremes; of those who crumple up at the first sight of danger, and of those of whom their fellows say, "He doesn't know what fear is." Neither will I forget the rare favourites of the gods whose fiery spirit is only soothed by the fury and clamour of a battle. Of such was General Picton of Peninsular fame. But the lot of the mass of mankind is to know fear, the decent fear of disgrace. Of such is the Young Soldier of *The Red Badge of Courage*. He only seems exceptional because he has got inside of him Stephen Crane's imagination, and is presented to us with the insight and the power of expression of an artist whom a just and severe critic, on a review of all his work, has called the foremost impressionist of his time, as Sterne was the greatest impressionist, but in a different way, of his age.

This is a generalised, fundamental judgment. More superficially both Zola's *La Débâcle* and Tolstoy's *War and Peace* were mentioned by critics in connection with Crane's war book. But Zola's main concern was with the downfall of the imperial regime he fancied he was portraying; and in Tolstoy's book the subtle presentation of Rostov's squadron under fire for the first time is a mere episode lost in a mass of other matter, like a handful of pebbles in a heap of sand. I could not see the relevancy. Crane was concerned with elemental truth only; and in any case I think that as an artist he is non-comparable. He dealt with what is enduring, and was the most detached of men.

That is why his book is short. Not quite two hundred pages. Gems are small. This monodrama, which happy inspiration or unerring instinct has led him to put before us in narrative form, is contained between the opening words I have already quoted and a phrase on page 194 of the English edition, which runs: "He had been to touch the great death, and found that, after all, it was but the great death. He was a man."

On these words the action ends. We are only given one glimpse of the victorious army at dusk, under the falling rain, "a procession of weary soldiers become a bedraggled train, despondent and muttering, marching with churning effort in a trough of liquid brown mud under a low wretched sky . . . ," while the last ray of the sun falls on the river through a break in the leaden clouds.

This war book, so virile and so full of gentle sympathy, in which not a single declamatory sentiment defaces the genuine verbal felicity, welding analysis and description in a continuous fascination of individual style, had been hailed by the critics as the herald of a brilliant career. Crane himself very seldom alluded to it, and always with a wistful smile. Perhaps he was conscious that, like the mortally wounded Tall Soldier of his book who, snatching at the air, staggers out into a field to meet his appointed death on the first day of battle—while the terrified Youth and the kind Tattered Soldier stand by silent, watching with awe "these ceremonies at the place of meeting"—it was his fate, too, to fall early in the fray.

Notes Toward an Analysis
of *The Red Badge of Courage*

by R. W. Stallman

Crane's style is prose pointillism. It is composed of disconnected images, which coalesce like the blobs of color in French impressionist paintings, every word-group having a cross-reference relationship, every seemingly disconnected detail having interrelationship to the configurated whole. The intensity of a Crane work is owing to this patterned coalescence of disconnected things, everything at once fluid and precise. A striking analogy is established between Crane's use of colors and the method employed by the impressionists and the neo-impressionists or divisionists, and it is as if he had known about their theory of contrasts and had composed his own prose paintings by the same principle. Their principle, as one writer defines it, is this: "Each plane of shade creates around itself a sort of aura of light, and each luminous plane creates around itself a zone of shade. In a similar way a coloured area communicates its 'complementary' to the neighboring colour, or heightens it if it is 'complementary.' "[1] In almost every battle scene in *The Red Badge of Courage* the perspective is blurred by smoke or by the darkness of night. Here is one example of the former contrast: namely, dark masses circled by light; and of the latter contrast: namely a luminous spot circled by darkness. (The former contrast is created in the first sentence of Crane's description, and the latter contrast in the second.)

"Notes Toward an Analysis of *The Red Badge of Courage*." Abridged from *The Houses That James Built* by R. W. Stallman (East Lansing: Michigan State University Press, 1961) and with emendations by the author. Originally "Introduction" to the Modern Library edition of *The Red Badge of Courage* (New York: Random House, 1951). The first part of this essay is reprinted by permission of Michigan State University Press. Footnotes 2 and 3 and the section beginning "*The Red Badge of Courage* is loaded with Biblical allusions . . ." on p. 137 © 1967 by R. W. Stallman.

[1] Cited in *Painting in France: 1895-1949*, by G. di San Lazzaro (1949), p. 28n.

The clouds were tinged an earthlike yellow in the sunrays and in the shadow were a sorry blue. The flag was sometimes eaten and lost in this mass of vapor, but more often it projected, sun-touched, resplendent [Chapter VI].

Crane's perspectives, almost without exception, are fashioned by contrasts—black masses juxtaposed against brightness, colored light set against gray mists. At dawn the army glows with a purple hue, and "In the eastern sky there was a yellow patch like a rug laid for the feet of the coming sun; and against it, *black and pattern-like,* loomed the gigantic figure of the colonel on a gigantic horse" (II). Black is juxtaposed against yellow (II) or against red (II, XIII). Smoke wreathes around a square of white light and a patch of yellow shade (I, XVIII). Smoke dimly outlines a distance filled with *blue* uniforms, a *green* sward, and a *sapphire* sky (XXIII). Further examples of color-contrast, particularly white versus black, occur throughout "The Open Boat," and blue is used symbolically in "The Blue Hotel." Crane had an extraordinary predilection for blue, which Hamlin Garland took to be the sign manual of the impressionists. It seems likely that Crane read Garland's *Crumbling Idols* (1894), but in any case he wrote a novel about an impressionist painter—the hero of *The Third Violet.* And in one of his sketches he wrote:

> The flash of the impression was like light, and for this instant it illumined all the dark recesses of one's remotest idea of sacrilege, ghastly and wanton. I bring this to you merely as an effect, *an effect of mental light and shade,* if you like; something done in thought *similar to that which the French impressionists do in colour;* something meaningless and at the same time overwhelming, crushing, monstrous (*Work,* IX, pp. 245-46).

Crane paints with words "exactly" as the French impressionists paint with pigments: both use pure colors and contrasts of colors. Black clouds or dark smoke or masses of mist and vapor are surrounded by a luminous zone; or, conversely, specks of prismatic color are enclosed by a zone of shade. Shifting gray mists open out before the splendor of the sunrays (XIV). Or, conversely, billowing smoke is "filled with horizontal flashes" (IV) ; "the mist of smoke [is] gashed by the little knives of fire" (XXIII) . Inside the surrounding darkness the waters of the river appear wine-tinted, and campfires, "shining upon the moving masses of troops, brought forth here and there sudden gleams of silver and gold. Upon the other shore a dark and mysterious range of hills was curved against the sky" (III; the same scene is duplicated in XIII). Cleared atmospheres, unimpeded vision or perspective, are rarely delineated; and where they occur the precision of vision is equated, symbolically, with revelation or spiritual insight. Dark mists and vapors represent the haze of Henry's unenlightened mind ("He, the enlightened man who looks afar in the dark, had fled because of his superior perceptions and knowledge"). Darkness and smoke serve as symbols of concealment and deception, vapors masking the light of truth. Sunlight and changing colors signify spiritual insight and rebirth. Henry is a color-bearer, but it is not until he recognizes the truth in his self-deception that the youth keeps "the bright colors to the front." In the celebrated impression of the red sun "pasted in the sky like a wafer" Crane is at once an impressionist painter and a symbolic artist.

Theme and style in *The Red Badge of Courage* are organically conceived, the theme of change conjoined with the fluid style by which it is evoked. The style, calculated to create impressions of confused motion and change, is deliberately disconnected and apparently disordered. Fluidity and change characterize the whole book. Crane interjects disjointed details, one *non sequitur* melting into another. Scenes and objects are felt as blurred; they appear under a haze or vapor or cloud. Yet everything has relationship and is manipulated into contrapuntal patterns of color and cross-references of meaning.

*   *   *

The Red Badge of Courage probes a state of mind under the incessant pinpricks and bombardments of life. The theme is that man's salvation lies in change, in spiritual growth. It is only by immersion in the flux of experience that man becomes disciplined and develops in character, conscience, or soul. Potentialities for change are at their greatest in battle—a battle represents life at its most intense flux. Crane's book is not about the combat of armies, it is about the self-combat of a youth who fears and stubbornly resists change, and the actual battle is symbolic of this spiritual warfare against change and growth. Henry Fleming recognizes the necessity for change and development, but wars against it. But man must lose his soul in order to save it. The youth develops into the veteran: "So it came to pass . . . his soul changed." Significantly enough, in stating what the book is about Crane intones Biblical phrasing.

The book begins with the army immobilized—with restless men waiting for orders to move—and, because the army has done nothing, with Henry disillusioned by his first days as a recruit. In the first picture we get of Henry, he is lying on his army cot—resting on an idea. Or, rather, he is wrestling with the personal problem it poses. The idea is a third-hand rumor that tomorrow, at last, the army will go into action. When the tall soldier first announced it, he waved a shirt that he had just washed in a muddy brook, waved it in banner-like fashion to summon the men around the flag of his colorful rumor. It was a call to the colors—he shook it out and spread it about for the men to admire. But Jim Conklin's prophecy of hope meets with disbelief. "It's a lie!" shouts the loud soldier. "I don't believe the derned old army's ever going to move." No disciples rally around the red and gold flag of the herald. The skeptical soldiers think the tall soldier is telling just a tall tale; a furious altercation ensues. Meanwhile Henry in his hut engages in a spiritual debate with himself; whether to believe or disbelieve the word of his friend, whom he has known since childhood. It is the gospel truth, but Henry is one of the doubting apostles.

The opening scene thus sets going the structural pattern of the whole book. Hope and faith (paragraphs 1-3) shift to despair or disbelief (4-7). The counter movement of opposition begins in paragraph 4, in the small detail of the Negro teamster who stops his dancing, when the men desert him to wrangle over Jim Conklin's rumor. "He sat mournfully down." This image of motion and change (the motion ceasing and the joy turning to gloom) presents the dominant *leitmotiv* and the form of the whole book in miniature. (Another striking instance of emblematic form occurs in Chapter VI, where Crane pictures a terror-stricken lad who throws down his gun and runs: "A lad whose face had borne an expression of exalted courage, the majesty of he who dares give his life, was, at an instant, smitten abject.") In Chapter I the opening prologue ends in a coda (paragraph 7) with theme and anti-theme interjoined. It is the picture of the corporal. His uncertainties (whether to repair his house) and his shifting attitudes of trust and distrust (whether the army is going to move) parallel the skeptical outlook of the wrangling men. The same anti-theme of distrust is dramatized in the episode that follows this coda, and every subsequent episode in the sequence is designed similarly by one contrast pattern or another.

Change and motion begin the book. The army, which lies resting on the hills, is first revealed to us by "the retiring fogs," and as the weather changes, the landscape changes, the brown hills turning to a new green. As nature stirs, the army stirs too. Nature and man are in psychic affinity; even the weather changes as though in sympathetic accord with man's plight. In the final scene it is raining, but the leaden rain clouds shine with "a golden ray" as though to reflect Henry's own bright serenity, his own tranquillity of mind. But now at the beginning, and throughout the book, Henry's mind is in a "tumult of agony and despair." This psychological tumult began when Henry heard the church bell announce that a great battle had been fought. Noise begins the whole mental melee. The clanging church bell and then the noise disorder his mind by stirring up legendary visions of heroic selfhood. The noisy world that first colored his mind with myths now clamors to Henry to become absorbed into the solidarity of self-forgetful comradeship, but Henry resists this challenge of the "mysterious fraternity born of the smoke and danger of death," and withdraws again and again from the din of the affray to indulge in self-contemplative moods and magic reveries. The walls of the forest insulate him from the noise of battle. In seeking retreat to absolve his shame and guilt, Henry, renouncing manhood, is "seeking dark and intricate places." It is as though he were seeking return to the womb. Nature, that "woman with a deep aversion to tragedy," is Mother Nature, and the human equation for the forest is of course Henry's own mother. Henry's flight from the forest sanctuary represents his momentary rejection of womblike innocence; periodically he rejects Mother Nature with her sheltering arms and her "religion of peace," and his flight from Mother Nature is symbolic of his initiation into the truth of the world he must measure up to. He is the deceived youth, for death lurks even in the forest sanctuary. In the pond a gleaming fish is killed by one of the forest creatures, and in the forest Henry meets a rotted corpse, a man whose eyes stare like a dead fish, with ants scurrying over the face. The treachery of this forest retreat, where nothing is as it seems, symbolizes the treachery of ideals—the illusions by which we are all betrayed.

Henry's mind is in constant flux. Henry's self-combat is symbolized by the conflict among the men and between the armies, their altercation being a duplication of his own. Like the regiment that marches and countermarches over the same ground, so Henry's mind traverses the same ideas over and over again. As the cheery-voiced soldier says about the battle, "It's th' most mixed up dern thing I

ever see." Mental commotion, confusion, and change are external-
ized in the "mighty altercation" of men and guns and nature herself. Everything becomes activated, *even the dead*. That corpse
Henry meets on the battlefield, "the *invulnerable* dead man," cannot stay still—he "*forced* a way for himself" through the ranks.
And guns throb too, "restless guns." Back and forth the stage scenery
shifts from dreams to "jolted dreams" and grim fact. Henry's illusions collapse, dreams pinpricked by reality.

Throughout the whole book *withdrawals* alternate with *engage-
ments,* with scenes of entanglement and tumult, but the same night-
marish atmosphere of upheaval and disorder pervades both the
inner and the outer realms. The paradox is that when Henry becomes activated in the "vast blue demonstration" and is thereby
reduced to anonymity he is most a man, and, conversely, when he
affects self-dramatizing picture-postcard poses of himself as hero he
is least a man and not at all heroic. He is then innocent as a child.
When disengaged from the external tumult, Henry's mind recol-
lects domestic scenes. Pictures of childhood and nursery imagery
of babes recur at almost every interval of withdrawal. Childhood
innocence and withdrawal are thus equated. The nursery limerick
that the wounded soldiers sing as they retreat from the battlefront
is at once a travesty of their own plight and a mockery of Henry's
mythical innocence.

> *Sing a song 'a vic'try,*
> *A pocketful 'a bullets,*
> *Five an' twenty dead men*
> *Baked in a—pie.*

Everything goes awry; nothing turns out as Henry expected.
Battles turn out to be "an immense and terrible machine to him"
(the awful machinery is also his own mind). At his battle task Henry,
we are told, "was like a carpenter who has made many boxes, making still another box, only there was furious haste in his movements." Henry, "frustrated by hateful circumstances," pictures himself as boxed in by fate, by the regiment, and by the "iron laws of
tradition and law on four sides. He was in a moving box." And
furthermore there are those purely theoretical boxes by which he
is shut in from reality—his romantic dreams, legendary visions
of heroic selfhood, illusions that the vainglorious machinery of his
own mind has manufactured.

The youth who had envisioned himself in Homeric poses, the

legendary hero of a Greek-like struggle, has his pretty illusion shattered as soon as he announces his enlistment to his mother. "I've
knet yeh eight pair of socks, Henry. . . ." His mother is busy peel-
ing potatoes, and, madonna-like, she kneels among the parings.
They are the scraps of his romantic dreams. The youthful private
imagines armies to be monsters, "redoubtable dragons," but then
he sees the real thing—the colonel who strokes his mustache and
shouts over his shoulder: "Don't forget that box of cigars!"

Spiritual change is Henry Fleming's red badge. *His red badge is
his conscience reborn and purified.* Whereas Jim Conklin's red badge
of courage is the literal one, the wound of which he dies, Henry's
is the psychological badge, the wound of conscience. Internal wounds
are more painful than external ones. It is fitting that Henry should
receive a head wound, a bump that jolts him with a severe headache.
But what "salve" is there to ease the pain of his internal wound of
dishonor? That is Henry's "headache"! It is the ache of his conscience that he has been honored by the regiment he has dishonored.
Just as Jim runs into the fields to hide his true wound from Henry,
so Henry runs into the fields to hide his false wound, his false badge
of courage, from the tattered man who asks him where he is
wounded. "It might be inside mostly, an' them plays thunder. Where
is it located?" The men, so Henry feels, are perpetually probing his
guilt-wound, "ever upraising the ghost of shame on the stick of their
curiosity." The unmistakable implication here is of a flag, and the
actual flag that Henry carries in battle is the symbol of his conscience. Conscience is also symbolized by the forest, the cathedral-
forest where Henry retreats to nurse his guilt-wound and be con-
soled by the benedictions that nature sympathetically bestows upon
him. Here in this forest chapel there is a churchlike silence as insects
bow their beaks while Henry bows his head in shame; they make a
"devotional pause" while the trees chant a soft hymn to comfort him.
But Henry is troubled; he cannot "conciliate the forest." Nor can
he conciliate the flag. The flag registers the commotion of his mind,
and it registers the restless movements of the nervous regiment—
it flutters when the men expect battle. And when the regiment runs
from battle, the flag sinks down "as if dying. Its motion as it fell was
a gesture of despair." Henry dishonors the flag not when he flees
from battle but when he flees from himself, and he redeems it when
he redeems his conscience.

Redemption begins in confession, in absolution—in a change of

heart. Henry's plight is identical with the Reverend Mr. Dimmesdale's plight in Hawthorne's psychological novel *The Scarlet Letter*. The mythology of the scarlet letter is much the same as that of
the red badge: each is the emblem of moral guilt and salvation. The
red badge is the scarlet letter of dishonor transferred from the bosom
of Hester, the social outcast, to the mind of Henry Fleming, the
"mental outcast." Henry's wounded conscience is not healed until
he confesses the truth to himself and opens his eyes to new ways;
not until he strips his enemy heart of "the brass and bombast of his
earlier gospels," the vainglorious illusions he had fabricated into
a cloak of pride and self-vindication, not until he puts on new gar-
ments of humility and loving-kindness for his fellow men. Redemption begins in humility—Henry's example is the loud soldier who
becomes the humble soldier. The loud soldier admits the folly of
his former ways. Henry's spiritual change is a prolonged process,
but it is signalized in moments when he loses his soul in the flux
of things; then he courageously deserts himself instead of his fellow
men; then, fearlessly plunging into battle, charging the enemy like
"a pagan who defends his religion," he becomes swept up in a delirium of selflessness and feels himself "capable of profound sacrifices." The brave new Henry, "new bearer of the colors," triumphs
over the former one. The enemy flag is wrenched from the hands
of "the rival color-bearer," the symbol of Henry's own other self,
and as this rival color-bearer dies, Henry is "reborn." [2]

Henry's regeneration is brought about by the death of Jim Conklin, his friend since childhood. He goes under various names. He
is sometimes called the spectral soldier (his face is a pasty gray) and
sometimes the tall soldier (he is taller than all the other men), but
there are unmistakable hints—in such descriptive details about him
as his wound in the side, his torn body and his gory hand, and even
in the initials of his name, Jim Conklin—that he is intended to represent Jesus Christ. We are told that there is "a resemblance in him
to a devotee of a mad religion," and among his followers the doomed

[2] Henry has sought redemption and thinks he has attained it, but Crane's
ambiguous imagery of sun-through-raincloud—at the end of the novel—both
affirms and simultaneously undercuts that affirmation. Seen from Crane's ironic
viewpoint, his mocked hero—a disciple in the Army of the Lord—has undergone
no true spiritual change or redemption. Henry's longing for "soft and eternal
peace" is just as unrealistic as his earlier code of Greek heroics, and so Crane's
hero is back where he started. The sunlight of his separate peace is obscured
and mocked by leaden rainclouds.

man stirs up "thoughts of a solemn ceremony." When he dies the
heavens signify his death—the red sun bleeds with the passion of
his wounds:

The red sun was pasted in the sky like a wafer.[3]

This grotesque image, the most notorious metaphor in American
literature, has been much debated and roundly damned by all Crane
critics (excepting Conrad, Willa Cather, and Hergesheimer, who
admired it, but failed to explain why), ridiculed as downright bad
writing—a false, melodramatic nonfunctional figure. It is, in fact,
the key to the symbolism of the whole novel, particularly the religious symbolism that radiates outwards from Jim Conklin. Like any
image, it has to be related to the structure of meaning in which it
functions; when lifted out of its context it is bound to seem artifi-
cial and irrelevant or, on the other hand, merely "a superb piece of
imagery." I do not think it can be doubted that Crane intended to
suggest here the sacrificial death celebrated in communion.

Henry and the tattered soldier consecrate the death of the spectral soldier in "a solemn ceremony." Henry partakes of the sacra-
mental blood and body of Christ, and the process of his spiritual rebirth begins at the moment when the wafer-like sun appears in the
sky. It is a symbol of salvation through death. Henry, we are made
to feel, recognizes in the lifeless sun his own lifeless conscience, his
dead and as yet unregenerated selfhood or conscience, and that is
why he blasphemes against it. His moral salvation and triumph are
prepared for by this ritual of purification and religious devotion
and, at the very start of the book, by the ritual of absolution that
Jim Conklin performs in the opening scene. It was the tall soldier
who first "developed virtues" and showed the boys how to cleanse
a flag. The way is to wash it in the muddy river. Only by experienc-
ing life, the muddy river, can the soul be cleansed. In "The Open
Boat" it is the black sea, and the whiteness of the waves as they pace
to and fro in the moonlight signifies the spiritual purification that
the men win from their contest against the terrible water. The ritual
of domestic comforts bestowed upon the saved men by the people

[3] The passage preceding this image reads: "The youth turned, with sudden,
livid rage, toward the battle-field. He shook his fist. He seemed about to deliver
a philippic. 'Hell—'" The critics who claim that the youth shakes his fist at
the battlefield have not noticed what the manuscript reveals: "He turned in
tupenny fury upon the high, tranquil sky. He would have liked to have splashed
it with a derisive paint" (in Chapter X of Manuscript SV).

on the shore, "all the remedies sacred to their minds," is a shallow
thing, devoid of spiritual value. The sea offers the only true remedy,
though it costs a "terrible grace." The way—as Stein said in Conrad's *Lord Jim*—is to immerse oneself in the destructive element.
Kurtz, in Conrad's "Heart of Darkness," washed his soul in the
Congo, and Marlow, because he had become a part of Kurtz, redeemed the heart of darkness by the same token. Conrad, like Crane,
had himself experienced his own theme, but Crane was the first to
produce a work based on it. Crane's influence on Conrad is apparent
in *Lord Jim*. Both *Lord Jim* and *The Red Badge of Courage* variously exploit the same thematic contrast of ideals versus realities.
In terms of religious symbolism they have further affinities. When
Lord Jim goes to his death, there is an awful sunset. Conrad's enormous sun—"The sky over Patusan was blood-red, immense, streaming like an open vein"—recalls Crane's symbolic red sun "pasted
in the sky like a wafer."

*   *   *

The Red Badge of Courage is loaded with Biblical allusions and
parallelisms. In a passage expunged from the final holograph Manuscript LV, Henry Fleming's mother says:

. . . and here's a little bible I want yeh to take along with yeh, Henry.
I don't presume yeh'll be a-setting reading it all day long, child, ner
nothin' like that. Many a time, yeh'll fergit yeh got it, I don't doubt.
But there'll be many a time, too, Henry, when yeh'll be wanting advice,
boy, and all like that, and there'll be nobody round, perhaps, to tell
yeh things. Then if yeh take it out, boy, yeh'll find wisdom in it—
wisdom in it, Henry—with little or no searching.

But Henry forgets the Bible and after Jim Conklin's death he
forgets the tall soldier whom he had known since childhood. However, Henry momentarily identifies with Tall Soldier Conklin when
he imagines that he too gets "calmly killed on a high place before
the eyes of all. He thought of the magnificent pathos of his dead
body." His vision of himself in the heroic role of the Tall Soldier
occasions Crane's ironic viewpoint about his duped and self-deceiving
hero: "For a moment he was sublime."

When Henry is wounded on the head, he goes "tall soldier
fashion," and thus again he cross-identifies with Conklin-Christ.
That bump on the head is ironically his sign of redemption, but it
is not even a true wound of battle. Dazed from the blow on his
head, Henry is met by the Cheery Soldier, an occurrence which has

(to quote Donald Thomas) [4] a suggestive parallel to the story of Christ on the road to Emmaus. In the Bible it occurs after the Resurrection:

> And, behold, two of them went that same day to a village called Emmaus, . . .
> And they talked together of all these things that had happened.
> And it came to pass, that, while they communed together and reasoned, Jesus himself drew near and went with them.
> But their eyes were holden that they should not know him (Luke 24:13-16).

Christ asks them questions, and "beginning at Moses and all the Prophets, he expounded unto them in all the Scriptures the things concerning himself" (Luke 24:17). These are Christ's anecdotes of himself, just as the Cheery Soldier's anecdotes are of himself. As the Cheery Soldier relates them, he indicates how confused the day has been for him: "There was shootin' here an' shootin' there, an' hollering' here an' hollerin' there, *in the damn darkness,* until I couldn't tell t' save m' soul which side I was on" (italics added here and below). The smoke of battle may have been heavy, but the "damn darkness" is a description of the darkness of the world at the time of Christ's death. It is no wonder that the Cheery-Soldier-as-Christ says, *"By dad,* I give myself up fer dead any number 'a times." The Cheery Soldier says: "It'll be a miracle if we find our reg'ments t'night," but the miracle is worked, for "in the search which followed, the man of the cheery voice seemed to the youth to possess a wand of a magic kind." To the wounded and confused youth the events of that night and the efforts of the Cheery Soldier might well seem amazing as he works his way through "mazes of the tangled forest with a strange fortune." To the Cheery Soldier "obstacles fell before him and became of assistance." Here is no ordinary soldier who leads this youth back to the Army of the Lord; here is divine guidance for one who is physically lost and for disciples who have lost their way. Many are obviously in retreat.

[4] What follows is recast from an unpublished short study by Professor Donald Thomas, drawn from his University of Connecticut doctoral thesis (1966), "The Long Logic: A Symbolic Interpretation of Stephen Crane's *The Red Badge of Courage.*" I am much indebted to Professor Thomas, for his discoveries buttress by 1950 reading of Crane's war novel in my Introduction to the Modern Library edition of *The Red Badge of Courage* (Random House, 1951). That reading was first reprinted in *Critiques and Essays on Modern Fiction,* edited by John Aldridge (1952); next in my *Stephen Crane: An Omnibus* (1952); and then in my *Houses That James Built* (1961).

At the start the Cheery Soldier took Henry's arm and said with a laugh: "I'm goin' your way. Th' hull gang is goin' your way." But in no literal sense is the whole gang going his way. In a symbolic sense the whole world is going the way of Christ. The Cheery Soldier substitutes as replacement for Conklin as Christ. In the Bible the story ends with the two disciples recognizing Christ: "Their eyes were opened, and they knew him; and he vanished out of their sight" (Luke 24:31). In both stories there is the sudden disappearance of the guide, the Cheery Soldier disappearing into the night. "As he who had so befriended him was thus passing out of his life, it suddenly occurred to the youth that he had not once seen his face." In this variant ending Crane's story differs from that of the Bible, but *that* is the way it happened when Crane walked back to Edmund's house at Lake View in the Spring of 1893 and was joined by a friendly stranger whose face he never saw.

The world revealed to Henry the next day is a new one: "When the youth awoke it seemed to him that he had been asleep *for a thousand years,* and he felt sure that he opened his eyes upon an unexpected world." During Henry's sleeping, as it were, there has occurred a thousand-year shift to the World of Revelation: the thousand years of Christ's rule on earth. "A heraldic wind" blows through the trees, and Henry sees the sleeping men around him as corpses in a charnel house and recognizes that "this somber picture was not a fact of the present, but a mere prophecy." A bugle is sounded. It is like the opening of the Book of Revelation (4:1): "The first voice which I heard was as it were of a trumpet talking with me; which said, Come up hither, and I will show you things which must be hereafter." In the course of battle Henry acquires humility: "New eyes were given to him. And the most startling thing was to learn that he was very insignificant." Since he is now humble, he is capable of being exalted and is ready for the new world revealed: "They had passed into a clearer atmosphere. There was *an effect like a revelation* in the new appearance of the landscape." In the battle that follows, Henry drives the troops to attack. "For him *the way seemed eternal,*" as indeed it is. The enemy is driven off, however, and the men discover they have come through another testing: "And they were men." The enemy attacks again, and Henry—involved in battle—becomes transported: "Sometimes he prattled, *words coming unconsciously from him in grotesque exclamations.*" He is now filled with the spirit as in the Bible: "And they were all filled with the Holy Ghost, and *began to speak with other tongues,* as the spirit gave them utterance" (Acts 2:4).

It is Peter in this section of the Bible who inspires the disciples and leads them, and it is Henry here who does the same: "He felt himself *the daring spirit of a savage religion-mad.* He was capable of profound sacrifices, a tremendous death." These same words described Conklin-Christ in an earlier chapter, and now Henry has become like him. As the troops retire victoriously from the field, Henry considers all that has happened. His performances in battle have earned him glory; his deeds are robed in "wide purple and gold," the royal colors of heaven. Henry remembers the praise of the Lieutenant, and he thinks of it as "a little coronation," which echoes the Bible's "crown of glory that fadeth not away (I Peter 5:4). Henry can now "look back upon the brass and bombast of his earlier gospels and see them truly. . . . He was a man." As he trudges "from the place of blood and wrath his soul changed." The Book of Isaiah is echoed in Crane's saying that Henry "came from hot plowshares to prospects of clover tranquilly."

Cosmic Pessimism
in *The Red Badge of Courage*

by Olov W. Fryckstedt

Let us turn to the first American edition [of *The Red Badge of Courage*] and see what Crane left of the theme of Fleming's revolt against the universe after the heavy excisions he made in the course of his work on the novel. Clearly he retained only one instance which could be termed [part of this revolt,] namely the famous scene at the end of Chapter IX where in a moment of indignation after Jim Conklin's death he shakes his fist in rage against the battlefield while the red sun is pasted as a wafer in the sky. Chronologically this scene precedes the other two occasions of rebellion which occur only in the manuscript text. The excised passages in Chapter X begin with what seems to be a direct reference to this scene. "Promptly, then, his old rebellious feelings returned . . . ."

Before we discuss this scene it might be useful to recapitulate briefly some of the events which lead up to it. As we know, the young soldier's rebellious feelings have their origin in the crisis he faced after his flight when he learns that his regiment has withstood the enemy attack. "A dull, animal-like rebellion against his fellows, war in the abstract, and fate grew within him." It is in this spirit that he penetrates into the forest away from the din of the battle front. His experiences in the forest are of great importance for our understanding of the moment of his revolt and despair, because they constitute important stages in his disillusionment with the universe.

Henry Fleming's withdrawal into nature in quest of peace and of answers to the ultimate questions of life strikes deep chords in

"Cosmic Pessimism in *The Red Badge of Courage*" (original title: "Henry Fleming's Tupenny Fury: Cosmic Pessimism in Stephen Crane's *The Red Badge of Courage*"). From *Studia Neophilologica*, XXXIII (1961), 265-281 (abridged). Reprinted by permission of *Studia Neophilologica* and the author.

American idealism. It was a thought dear to Americans that they could always take refuge in the vast expanses of untouched and innocent nature away from the ills and limitations of human society. The transcendentalists had added a new dimension to man's relation to nature. To them the natural phenomena were keys to spiritual realities: through nature man could commune with God and in her face he could read the laws of right and wrong.

Crane satirizes the youth's naïve belief in the innocence and peacefulness of nature; his belief is nothing but the romantic view reduced to absurdity:

> This landscape gave him assurance. A fair field holding life. It was the religion of peace. It would die if its timid eyes were compelled to see blood. He conceived Nature to be a woman with a deep aversion to tragedy.

In the episode with the squirrel Crane also pokes fun at the transcendentalist and romantic view that nature could give man direct answers to his petty problems. Henry Fleming takes the squirrel's flight after the pine cone has been thrown at it as nature's way of endorsing his own flight by demonstrating that his behavior as well as that of the squirrel was part of a general natural law. Thereafter moving deeper and deeper into the heart of nature's mystery, he finally comes to the innermost part of the forest cathedral. When suddenly confronted with the decomposing corpse upon whose face ants are eagerly feeding he realizes with a shock of terror the real law that governs nature. All life exists upon death, "eating ravenously, stuffing itself with the hopes of the dead," as Crane wrote in the manuscript. Nature could offer him no escape or relief from life on the battlefield; in fact he had found that the laws which governed nature were not too different from those which seemed to rule on the battlefield. The corpse in the forest cathedral blocked his retreat away from men and forced him back.

Fresh from the agonizing discovery in the forest Fleming meets the endless stream of wounded men and finally witnesses his friend Jim Conklin's gruesome death struggle. Throughout his excruciatingly painful death pangs Jim Conklin moves and acts as if he were taking part in some kind of grotesque ritual. The two spectators, Henry Fleming and the tattered soldier, are terrified and inspired by "thoughts of a solemn ceremony." But they also sense that this grotesque ritual, born of pain and terror, has little to do with traditional religion. It seems rather to mock religion and reduce its teachings to nonsense; it is religion gone mad. Jim Conklin resembled "a devotee of a mad religion, blood-sucking, muscle-wrenching, bone-crushing." His senseless pangs seem rather to spring from the brutal and unfeeling laws of nature whose full meaning was revealed to the young soldier in the religious half-light of the forest cathedral. Jim Conklin appears to be the innocent and unknowing victim of some ravenous animal. When he has finally succumbed to death, his wounded side looks as if it had been chewed by wolves. Fleming's intense suffering at the sight of his friend's death struggle is enhanced by his growing realization that it is totally meaningless and that its cruelty serves no purpose. His feelings of outrage and indignation reach a climax when he stands over Jim Conklin's dead body with its cruel wound and its stupidly grinning face. Turning toward the battlefield in livid rage he shakes his fist at it in a pathetic and ineffectual gesture. All he can say is "Hell." A fiercely red sun shines over the scene. Here as elsewhere in the book the sun is a symbol of impassive nature. It has now assumed the color which in other places in the book symbolizes war, blood, violence, and fear. It is characteristic that Crane considered using the word "fierce" in no less than two places in the sentence: "The [fierce—canceled in the first version] red sun was pasted in the sky like a [fierce—canceled in the second version] wafer." Once before during the brief lull in his first battle, Fleming had become aware of the sun in a clear blue sky: it had then surprised him that "Nature had gone tranquilly on with her golden process in the midst of so much devilment." The appearance of the blood-red sun at this moment of despair and grief confirmed the violence and brutality of the processes of nature.

Jim Conklin's death scene is a climactic moment in the book. We are made to see man's insignificance and the relentlessness of the laws governing the universe. Although Fleming cuts a rather pitiful figure under the towering sky, Crane's intention is not satirical. In fact this is one point in the book where the author seems to identify himself wholly with his character. The youth's moment of rage and despair recalls a prevalent mood in *The Black Riders*. And the horror of a world without a god is a theme which recurs in both Crane's prose and poetry. A newly discovered poem, quoted by Daniel Hoffman in his study of Crane's poetry, describes this nihilistic wasteland:

> A row of thick pillars
> Consciously bracing for the weight
> Of a vanished roof
> The bronze light of sunset strikes through them,
> And over a floor made for slow rites.
> There is no sound of singing
> But, aloft, a great and terrible bird
> Is watching a cur, beaten and cut,
> That crawls to the cool shadows of the pillars
> To die.

Jim Conklin's final struggle parodies the rites of a religion in order to bring out the cruel irony of death's total lack of significance in an indifferent naturalistic universe. Under these circumstances any protest against the order of things is futile. "When it occurs to a man," Crane wrote in "The Open Boat," "that nature does not regard him as important, and that she feels she would not maim the universe by disposing of him, he at first wishes to throw bricks at the temple, and he hates deeply the fact that there are no bricks and no temples." . . .

Throughout his work on *The Red Badge of Courage* Crane considered the theme of Fleming's revolt against the universe as intimately related to his war story. The explanation of this is obviously to be found in the fact that war as a subject appealed to Crane precisely because it seemed an excellent vehicle for him to express the ideas about human life which preoccupied him at this time. War dramatized to perfection his naturalistic conception of human existence. Through this medium Crane was able to objectify his own feelings of anxiety and despair. In this war story Crane was thus manipulating two levels of meaning: one—more obvious and concrete—concerned the record of the hero's war experiences and the other—more elusive and somewhat submerged—concerned the theme of man's place in the universe. The extensive cuts in the manuscript, all of which relate to the theme of Fleming's revolt against the universe, indicate that Crane was most anxious not to let the philosophical implications of his story become too conspicuous and thus break the unity of tone and plot. He was writing a war story, not a philosophical tract.

His artistic problem was to make scenes, events, and descriptions subtly suggest a wider perspective on human reality, an awareness of a larger tragedy than the one witnessed on the battlefield. Much of the peculiar tone of dreamlike strangeness and terror which prevails in the book was no doubt due to the genesis of the work: as Crane was imagining the war scenes in the novel, on the basis of rather extensive research and reading, he saw them bathed in the light of his naturalistic pessimism; they assumed the color of his despair over man's situation in the universe. *The Red Badge of Courage* is not meant to be read as straight allegory or as a sustained parable. It is not consistently symbolical. The metaphysical perspective is not insistent but nevertheless subtly pervasive. There is a faint suggestion that the soldiers are involved in a more desperate struggle than the actual fighting, that the apparent meaninglessness of the war is readily surpassed by a greater and more terrifying emptiness. This atmosphere of despair, of mystery, of terror haunts us throughout the book.

Homer and Stephen Crane

by Warren D. Anderson

The whole story of Private Henry Fleming [in *The Red Badge of Courage*] requires only about 160 pages in the telling; Crane called it an episode. He is concerned not with *mênis*, the smoldering anger of a grudge such as Achilles nursed, but with a quality of spirit for which English has no single word. The Homeric poems speak of it as *menos*, and it often refers to the transfiguring battle-rage of the brave fighter. Its opposite is fear; the relationship between the two opposites powerfully informs Crane's novel. One notes that in the formal presentation of his theme he has divided this strikingly short work into twenty-four chapters, their average length only about a half-dozen pages. The end of a chapter, moreover, does not necessarily mark a break in the action. It would seem difficult to account for this wealth of chapters, which the newspaper serialization arrangements did not require, unless perhaps it hints at the traditional division of *Iliad* and *Odyssey* into twenty-four books each.

At all events, Henry Fleming and his adventures have their Homeric counterparts. Though he acts from very different motives, Achilles too retires from battle, is profoundly affected by the death of a comrade, and returns to overwhelm the enemy with a furious attack. Telemachus gains a courage (*menos* as boldness of spirit) that brings him from adolescence to the full stature of young manhood. At the climactic moment of his life, Hector finds himself obeying impulses more primordial than the civilized imperative that calls us to render our duty. Moreover, both Homeric poems have been thought to deal with self-discovery, which for Achilles at least

"Homer and Stephen Crane." From *Nineteenth-Century Fiction*, XIX (June 1964), 77-86 (abridged). © 1964 by The Regents of the University of California. Reprinted by permission of The Regents of the University of California and the author.

means discovering the true nature of heroism (*aretê*) without illusion.

Like Homer, Crane treats various kinds of non-mortal entities as immediate and potent factors in war. Such epic fixtures are creations, even aspects, of man's mind; here the difference between the two writers may lie chiefly in the degree of awareness. But what matters is that Crane gives the impression of consciously following Homeric and Vergilian precedent. He lends an objective vividness to these subjective qualities by presenting them in the form of gods or goddesses, demons or witches. Actually he recognizes, within the frame of illusion, only one god and one goddess. The dominant entity, almost the center of a battle-spawned monotheism, is the war-god. He is repeatedly suggested as being swollen and red, not majestic but animal-like. Homer had created a double Ares, anthropomorph and battle-spirit; Crane grants neither human form nor abstract status, suggesting instead the arcane bestiality of a Moloch. Unlike the war-god, the goddess of *The Red Badge of Courage* does have an epiphany. She is the battle-flag, the symbol and prize of valor that floats untouched above the fighting. She appears but once, nevertheless, and then as a mere image in the excited mind of Henry Fleming. Clearly *Nikê* does not have the stature of *Polemos*: victory is relative and ephemeral, war a grim enduring absolute.

Terror, rout, and the fear that leads to flight all take personified form in the *Iliad*; so Henry Fleming, lying awake on the night before his first battle, saw in the darkness "visions of a thousand-tongued fear that would babble at his back and cause him to flee" (Chapter II) ; and the next day (III), as action became imminent, his old fears "reassailed him, but . . . he doggedly let them babble." Later (XI), in a surge of theoretical bravery, Henry imagines himself rushing to the front "to seize and throttle the dark, leering witch of calamity."

We are familiar with the elaborate and bizarre personification of rumor in *Aeneid* 4. Homer had already set the precedent; the idea of swift, towering growth into the heavens comes, moreover, from his image of *Eris*, quickly-spreading Strife. Vergil's special contribution consists in presenting *Fama* as a bird. Whether he maintains the tradition consciously or not, Crane writes (IV) that the Union troops "mouthed rumors that had flown like birds out of the unknown"; on a later occasion (XVI) "Among the men in the rifle pits rumors again flew, but they were now for the most part black creatures who flapped their wings drearily near to the ground and refused to rise on any wings of hope." This second comparison, free from Vergil's extravagance, achieves as great an effectiveness. Elsewhere (V and XXIII) bird imagery once or twice describes the flags, which seem to Henry Fleming "like beautiful birds strangely undaunted in a storm," or the battle shock itself—he expects "an encounter of strange beaks and claws, as of eagles."

Obvious borrowings from antiquity almost never appear in *The Red Badge of Courage*. One striking and beautiful exception (III) : as the morning sun burns away the mist "regiments burst into view like armed men just born of the earth." When Crane writes in the same chapter that "the insects, nodding upon their perches, crooned like old women," the reader of Homer remembers the old men on Troy's wall, piping like cicadas, though the resemblance may be a matter of coincidence. More difficult to dismiss is the incident (VII) in which Henry, after running from the fighting, chases away an inquisitive squirrel and takes its flight as "a sign" justifying his own behavior. One wonders too at the way Henry, stumbling with head bowed in an oblivion of pain, is quickly and surely guided to his own unit by a stranger identified only as "the man of the cheery voice." He "seemed to the youth to possess a wand of a magic kind," says Crane (XII), and "threaded the mazes of the tangled forest with a strange fortune." As he left Henry "it suddenly occurred to the youth that he had not once seen his face." So in the *Iliad* a god will spirit a wounded fighter away to safety without revealing his own nature. It must be noted that Crane took this particular incident from a similar but less dramatic boyhood experience; his reason for using it is perhaps another matter.

The most remarkable parallel with Homer does not consist in any of these particulars; it may be found throughout the novel, in Crane's use of similes. The sheer quantity of them (about 160, without including instances in dialogue) is impressive, but what interests a classicist reader is the way they are handled. Most often Crane compares men in war to animals, though an occasional vignette will be taken from peacetime life. Fleeing troops are likened to helpless sheep or chickens; when they attack, however, they become maddened horses, fierce hounds, wolves, eagles, panthers. Troop columns are dragons, winding serpents, moving monsters with many feet. A shattered line of charging men buckles slowly like a toppling wall, it curls and writhes like a snake trodden underfoot.

John Berryman has said of Crane: "His animism is like nothing else in civilized literature. Mountains, trees, dogs, men, horses, and boats flash in and out of each other's identities."[1] The second statement is profoundly true. The first is not, unless Homer be thought uncivilized, for essentially the same unreflecting sense of man's oneness with the natural creation underlies the greater part of Homeric simile. This sense disappears early in the development of a culture— the seventh-century lyric poet Alcman seems still to have it, for example, whereas Euripides and Vergil clearly do not—and when it has gone its place is taken by a conscious dealing with nature (the capitalized form, Nature, now begins to have appropriateness) that betrays the sense of disjunction. The *Iliad* can compare fighting men to wolves or again to donkeys or wasps as the occasion demands, quite without ludicrousness: the comparison rests upon a basis of community. The Romantic poets could not work from any such presupposition, and there is a certain shock in the realization that *The Red Badge of Courage* came only four decades after the death of Wordsworth. Yet once in a great while a writer appears who celebrates the ancient union as if it had never been dissolved. Such very likely is Nikos Kazantzakis in his *Sequel* to the *Odyssey*; such was Stephen Crane beyond all doubt, and his similes are more truly Homeric than those of Kazantzakis.

For proof, one may consider their distribution. It directly reflects the immediacy and intensity of battle. Only two chapters out of the entire twenty-four use a large number of similes for any other purpose: these are the second, in which the description of a regiment marching toward battle sets the novel's tone, and the ninth, which records the death of Jim Conklin. Everywhere else similes become more frequent in proportion as the fighting becomes more savage. By the same token they occur only rarely during lulls in the fighting, and they are wholly absent from the two chapters (the tenth and the fifteenth) which deal exclusively with inner moods and personal relationships. Such technique may justifiably be called Homeric. The main strategy is clearly that of the *Iliad*; and Crane parallels Homer even on the more immediate level of tactics, for he deploys his similes at various times to mark a crisis or transition or to render in depth the several aspects of a given situation. Though one or two instances seem to echo particular similes applied to Ajax and Hector, there is no need to labor these parallels.

[1] *Stephen Crane* (New York, 1950), p. 268.

"The Open Boat" and The Absurd

by William Bysshe Stein

"The night of the jungle" is the dark metaphor of Crane's sensibility. Like the *Weltnacht* of modern existentialism, it controls his vision of human destiny. Beginning with *Maggie,* his requiem for the God of Christianity, he commits himself to record the anxiety, the frustration, the despair, the irrationality, and the absurdity of existence. In this perspective both life and death are emptied of meaning, and, as a consequence, man is denied the catharsis of tragedy. He is always doomed to play the role of a clown, but most of the time without the self-awareness of the clown. This fact perhaps explains why the occurrence of death in Crane's fiction is always touched with macabre humor. It may seem on occasions that some of his heroes or characters, after a crisis of experience, achieve an understanding of themselves in terms of acceptable ideals and values. But in cases like these—the terminal vows of Henry Fleming in *The Red Badge of Courage* serve as a good example—the reader must ask himself whether the individual has reached his new wisdom through an assimilation of the contradictions that he discovered in his thoughts, feelings, and actions in the course of a specific ordeal. If he has not, then we must conclude that he is the victim of self-deception. In line with Crane's belief that "Preaching is fatal to art in literature," his stories tell themselves. One does not find the theme crystallized in isolated episodes or images; the total report of a pattern of action is the meaning of a story. If there are moral lessons to be learned, they are defined ceremonially, in the sequence of connected events that constitutes a hero's initiation into the ludicrous "pathos of his situation." (This phrase from "The Open Boat" has, one cannot deny, at least a verbal similarity to the existential lamentation, "the pathos of existence.") . . .

" 'The Open Boat' and The Absurd." From "Stephen Crane's *Homo Absurdus*" in *Bucknell Review,* VIII (May 1959), 168-188 (abridged). Reprinted by permission of *Bucknell Review* and the author.

["The Open Boat"] objectively registers the absurdity that envelops any encounter with contingent death. It filters into man's thoughts, it dominates man's feelings, and it informs the world of man's existence. The men in the boat, particularly the correspondent, try desperately to justify their survival in the struggle against the sea, but the value categories of their culture fail to serve them in their predicament. The idealistic virtues of bravery, fortitude, and integrity possess no meaning in a universe that denies the importance of man. And Crane, like a Sartre or a Camus, traces this condition to the withdrawal of God from the province of humanity. In His absence or death His place has been usurped by the idiot forces of nihilism:

> . . . 'if I am going to be drowned, *why,* in the name of the seven mad gods who rule the sea, was I allowed to come thus far and contemplate sand and trees? Was I brought here merely to have my nose dragged away as I was about to nibble the sacred cheese of life? *It is preposterous.* If this old ninny-woman, Fate, cannot do better than this, she should be deprived of the management of men's fortunes. *She is an old hen who knows not her intention.* If she has decided to drown me, *why* did she not do it in the beginning and save me all this trouble? *The whole affair is absurd.'* [My italics.]

Crane here asks the same questions implicit in Trescott's enumeration of the cups [in *The Monster*]. Pathetically, they are all negative in content, for they cannot be answered. In effect, man cannot construct a rational picture of the world out of his own experience. He knows only that he is the victim of forces beyond his control, that he suffers without apparent justification, that he confronts the reality of nothingness. As opposed to the abstract and the possible, this is the real and the concrete—the existence that defies understanding in terms of essence.

Crane next carries this phase of the correspondent's subjective dialectic to its logical conclusion, applying the lesson of divine treason to a redefinition of the meaning of good and evil. How ridiculous it is, he argues, to fret about the transcendent realm of values if these are not to be realized here and now under the stress of human problems:

> [The wind-tower] represented in a degree . . . the serenity of nature amid the struggles of the individual—nature in the wind, and nature in the vision of men. She did not seem cruel to him then, nor beneficent, nor treacherous, nor wise. But she was indifferent, flatly indifferent. It is, perhaps, plausible that a man in this situation . . .

should see the innumerable flaws of his life, and have them taste wickedly in his mind, and wish for another chance. *A distinction between right and wrong seems absurdly clear to him,* then, *in this new ignorance of the grave-edge,* and he understands that if he were given another opportunity he would mend his conduct and his words, *and be better and brighter during an introduction* or at a tea. [My italics.]

In addition to parodying the old wives' tale that man, on the brink of death, is involuntarily forced into an audit of his spiritual resources, Crane debunks the moral function of the categories of good and evil. Since the world has been stripped of causality, there is no one to whom man is responsible for his individual behavior. Only the gods of the properties have any visible existence, and to these the correspondent turns in burlesque adoration. Here, ostensibly, society has learned to distinguish between right and wrong in a manner that touches human needs and desires, however petty and futile they are. This *reductio ad absurdum* of moral authority, interestingly enough, has its analogue in Camus's *The Stranger.* Meursault cannot feel sorry for himself or for the man whom he murdered, for he is beyond good and evil. He is the unregenerate "outsider" who has lost his identity in the world. Any effort at all to combat this state of affairs would be wasted. Hence he passively accepts the rule of chaos. This knowledge, it would seem, is not unlike the correspondent's "new ignorance."

At least one gathers this impression from Crane's description of the correspondent's sudden immersion in the sea. In his alienation from God and nature, he finds himself hopelessly confused. His sense of being is disjointed, for he cannot coordinate thought, feeling, and action. Instead of worrying about drowning, he bewails the temperature of the water: "The coldness of the water was sad; it was tragic. This fact was somehow mixed and confused with his opinion of his own situation, so that it seemed almost a proper reason for tears. The water was cold." And instead of concerning himself with the necessity of preserving his strength, he hails his weariness as a chance to make a truce with his fear of physical pain: "he reflected that when one gets properly wearied drowning must really be a comfortable arrangement . . . ; and he was glad of it, for the main thing in his mind for some moments had been horror of the temporary agony. He did not wish to be hurt." These contradictory responses to the crisis of death parallel a basic premise of existential philosophy. The sense of the absurd originates in the human mind, and it grows directly out of the irrationality of experience. In the process an irreconcilable conflict between consciousness and reality is engendered. For, as in the behavior of the correspondent, man cannot adjust himself to the conditions of existence. Significantly, these incongruities of experience contrast with his earlier convictions about the meaning of the collective ordeal. I refer to "the subtle brotherhood of men" that the correspondent predicates for the group in the boat. This fleeting apprehension, I submit, is merely self-deception—man torturing his imagination to find purpose in purposelessness, nobility in ignobility, dignity in degradation. This supposition of meaningful human unity, if one is to accept its validity, must be correlated with the outcome of the experience. The brief comradeship is unpityingly dissolved by contingent circumstance, for the oiler perishes in the turbulent waters. Is not this the message of "the great sea's voice" that the survivors are left to interpret? Is not this what Sartre calls the triumph of the absurd—the appalling realization that "every existing thing is born without reason, prolongs itself out of weakness and dies by chance?" This is the pathos of existence that the correspondent first discovers in his memory of the soldier dying at Algiers: "it was an actuality—stern, mournful, and fine," and he "was moved by a profound and perfectly impersonal comprehension." Related to the terminal episode of the story, the respective fates of the men are as inexplicable as the death of the soldier. To die is simply to die. To live is to be absurd—in chilled solitude to watch all trusted hopes and anticipations dissipate. This idea is, I believe, firmly crystallized in the correspondent's comical theophany just a few minutes before he discovers that his companion in the ordeal has died: "he was naked—naked as a tree in winter; but a halo was about his head, and he shone like a saint." If, as some readers insist, this vision of one of the rescuers is a symbol of moral regeneration, then Crane is here leaping the void of the absurd, hand in hand with Kierkegaard.

"The Blue Hotel":
A Psychoanalytic Study

by Daniel Weiss

"The Blue Hotel," as an intensive study of fear, is perhaps the
finest thing Crane has done, if it is not the finest thing any American writer has produced on this subject. Behind it lie the images of
terror and violence which make *The Red Badge of Courage* a masterpiece of intuition. Behind it lies the uneasy sense of invulnera-
bility that drove Crane to test his own courage, to advance from his
literary dream of "broken-bladed glory" to become in his own right
the foolhardy war-correspondent who, during the Cuban war, "let
himself quietly over the redoubt, lighted a cigarette, stood for a
few moments with his arms at his sides, while the bullets hissed past
him into the mud, then as quietly climbed back over the redoubt
and strolled away." [1]

A psychoanalytic study of "The Blue Hotel" is best made within
the context of Crane's other works, principally *The Red Badge of
Courage*, but including subsequent war and adventure fiction. The
principle of selection involves Crane's treatment of the protagonist.
It is the introspective and analytic mind of Henry Fleming, or Nolan,
or the New York Kid which may provide us with the keys to the
beautifully articulated but hermetically sealed imagination of the
Swede.

If we approach *The Red Badge of Courage* as the reconstruction
on Crane's part of an emotional rather than an historical event, we
emerge with an inventory of regressive aims and fantasies whose

"'The Blue Hotel': A Psychoanalytic Study." From *"The Red Badge of
Courage"* in *The Psychoanalytic Review*, LII (Summer and Fall 1965), 32-52,
130-154. Reprinted by permission of the National Psychological Association for
Psychoanalysis. An abridgement was prepared especially for this volume by
the author.

[1] John Berryman, *Stephen Crane* (New York, 1950), p. 222.

main fixtures are a variety of defenses against anxiety, and a displacement, on to the army, of parental and sibling identifications. Henry Fleming's career is a series of strategies by which he denies the existence of personal danger; these are describable in terms of counterphobic defenses, regressive magical formulae, a recourse to those mental processes which either ignore reality, or finally substitute a system of delusions linked to reality only as magical formulae are linked to the phenomena they presume to control.

To defeat anxiety one must persuade oneself that there is no cause for it. In the beginning Fleming denies danger by projecting it into the past or seeing it as a game—a "Greeklike struggle," or a "blue demonstration." Next, he denies his own fears by projecting them on to others, his mess-mate Wilson, for example, when he fortifies himself by the disparagement of others. Again, he may seek his security in the passive dependence on institutionalized parent-figures who stand omnipotently on guard over him. Fleming takes refuge within the collective maternal figure of the regiment itself, enclosing whole pods of siblings in a "moving box," the "battle brotherhood," or in the paternal shadow of the authoritarian officer on his great black horse.[2]

The movement of the novel involves in great part the failure of these illusionary defenses to sustain him against what is essentially an intra-psychic problem. The maternal regiment confuses death with self-forgetfulness; the paternal officer awakens the self-reproaches of a hostile superego, and one's fellow siblings compete for the favors of authority if they do not actually threaten one's own safety.

In the main, Henry Fleming's counterphobic techniques may be described as alternating "flights" to activity and passivity. The flight to activity involves the primitive logic of becoming the thing or person one fears and then proceeding to intimidate others. Reassurance is bound up with the obsessive display of fierceness; seeming *is* being, pretensions are genuine. At such moments tensions clamoring for discharge convert fear into anger, hatred and aggres-

[2] Relevant discussions of anxiety, defense mechanisms, and the psychology of combat are to be found in the following works: Otto Fenichel, *The Psychoanalytic Theory of Neurosis* (New York, 1945), pp. 122, 126; H. W. Frink, *Morbid Fears and Compulsions* (London, 1925); A. Kardiner and H. Spiegel, *War Stress and Neurotic Illness* (New York, 1947); "Real Warfare," in *The American Soldier, Combat and Its Aftermath* (Princeton, 1949), Vol. II; and Gregory Zilboorg, "Fear of Death," *Psychoanalytic Quarterly,* XII (October 1943).

sion. In *The Red Badge of Courage* the flight to activity manifests
its primitive nature by the blind and objectless rage Fleming manifests on the firing line. Of the two flights it is the more truly moti-
vated by anxiety and anxiety alone.

The flight to passivity is describable in terms of Henry Fleming's
readiness to accept protection, to yield rather than to advance, to
depend on the "cheery man" who leads him back to his bivouac,
and to engage finally in a *fraternal* competition for the love, protection and esteem of *both* parent-symbols. His role is qualified by
its being exclusively filial and submissive. His flight to passivity
acquires an ethical dimension. This does not at first seem apparent
until we measure his new-found valor against his new-found pro-
tectress, the flag, in terms of his inner satisfaction.

After resolving to die in the sight of the angry officer, the novel
ends with Fleming's choice of role as flag-bearer, a role which is
thenceforth that of the spectator among scenes of violence. It is of
interest to note that when Crane finally got to see *his* war, it was
not as a combatant but as a war-correspondent, a *spectator*. *His* behavior under fire was, as his biographer points out, "somnambu-
listic," passive, made up of useless gestures. The essential nature of
his description of war changed but little. Thus the equation evolves:
Henry Fleming, color-sergeant = Stephen Crane, war-correspondent.
Having beaten his pen into a sword in *The Red Badge of Courage*,
he subsequently beats it back into a pen. Yet, in his fiction, the same
bronze father-images stand guard, and the same passive neophyte
(behind whom now stands the war-correspondent) remains the
ironist of his ordeal.

Subsequent works of fiction attest to the permanence of Crane's
initial insights. "The Price of the Harness," written out of the Spanish-American War, contains familiar elements: "The whole scene
would have spoken to the private soldiers of ambushes, sudden flank
attacks, terrible disasters if it were not for those cool gentlemen
with shoulder straps and swords, who, the private soldiers knew,
were of another world and omnipotent for the business." The hero
of the story, Nolan, combines in his character and the effect of his
death on his comrades qualities inherent in both Jim Conklin and
Henry Fleming. He is at once the passive spectator and the good
soldier. Crane describes him as if, having overlaid his original fantasy with fact, he could not for the sake of integrity obscure either.
Nolan, actively engaged in the charge which costs him his life,
thinks:

He had loved the regiment, the army, because the regiment, the army, was his life. He had no other outlook; and now these men, his comrades, *were performing his dream-scenes for him. They were doing as he had ordained in his visions.* It is curious that in this charge he considered himself as rather unworthy. . . . His part, to his mind, was merely that of a man who was going along with the crowd. [My italics.]

"The Five White Mice" illustrates with more intimate directness the relationship between fraternal competition and parental omnipotence than their institutionalized equivalents in *The Red Badge of Courage*. The New York Kid, whose companion, the drunken 'Frisco Kid, has jostled a proud Mexican, is challenged to fight. He has just bluffed his way out of losing a bet on a throw of the dice, and now his bluff is being challenged in an invitation to mortal combat. Again, as in *The Red Badge of Courage*, the same massive inhibitions against self-assertion and aggression turn the Kid's gun into an "impotent stick." The gun he draws feels "unwieldy as a sewing machine. . . . Some of the eels of despair lay wet and cold against his back." At the same moment he thinks of his father:

He witnessed the uprising of his mother and sister, and the invincible calm of his hard-mouthed old father, who would probably shut himself in his library and smoke alone. Then his father would come, and they would bring him here, and say: "This is the place." . . . He pitied his old financing father, unyielding and millioned, a man who commonly spoke twenty-two words a year to his beloved son. The Kid understood it at this time. If his fate was not impregnable, he might have turned out to be a man and have been liked by his father.

Behind the passage is Henry Fleming, who has decided to die, a "salt reproach" to the colonel, exchanging a plausibly heroic death for a speculative manhood. With this flashback in his mind the New York Kid draws his pistol, convinced that he will be killed. The Mexican and his friends step back in fear, and the Kid realizes that the "tall," "stout" Mexican, "a fine and terrible figure," is vulnerable:

He had never dreamed that he did not have a complete monopoly of all possible trepidations. . . . Thus the Kid was able to understand swiftly that they were all human beings. . . . He was bursting with rage because these men had not previously confided to him that they were vulnerable. . . . He had been seduced into respectful alarm by the concave attitude of the grandee. And after all there had been an equality of emotion—an equality!

"Had he not resembled my father as he slept," says Lady Macbeth (her dagger as "unwieldy as a sewing machine"), "I had
done't." We can, with Crane's heroes, postulate a closed season on
fathers. The Kid's flight to activity (so out of character with the
gambling man Crane has described) is inhibited by his recognizing
in the "Spanish grandee" the authoritarian figure of his "unyielding and millioned" father. The inhibition is released when he realizes that he has only to deal with a vulnerable sibling like himself. Here, rage is the equivalent of laughter, a violent release from
tension.

In considering "The Blue Hotel" in its psychological affinities
with Crane's other fiction of war and physical danger, we face first
of all an archeological problem. Excavating for the characterologi-
cal sources of Henry Fleming's or Nolan's or the New York Kid's
actions, we have run across a structure that is obliquely but intrinsically a part of the counterphobic techniques examined in those
works. Digging on the battlefield of Homeric Troy we have found
a city below the war-torn site.

The Red Badge of Courage presented a reasonably normal youth
making a tolerable adjustment to an unreasonably tough situation.
His anxieties were finally and convincingly assuaged when certain
psychic imperatives found satisfaction under the shelter of the flag.
Certain shadowy relationships, parental and sibling, resolved themselves in the process with nothing more untoward in their nature
than would be compatible with the ambivalences of adolescence—
identifications and projections and flights, all in the service of an
urgent adjustment to danger. In "The Blue Hotel" the firm ligature
of counterphobic defense techniques unites the story with the others
that have been considered, but now they are in the service, not of a
real danger situation, but of a paranoid delusional system and all
that such a system implies. *The Red Badge of Courage* can be called
a strategic fantasy of fear overcome. "The Blue Hotel" is a nightmare.

The rational framework of "The Blue Hotel" is trivial, perhaps
a weakness. The widespread, half-comic assumption on the part of
Easterners and Europeans in the nineties that the western United
States were inhabited solely by cowpokes, Indians, and bandits, is
used by Crane as a foundation for the Swede's immediate suspicion
of everyone. But the Swede, like Bartleby the Scrivener, is too aus-

tere an "isolato," the very mask of fear, to be measured by ordinary standards. He ennobles the trumpery plot.

The Swede, with some other travelers, arrives at the Palace Hotel, Nebraska, convinced from the start that he will be robbed and murdered by the proprietor, Pat Scully, his son Johnnie, or one of the cowboy transients about the place. At first he is timidly apprehensive, then hysterically frightened. Scully calms him down and invites him to play a friendly game of cards with the group. The Swede now undergoes a complete change of personality. He plays cards with manic verve, "board-whacking" as he takes his tricks. The card game is upset when he accuses the proprietor's son, Johnnie, of cheating, and then beats him in a fist fight. Flushed with this triumph he extends his circle to the local saloon where, trying to browbeat the local gambler into drinking with him, he meets the death he has long feared. The Easterner speaks the epilogue. Johnnie, he says to the cowboy, *was* cheating. "And you—you were simply puffing around the place and wanting to fight. And then old Scully himself! We are all in it. . . . Every sin is the result of a collaboration. We, five of us, have collaborated in the murder of this Swede."

In discussing *The Red Badge of Courage,* I touched upon Henry Fleming's attempts, first and last, to still his excitement by seeing the war first as a "blue demonstration" and finally as a "matched game." As a defense against a danger situation, either one's own rebellious impulses or an environmental threat, the game satisfies the compulsion to repeat in a mitigated, controlled form an experience which was originally terrifying. Children's games often play out deaths, murders, mutilations, with the child playing the active role in a drama which originally cast him as its passive, frightened victim. Such games, as we all know, are played with a frantic joy that comes close to being pain. It is, in fact, a joy that celebrates a release from painful anxieties.

There is, in the stories we have considered, a sort of "game syndrome" that operates in this way. We have seen it in the imagery of the "matched game" of *The Red Badge of Courage.* It shows itself briefly in "The Price of the Harness" in Nolan's relegating the charge he is engaged in to a level of "dream-scenes." In "The Five White Mice" the game is more ambitiously employed: it is an analogous foreshadowing of the main action. The New York Kid in a friendly dice game in the Mexican bar puts fifty dollars, sight unseen, on a die. There are no takers; the die is a low number; he would have lost. The same bluff and backing-down takes place in

the street, in what the Kid thinks of as the "unreal real." This time
it is the Kid himself who is the losing die, and the Spanish grandee
is the timid bettor who will not call the Kid's bluff. The full psychological function of the game as a release from anxiety is subordi-
nated to its value as a symbolic statement of self-evaluation. The Kid
says, in effect, "I am not what I seem to be, but only my father will
call my bluff."

In "The Blue Hotel" the play's the thing, and Crane apparently
knew it, the same way he knew something about the Swede's mind,
somewhere between a conscious and an intuitive level of insight.
As a man the Swede is past redemption; the game of cards is not his
undoing. It merely serves as the last scrap of reality on which he
can found his delusions of persecution.

When the Swede enters the hotel, Scully's son Johnnie and an old
farmer are playing cards for fun. Serious money-gambling is too
close to reality for mock-hostility to function as it does in child's
play. Playing for fun, Johnnie and the old man are engaged in serious quarrels over their game. Following each such outburst the
Swede laughs nervously, and makes some remark about the dangers
of Western life, incomprehensible to the others. When he is first
invited into the game, he plays nervously and quietly, while the
cowboy is the "board-whacker." "A game with a board-whacker in
it is sure to become intense," and for the Swede the intensity, because all occasions inform against him, becomes unendurable, and
he voices his fears: "I suppose I am going to be killed before I can
leave this house!"

Old Scully, with a fine sense of the problem, exhibits the domesticity of his life to the Swede, pictures of his wife and dead daughter, an account of his sons and the life of the town. He draws the
Swede into the circle of fraternal fellowship to which his son, the
cowboy, and the transients of the Palace Hotel belong. The Swede,
finally induced to take a drink (which he first rejects, as Scully says,
because he "thought I was tryin' to poison 'im"), discharges all the
energy that was a part of his anxiety in an outburst of false relief.
He becomes a part of the family with a vengeance, presiding over
the supper table with a joyless, feverish joy: "The Swede domi-
neered the whole feast, and he gave it the appearance of a cruel
bacchanal. He seemed to have grown suddenly taller; he gazed,
brutally disdainful, into every face. His voice rang through the
room."

When he plays cards again with the group he becomes the "board-

whacker" while the cowboy is reduced to a sad silence. It is the discovery of Johnnie's cheating which precipitates the catastrophic
sequel. The Swede is mad; he "fizzed like a fire-wheel"; but the
game of cards is a benign way for him to work off his aggressions
harmlessly, his hostilities intelligently displaced to the card table.
Ironically, however, the game is denied its therapeutic value. The
scrap of reality that will revive the Swede's original delusion, which
he has not relinquished, merely mastered, is provided by the fact
that Johnnie is *really* cheating. *Real* cheating in a game for fun violates the make-believe, like acid in a water-pistol. For the Swede
the cheating restores the game to the world of outlaws, professional
gamblers, and gunmen. It then follows, with maniacal logic and
poetic justice both, that the next and last victim of the Swede's at-
tentions should be the town's professional gambler, whom the Swede
unwittingly but unerringly singles out. He is the institutionalized
reality of which Johnnie was merely the precursor.

I have reviewed here the elements which relate most apparently
to Henry Fleming's actions in *The Red Badge of Courage*. The
Swede exhibits, albeit madly, alternate flights to passivity and activity. Wary apprehension succeeds to panic and a passive acceptance
of annihilation, to be succeeded by a triumph of mastery, an identification with the aggressor, the pursuer and no longer the pursued.
And above all, there is the framework of the game, danger passing
off in play, only to return again as danger.

There are other resemblances, however, obscured, not by their
existing in "The Blue Hotel" as traces, but because in "The Blue
Hotel" these elements are more intense. They have the vividness
of mania.

The inference in connection with paranoid delusions of persecution is that the subject is defending himself against his own homo-
sexuality. In his relations with other men he denies his love by sub-
stituting an equally dynamic attraction—that of hate. He then denies the hate itself, since it lacks any foundation in reality, and puts
upon him, moreover, the guilty burden of aggression, and projects
his hatred upon the object of his original desire. The ego in such
cases regresses from its ability to test reality to the archaic delusional
systems, the animistic world of childhood, in which all nature is
equally sensate. Thus the wish to be the passive victim of some
homosexual violation may express itself in the fear of such violation
—which displaces itself to other bodily openings. The fears arise
in connection with being poisoned, invaded by dangerous rays,

brainwashed, etc. What may also result is that the paranoid may identify *with* his persecutor in order actively to do *to* him what he might otherwise have suffered himself. The transformation of the repressed erotic attraction in favor of an overt sadistic aversion finds its literary expression in such relationships as Prince Hal's and Harry Hotspur's, "I will embrace him with a soldier's arm," or Claggart's persecution of Billy Budd in Melville's novel.

The Swede's emotional swing from apprehensive depression to manic elation reflects, internalized, the same battlefield as that on which Henry Fleming fought his fears. The problems of self-esteem, alienation, and reunion with the omnipotent superior present themselves, along with the techniques of mastery involved. We can only add, tentatively, in view of the Swede's paranoid delusions, that the Swede's anxieties involve the mastery of his own homosexual aggressions rather than a threat from the external world.

Anyone arriving in a strange town will experience that sense of narcissistic starvation that comes with the feeling that one is a social cypher in the life of the community. The Swede, psychotic to begin with, arrives, already prejudiced, in the small Western town, bringing with him a massive and insatiable need for reassurance against his own unfathomed wishes.

"We'll git swallowed," says a soldier meekly, just before a charge in *The Red Badge of Courage*. It is perfectly descriptive of the oral level of fixation that prevails in a raging battle. Eat or be eaten. The Swede's repressed oral fixations involve "swallowing" the world in order to be reunited with omnipotence, the way a hungry child cleaves savagely to the breast that comforts it. But the obverse side of the coin is his manifest fear that the world will just as savagely attack him.

In this spirit he refuses the first drink Scully offers him as if Scully's teeth were at his throat. But Scully's kindness and the drink itself, once he has swallowed it and found it harmless—experiences which would, with a rational man, effect a pleasant reunion with society—return the Swede's impulse to its original, uninhibited form. Scully behaves like a father toward the Swede. What is more he offers him the oral satisfaction of a drink. " 'Drink,' said the old man affectionately. . . . The Swede laughed wildly. He grabbed the bottle, put it to his mouth; and as his lips curled absurdly around the opening and his throat worked, he kept his glance, *burning with hatred*, upon the old man's face" [my italics]. The image is the image of a fierce baby, its feeding time long overdue, glaring over the nipple at the source of its relief.

The combined gestures are the symbolic fulfillment of a deeply repressed fantasy. Scully has, in effect, "adopted" the Swede, whose exaggerated need for assurance and oral sadistic drives will extend themselves to the absorption of everything and everyone in sight. His foster father, Scully, he swallows at one gulp. A few minutes after he has drunk he is contradicting Scully "in a bullying voice," or has "stalked with the air of an owner off into the executive parts of the hotel." He must enter into this cannibalistic relationship with everyone at once. In the card game he takes all the tricks. At supper he almost impales the Easterner's hand as they reach for the same biscuits. His fight with Johnnie is a still more intimate encounter, a sibling struggle for the attention of the same father, the translation into sadistic (and therefore socially plausible) activity of the Swede's repressed homoerotic drives. There is no clear line here between the various components which move the Swede to action. His mind is a graveyard of decaying realities, baseless fears, disguised desires, and futile strategies.

Manic elation is the literal rendering of the ancient "Whom the gods destroy they first make mad." Its shrill laughter and high spirits and sense of unlimited power are a celebration of the release of the ego from the bonds of a self-derogatory conscience. Now the ego has become the lord of its own misrule and embarks on defiant pursuit of forbidden pleasures, which here involve the aggressive humiliation of other men. The Swede discharges his new, liberated energies in cards, drinking, and fighting. He has achieved his reunion with omnipotence at the expense of his intellect. He had begun in self-effacing humility by fearing for his life; he ends, bloated with his triumph over his imagined persecutors. He *is* the group. His commanding the gambler to drink with him, the sadistic counterpart to Scully's earlier, kinder command, is his moment of *hubris*. He has become the manic travesty of the father. The gambler knifes him, the knife itself a translation (and therefore socially acceptable, more so, at least, than its phallic equivalent) of the Swede's repressed wish for sexual violation; and like an enchantment dispelled, the Swede reverts to his former role of the passive, helpless victim of another man. "The Blue Hotel" has, incidentally, been compared with Hemingway's "The Killers." And this is interesting, because psychologically, they are diametrical opposites meeting only at the

antipodes, in fear itself. Ole Andreson, in "The Killers," exemplifies in almost pathological terms the flight to passivity, the "strategic abandonment of hope," in his fatalistic resignation to death.
The Swede is the other side of the coin, a pathological flight to activity.

The Easterner's self-accusatory indictment of all of them as murderers—"Every sin is the result of a collaboration"—is too oriental,
too transcendental a statement to be confined within a blue hotel
or a platitude of social consciousness. It has karmic ramifications,
whose psychological equivalents are consistent with that omniscient
"Indefinite Cause" which threatens to seal Henry Fleming's doom,
that fascinated dread and disbelief with which Crane's characters
enter on to the stage as spectators and actors both. In summing up
"The Five White Mice" John Berryman writes, "The Kid's faith,
in substance—Crane's new faith—is in Circumstance as *not* making
impossible the individual's determination of his destiny." [3] It is, we
may say, Crane's vision of normality, a mind turned outward upon
the world, away from its crippling presentiments. The Easterner's
epilogue, as it gestures inward towards an infinity of secret causes,
is Crane's cry of resignation.

[3] Berryman, p. 110.

The Crucible of Childhood

by Eric Solomon

Stephen Crane's *Whilomville Stories* deserves to be bracketed
with Mark Twain's *Adventures of Huckleberry Finn* as a book ostensibly about boys and actually about the human condition. Like
Huckleberry Finn, Crane's volume of childhood tales has a more
mature vision and serious purpose than most American boyhood
stories, and it parodies the usual formulae of sentimental, nostalgic,
dreamy, and happy childhood tales. Despite the warmly humorous
anecdotes of boyhood that make up the outer shell of *Whilomville
Stories,* Stephen Crane was anticipating the techniques employed
in Richard Hughes' *High Wind in Jamaica,* William March's *The
Bad Seed,* and William Golding's *Lord of the Flies.* These novelists
construct extreme situations through which they can portray young
children displaying destructive behavior that parallels, in the authors' view, that of adult society. Stephen Crane's children are at
once young and old, reflecting the values of the mature world and
prefiguring the actions that such a world will demand. Parody and
pain combine in *Whilomville Stories* to offer in the guise of a childhood idyl a bitter version of man in society. Beneath the concrete
evocation of small-town America lurks the trenchant criticism of the
universe that Crane called forth in his more clearly adult fiction.
Crane both mocks the familiar boyhood idyls and uses the form to
disguise his savage attacks on his society. Guilt and innocence,
freedom and authority, appearance and reality, isolation, fear, the
rigid codes of a stratified society, the demand for conformity, the
harshness of organized religion—all cohere to make *Whilomville
Stories* a serious work of fiction.

Whilomville: the word coined by Crane points to a town that

might have existed "once upon a time" or one that did exist at some past time. The deliberate ambiguity of the title separates Crane's book from the boyhood volumes written by his contemporaries, stories that used such obvious titles as *Peck's Bad Boy and His Pa* (George W. Peck), *The Story of a Bad Boy* (Thomas Bailey Aldrich), *Being a Boy* (Charles Dudley Warner), *A New England Boyhood* (Edward Everett Hale), *A Boy's Town* (William Dean Howells), or simply *Penrod* (Booth Tarkington). In a series of tales that appeared in *McClure's* in 1898, the same year that the magazine published the first of Crane's boyhood tales, William Allen White employed a similar title, *The Court of Boyville*. Although White's stories are often sentimental and use the slapstick humor that authors from Peck to Tarkington depended on, White insists on the alien quality of Boyville; but, unlike Crane, White regrets his exile from this ideal world that has laws going back to the beginning of time. Neither he nor Tarkington conceived of a boy's existence as a caricature of adult behavior. . . .

One must understand Stephen Crane's aim in order to grasp the true value of *Whilomville Stories*; more than in any of his other works, the parodic principle is operative here. If one considers the tales as fundamentally about children, then one must reject the volume as a failure of tone because of the disparity between the sophisticated form and diction and the seemingly naïve content. Yet Crane was far too aware of the modes of childhood thought not to realize that stories for children should be cast in a simple form. "Does anybody know how a child thinks? The horrible thing about a kid is that it makes no excuses, none at all. They are much like breakers on a beach. They do something, and that is all there is in it." . . . As in his best parodic-realistic fiction, Crane sustains a double vision in *Whilomville Stories*: Jimmie Trescott and his friends often act from childish motives in childish ways; but these motives and actions are not very different—and are sometimes not at all different—from those of the adult world. The stories most often reproduce grownup behavior on the level of children's actions, as in *Lord of the Flies*, and at the same time indicate how the child's world may be in some ways better than that of his elders. The child's actions many times travesty those of the mature members of the community; as in *Tom Sawyer*, adult morality is a prime target. As among adults, for example, a newcomer must establish himself in society according to a formal code. The children never equal in sheer awfulness, however, adults such as Crane's Sunday-school superintendent, "one who had never felt hunger or thirst or the wound of the challenge of dishonor; a man, indeed, with beautiful flat hands who waved them in greasy victorious beneficence over a crowd of children."

Crane's children mimic the problems of adulthood, and these parodied problems appear in stark clarity because the façade of pretense and verbiage that covers grownup life is much less sophisticated among children. According to Booth Tarkington, "Boys are just like people, really. . . . Only they're not quite so awful, because they haven't learned to cover themselves all over with little pretences." [1] Like Tarkington, Crane analyzes the psychology of the child in a book written for adults; unlike Tarkington, Crane moves beyond the child's mind to expose man's moral deficiencies. It is when the worlds of childhood and adulthood coalesce that *Whilomville Stories* engages the reader's mind as well as his emotions and is most profound. Howells showed how a boy's world could be used, as the more bitter Crane would use it, to anatomize society. He insisted that the boy's society was as strict as any other through its "unwritten usages . . . binding through all personal vicissitudes, upon the great body of boys between six and twelve years old. No boy can violate them without losing his standing among the other boys. . . . It has its own ideals and superstitions, and those are often of a ferocity, a depravity, scarcely credible in after life." [2] Stephen Crane comprehended that the after life of men and women was just as ferocious as the world of boys and girls, and usually more so; thus in *Maggie* he resorts to the same war imagery that appears in *The Red Badge of Courage*, indicating that both the slum child and the Civil War soldier live in a state of warfare. In the village of Whilomville run the same savage currents that define Sherwood Anderson's Winesburg; growing up in America is a battle for survival.

Stephen Crane wrote the thirteen stories that make up the Whilomville volume during the last year of his life. A year earlier, in *The Monster,* he had experimented with a mordant view of life in a small-town setting. But in that short novel, set though it is in the village of Crane's childhood, the adults of the Trescott family are central, while the small boy Jimmie is something of a peripheral figure, observing action without comprehension. The later stories

[1] Booth Tarkington, *Penrod* (New York, 1914), p. 313.
[2] William Dean Howells, *A Boy's Town* (New York, 1890), p. 67.

concentrate on Jimmie, who remains an innocent eye sharing his
parents' weaknesses and often himself repeating or being victimized
by adult behavior. Although *The Monster* ends in defeat for the
idealistic doctor (as will many of the stories), the boy is scarcely affected. A tale much closer to the technique of *Whilomville Stories*
appeared in *McClure's* in 1898. Crane's "His New Mittens" treats a
youth named Horace who is in mild revolt against his family.
The boy refuses to wear clothing that he thinks will make him an
outcast in his society, runs away, and eventually returns to his for-
giving mother and aunt. Written with some humor and more sentiment, the story anticipates the Whilomville series in setting and
in its theme of the pressures on the individual to conform.

When Crane turned again to Whilomville, he was writing against
time and for money. He turned out the stories hastily; some were
obviously based on his own memories, others on those of his wife,
Cora—who appears, under her own name, in two tales. His dark
view of mankind, aggravated by his illness and his frantic need for
cash, made *Whilomville Stories* far different from the usual nostalgic memoir.

A close study of these stories reveals three important facts. First,
the stories were clearly conceived as a series. They appeared in suc-
cessive issues of *Harper's* for thirteen months from August 1899
through August 1900 (two months after the author's death) and
when published in book form in 1900 were kept in the same order. Second, the tales follow a chronological pattern, moving from
summer to summer and including two Christmases to cover a two-
and-one-half-year cycle. Obviously *Whilomville Stories* is not a random collection of fugitive pieces like Crane's other short-story volumes, *The Little Regiment* and *The Open Boat*. He thought of the
book as a book, and it has a clear pattern of developing seriousness.
From the early stories that show youthful innocence bruising its
high spirits against the restrictions of the official culture, the narratives grew more bleak until at the end Jimmie Trescott displays
all the hypocrisies of the adult world. Third, each story represents
a flaw in man. Beneath the childish play and humorous situation
constantly runs Crane's disappointment with man's puny—childish
—ambitions and behavior. All of the seven deadly sins, with the
obvious exception of lechery, appear in the volume. As we shall
see, the book commences with a story about an "angel" and closes
with a devilish perversion of the spirit of Christmas.

Of course, the thirteen stories are neither of a uniform level of

The Crucible of Childhood

achievement nor of an equal seriousness of tone. And Crane adheres to the usual formal requirements of the boyhood story. *Whilomville Stories* is rich in remembered detail, the local color of upstate New York, the aspects of a boy's life at home, in school, at play. The backdrop is idyllic: ". . . nothing was finer than the cool sheen of the hose sprays over the cropped lawns under the many maples in the twilight." The town, as pictured in Peter Newell's illustrations in *Harper's,* is pleasant, tree-shaded, comfortable; the surrounding area is a boy's haven of fields and woods in summer—"The breeze was heavy with the smell of sweetfern. The pines and hemlocks sighed as they waved their branches. In the hollows the leaves of the laurels were lacquered where the sunlight found them"; and in winter, "From time to time an enwearied pine bough let fall to the earth its load of melting snow, and the branch swung back glistening in the faint wintery sunlight. Down the gulch a brook clattered amid its ice with the sound of a perpetual breaking of glass."

In such an atmosphere the youth of Whilomville find their pleasures. They hunt, pretend to be bandits or pirates, wrestle and box, ride their velocipedes, throw rocks at carriage lamps, go on picnics. Jimmie Trescott's home is secure: a comfortable house, a hearty cook, a colorful Negro coachman (named Peter Washington in this version of the Trescotts' domestic economy) , an adoring mother, a strict but humorous father. School exists primarily for recess and sport. The world is full of interesting places, candy stores, barber shops, stables. There are many novelties to keep a child from boredom; the seasons vary, new neighbors appear: "Then, near the first of April, would come along a wagon-load of furniture, and children would assemble on the walk by the gate and make serious examination of everything that passed into the house." As for the adults, they farm, vaguely pursue professions as doctors or artists, give tea parties, argue. There are Negro slums, but the atmosphere is jolly and silly, poverty is unreal. In the Whilomville environment, a youth's mind is free to release its imaginative force. "Each boy had . . . a conviction that some day the wilderness was to give forth to him a marvelous secret. They felt that the hills and the forest knew much, and they heard a voice of it in the silence. It was vague, thrilling, and altogether fabulous. . . . they lived there, in season, lives of ringing adventure—by dint of imagination." And a boy's psychology makes life appear relatively simple. "The long-drawn animosities of men have no place in the life of a boy. The boy's mind is

flexible; he readjusts his position with an ease which is derived from
the fact—simply—that he is not yet a man." Surely this world seems
similar to those of the boys who gambol through the pages of Aldrich and Peck, White and Howells. Yet there is a difference that
becomes manifest when the theme and tone of each story is fully
ascertained. A close reading is necessary since here, departing from
his earlier handling of parodic frames, Crane accepts the traditional
techniques and manners throughout, but mocks with equal consistency the didactic undertones of the genre.

The first of the *Whilomville Stories*, "The Angel Child," is essentially comic. Jimmie Trescott's cousin Cora, beautiful and im-
perious, uses five dollars absent-mindedly given her by her artist-
father to lead astray Jimmie and his friends—who represent "the
families of most excellent people." After gorging themselves on
candy, the children follow Cora to the barber shop, and all lose
their shining childhood tresses. The outcome of this shearing is,
naturally, parental horror, anger, and blame. The source of humor
is obvious, but underneath the "cute" story move disturbing currents. The tale is about pride: the pride of Cora that comes from
the corrupting forces of money, beauty, and the need to be a queen
who rules "with an iron grip." The tale is about mob hysteria, as
the children blindly struggle to attain the barber's chair, ignoring
the obvious consequences. "Little did they know if this were fun;
they only knew that their small leader said it was fun." The tale is
about the childish, hysterical attitudes of the adults who screech,
form a giddy whirl, talk of mob revenge, of destroying Cora's family
or the idiotic barber. Crane's diction heightens the absurdity of
the supposedly mature social leaders whose response cannot be dif-
ferentiated from those of their children. They "storm," cry for "mid-
nightly massacre," for dipping "arms in blood to the elbows." While
reason eventually prevails, Crane's story presents the narrow line
that separates childish from adult action, as well as the corrupting
effect of money, the postures of group conformity, and the force of
pride. And, incidentally, "The Angel Child" touches on the question of guilt and innocence. Cora escapes the opprobrium that falls
upon her unworldly father, that dreamy man who does not understand the nature of a five-dollar bill (surely a sin in the gilded age
of American prosperity). A man "never energetic enough to be ir-
ritable unless someone broke through into that place where he
lived with the desires of his life," he is charged, with conscious in-

congruity on the author's part, "in the most biblical way" as "the guilty one—he!" "The Angel Child" is not a complex story; it is a humorous tale about children's behavior that carries manifold overtones of serious comment about human behavior in general. The story serves to alert the reader that even the safe, comfortable world of Whilomville children is a part of the savage universe that the author most often chronicles in a style heavy with irony.

The second story, "Lynx-Hunting," is one of the most interesting in the volume. Here it is not necessary to seek far beneath the surface for Crane's meanings; form and content coalesce in a tense précis of man's corruptibility in society. As the story opens Jimmie feels guilty because he wants to borrow his father's rifle. He needs this symbol of manhood since he has told his friends the "black lie" that he, like Willie Dalzel, who has a gun that makes him "superior in manfulness," can also use his father's weapon. Thus at the very start of the story a foolish pride has driven Jimmie to lie "as naturally as most animals swim."

Crane's language forces the reader to make the imaginative leap that will enable him to realize that this boy's story is about society in general. Jimmie's companions are called distinguished; he is pompous. The social demands of the situation, the rules for conduct, force Jimmie to persist in his easily detected falsehood and, "backed into an ethical corner," to prevaricate "as stupidly, as desperately, as hopelessly as ever lone savage fights when surrounded at last in his jungle."

The boys go off to hunt a lynx, a fabulous beast known only to adults (and described in a school text), which, again in order to conform, the young hunters must lie about and pretend to have seen themselves. Crane stresses the boys' lack of respect for the truth; they all lie carefully about their courage, they play games of make-believe, as boys are "willed" to do. As they pretend to be smugglers, they parrot terms of subliterature without any comprehension of their meaning. "Once aboard the lugger, Bill, and the girl is mine. Now to burn the chateau and destroy all evidence of our crime"— these phrases mean no more than the word "lynx." Like the Swede in "The Blue Hotel," they live in an imaginative world informed by the "fine words" of dime-novel rhetoric, that of Tom Sawyer's "best authorities." The contrast between illusion (the fabulous beast that they hunt) and reality (an innocent bird that they blow into a rag of wet feathers) is clear. When it is Jimmie's turn with the gun, he aims at a chipmunk—a beast no more fabulous than the defunct bird—and hits the least romantic and most domestic of all animals, a cow. Although Jimmie does not want to fire the weapon in the first place, he cannot withstand the pressure of the group; "if he refused to shoot he would lose his caste, his scalp-lock, his girdle, his honor." The words are important because the remainder of the story will question the meaning of such abstractions as honor and faith. Had the story ended here, leaving Jimmie secure in the egoistic pride that the first shot of his life brings forth, and focusing on the mistaken target bellowing across the pasture, "Lynx-Hunting" would be no more than an account of the desire to conform that brings on lies and illusions. Crane is not willing, however, to let his little men off easily.

Just as in *The Red Badge of Courage*, the results of one's actions are at least as important as the action itself. Interestingly enough, it is the hero of the war novel, Henry Fleming grown older, who insists that the boys pierce through their illusions and accept the responsibility for their actions—the same Henry Fleming who started his battle of life as both a coward and a liar. Suddenly the boys are no longer smugglers and lynx hunters; they are fleeing miscreants whom a gigantic Swedish farm hand captures and drags to Farmer Fleming for judgment. Again, Crane's diction demands notice. An Old Testament wrath threatens the boys as the land appears to them black and the farm hand seems to come from the heavens. Caught by this chastiser, who beats them as blindly as does the god in Crane's poem "A god in wrath was beating a man," the boys collapse completely. Their illusions of truth, courage, and loyalty break down to the realities of lies, cowardice, and betrayal. "They begged like cowards on the scaffold, and each one was for himself. 'Oh, please let me go, mister! I didn't do it, mister! He did it!' "

Crane does editorialize to indicate that these betrayals result from the boys' terror and their youthful belief that for boys there are no such events as accidents; since they are caught, they must be guilty. These sinners in the hands of an angry god—Henry Fleming, flourishing a cruel whip—are already in Hell, but a Hell of their own making. "At his approach the boys suffered the agonies of the fire regions." This kind old man, however, cares for boys, and the whip is in his hand by chance; it is simply their guilt that drives them into tearful and clamorous denials as if they were martyrs at the stake. The comparison emphasizes once more that the human being is a wretched creature, and makes his Hell on earth by his fear.

The story closes on a carefully conceived anticlimax. Jimmie admits that he shot the cow and gives as his excuse the story that he thought the cow was a lynx. This admission reduces Fleming and the Swede to helpless laughter, and the story ends on this note. But the finish provides an additional irony: Jimmie may have imagined that he was aiming at a lynx, but he was actually shooting at a chipmunk when he hit the cow. Boys do not know what is truth, and the amused farmers do not care to wait for the correct answer.

In Crane's next story, "The Lover and the Telltale," Jimmie Trescott violates the mores of the children's society by staying in school during recess and writing a love letter to the angel child. This motif is a staple in nearly every boys' book from Aldrich to Tarkington, but only Crane uses the commonplace plot device to comment on the savage behavior of society—"wolflike" is Crane's adjective —toward one who goes his own way. Again, there is plenty of incidental humor in "The Lover and the Telltale" as Jimmie struggles with his letter, in which the language reduces to absurdity conventional lovers' rhetoric. "My dear Cora I love thee with all my hart oh come bac again, bac, bac gain for I love thee best of all oh come bac again When the spring come again we'l fly and we'l fly like a brid." Nevertheless, the burden of the story is a stern rejection not only of childish society but most particularly of the adult society that is mirrored in youth's parody of elders' acts.

The child is father to the man: Jimmie is accustomed to prey on his younger companions "with all the cruel disregard of a grown man." If in the first two stories the children prefigure adult behavior, here the children clearly imitate the weaknesses of the older generation. Crane is most explicit. The villainess, little Rose Goldege (who is no flower and from no golden age), is in a position to spy on Jimmie because she is consciously parodying her elders, staying in the classroom to play house, pretending to be a matron "dramatizing her idea of a household." But what is her idea of a household? And why does she betray Jimmie's secret? Because, says Crane, she is the imitator of her family's customs, she must reflect all the bitterness of a provincial household without men, of a middle-class family whose source of income has disappeared, of a group of women, in short, who resort to vicious gossip to lower their neighbors' reputations. Stephen Crane embarks on one of his most

serious and sustained analyses of social behavior in his description
of the girl's environment.

> It contained now only a collection of women who existed submis-
> sively, defiantly, securely, mysteriously, in a pretentious and often
> exasperating virtue. It was often too triumphantly clear that they
> were free of bad habits. However, "bad habits" is a term here used
> in a commoner meaning, because it is certainly true that the principal
> and indeed solitary joy which entered their lonely lives was the joy
> of talking wickedly and busily about their neighbors. It was all done
> without dream of its being of the vulgarity of the alleys. Indeed it was
> simply a constitutional but not incredible chastity and honesty ex-
> pressing itself in its ordinary superior way of the whirling circles of
> life, and the vehemence of the criticism was not lessened by a further
> infusion of an acid of worldly defeat, worldly suffering, and worldly
> hopelessness.

Rose is "typical" of this harsh world; she spends her evenings
listening to her mother and a group of spinsters gossip around the
stove. "Thus all her home teaching" prepares her to flush out Jimmie's secret and to broadcast it to the world. And Jimmie, the sensitive poet, is thrown upon the mercies of the tribe whose codes he
has been ignoring. Crane's double vision of the two worlds of child
and adult enables him to show Jimmie reacting as a child to a child's
dilemma that is also an adult one. He scuffles with Rose, accepts
the word of the teacher as law, and leaves the classroom to confront
his fate in the schoolyard among the "barbarians," the "yelping
demoniac mob." Friends and enemies alike (as in *Lord of the Flies*)
revert to animal behavior, that of "little blood-fanged wolves."
Shocked out of his previous stance of romantic lover, Jimmie too
reverts to the tribal code and fights for his place in society, striking
out blindly at whoever comes within his reach. For all the violence
and the blood-stained shirts in the noisy schoolyard that sounds
"like a pine tree when a hundred crows roost in it at night," the
children are *not* animals. As in the end of Golding's novel, when
the atavistic hunt for Ralph ceases at the appearance of an adult
naval officer, so the pealing school bell returns these boyish fighters
to order. "It was a bell that these children obeyed, even as older
nations obey the formal law which is printed in calfskin." Such
wording would seem pretentious if "The Lover and the Telltale"
were simply a child's story. But the phrase fits Crane's version of a
world where children repeat the age-old unpleasant roles of mob
and victim. Crane's dark parody lets him use the simple form as a

frame and add an overall realism of motive and action in language suitable to the mocked adult world.

As usual, the story ends quietly, on a muted bit of irony. The two worlds separate when the teacher cannot understand Jimmie's inability to distinguish his antagonists. Society can never understand what it does to the rebel; it can only punish. The imagery joins the blind ruler—the teacher—with the conscious villainess—Rose; the teacher "blazes," disintegrates into "flaming fagots of anger," while the "Satanic eyes" of the girl gloat at Jimmie's discomfiture. Although the adult world finds a reflection in the childish one, the characters do not comprehend the relationship—such knowledge belongs to Crane and his readers.

*   *   *

Jimmie Trescott . . . meets defeat in the final Whilomville story, "A Little Pilgrimage." Set in a pre-Christmas atmosphere, the tale provides a suitable conclusion to the book. The Christmas spirit turns out to be a compound of hypocrisy and greed; religion is mocked; and Jimmie is no longer the innocent he was at the start of *Whilomville Stories*. He is now able to carry out the same kind of conscious deceptions that his parents use. If the book started with an angel child, it ends with Jimmie playing the devil's game. In a virtuous burst the children of the Presbyterian Sunday school vote to forgo their usual Christmas tree and to send the money to aid the victims of the Charleston earthquake. This decision is taken a long time before Christmas, however. Pride and cupidity prevail over the Golden Rule in Jimmie's heart, and he deceptively persuades his father that the Big Progressive church has a Sunday school with stronger spiritual appeal.

The Sunday school itself contains images of the entire Whilomville community: oily superintendent, authoritarian teachers, confused children. The meaning of the lesson, from Jeremiah, is beyond the grasp of all of them. Perhaps the key passage of the volume is Crane's analysis of the child's response to the biblical definitions of good and evil. "This thing of being good—this great business of life—apparently it was always successful. They knew from the fairy tales. But it was difficult, wasn't it? . . . And the angels, the Sunday-school superintendent, and the teacher swam in the high visions of little boys as beings so good that if a boy scratched his shin in the same room he was a profane and sentenced devil." The deviltry is as ironic as the angelicism at the volume's start. Neither children nor their elders have the slightest understanding of the abstract words virtue and sin. The authorities for moral behavior in both worlds—fairy tales and Bible—are equally misleading and laughable.

If Jimmie is a hypocrite in choosing a new Sunday school for venal reasons, the school betrays him by renouncing its Christmas tree also. There are no rewards, not even for the hypocrite. The world is a grim and empty place. As for "religion," if Jimmie "remembered Sunday-school at all, it was to remember that he did not like it." Jimmie dislikes the adult world of hypocrisy, gossip, and false pride, but he is admirably prepared to enter it. He leaves the Sunday school to grow up in Whilomville, a town that exists sometime and all the time, for it represents a state of mind, of spiritual vacuity. *Whilomville Stories* is a coherent work of fiction that examines and considers the developing consciousness of a boy in a nineteenth-century American town that stands for the bleak world in which all men, adults and children alike, must live and die.

Chronology of Important Dates

1871	Stephen Crane born November 1 in Newark, N.J., fourteenth and last child of the Reverend Jonathan Townley Crane, a Methodist minister and author (d. 1880) and Mary Helen (Peck) Crane, later a reporter of church activities for various newspapers (d. 1891).
1878	Family moves from Paterson, N.J. (1876) to Port Jervis, N.Y., the "Whilomville" of Crane's later tales. Schooling begins.
1882	Family moves to Asbury Park, N.J.; Crane attends school there until 1888.
1885	Writes first complete story, "Uncle Jake and the Bell Handle," at 14; many juvenile fragments in the mid-'80s.
1891	Attends Syracuse University during the spring semester, after similarly brief schooling at Hudson River Institute, Claverack, N.Y. (1888-90) and Lafayette College (1890). Publishes first story, "The King's Favor," in Syracuse *University Herald,* writes first draft of *Maggie* in Delta Upsilon fraternity house, and plays baseball superlatively.
1892	Publishes five "Sullivan County Sketches" in New York *Tribune* and one in *Cosmopolitan* (December), his first magazine appearance. After several years of assisting brother Townley in reporting shore news from Asbury Park, is fired for his report of a labor parade.
1892-94	Boarding-house years in New York City; explores the Bowery.
1893	Publishes *Maggie: A Girl of the Streets* (February or March) under pseudonym "Johnston Smith," after completing novel in winter of 1892-93. No sales and few reviews, but encouragement from Hamlin Garland and William Dean Howells. Begins *The Red Badge of Courage* and probably completes full-scale revision.
1894	Sells only a dozen sketches. *The Red Badge* appears in an abridged newspaper version (December).
1895	Trip to the West and Mexico as syndicate feature writer (January to May); meets Willa Cather. First volume of poems, *The Black Riders and Other Lines,* comprising poems written mostly the previous year, published (May) and widely noticed. Romantic attachment to Nellie Crouse, to whom he writes some of his most important letters. Writes *The Third Violet* during fall at Hartwood, N.Y. *The Red Badge of Courage:*

An Episode of the American Civil War published (October), and acclaimed in both the United States and England.

1896   At age 24 now a well-known and to some even notorious figure after years of obscurity. A revised version of *Maggie,* together with *George's Mother,* another novel of the New York period (1894?), published (both in June). *The Little Regiment and Other Episodes of the American Civil War* (December) capitalizes on the success of his war novel. Harassed by New York police. Meets Cora Taylor, five years his senior, proprietress of a Jacksonville, Florida house of assignation in November, en route to cover filibustering expeditions to Cuba.

1897   Shipwrecked January 2 off coast of Florida when his ship, the *Commodore,* sinks; "The Open Boat," based on this incident, published in June. With Cora, covers Greco-Turkish War (April to May) as correspondent for New York *Journal* and *Westminster Gazette;* "Death and the Child" and the novel *Active Service* come out of this experience. *The Third Violet* published (May). Settles with Cora as man and wife in Oxted, Surrey, and becomes acquainted with Joseph Conrad.

1898   *The Open Boat and Other Tales of Adventure* published (April). Spanish-American War correspondent in Cuba and Puerto Rico for New York *World* and New York *Journal* (April to November); excellent dispatches, among the best of Crane's long newspaper career. Major stories appear in periodicals: "The Bride Comes to Yellow Sky," "Death and the Child," *The Monster,* and "The Blue Hotel."

1899   Publication of *War Is Kind,* second volume of poems, many dating back to at least 1895 (May); *Active Service* (October); and *The Monster and Other Stories* (December). Residence at Brede Place, Sussex, with Cora; extravagant hospitality and feverish writing to pay off debts. Begins *The O'Ruddy,* an historical romance, and a novel on the American Revolution of which only a sketch survives.

1900   After protracted illness, dies of tuberculosis in a sanitorium in Badenweiler, Germany on June 5, aged 28, faithfully tended by Cora. Buried in Hillside, N.J. *Whilomville Stories* and *Wounds in the Rain,* his Cuban stories and sketches, appear posthumously (August and October).

1901   *Great Battles of the World,* a series of historical sketches. Cora returns to Jacksonville (d. 1910).

1902   *Last Words,* a miscellany of early and late stories and sketches compiled by Cora.

1903   *The O'Ruddy: A Romance,* completed by novelist Robert Barr.

Notes on the Editor and Authors

MAURICE BASSAN, the editor, is Assistant Professor of English at San Francisco State College. He has written a number of studies of Crane and other American writers, including Hawthorne and Faulkner, and recently published *Stephen Crane's* Maggie: *Text and Context.* He is writing a full-length study of Crane's early career.

WARREN D. ANDERSON, Chairman of the Department of Greek and Latin at the College of Wooster, is the author of *Matthew Arnold and the Classical Tradition* and *Ethos and Education in Greek Music.*

JOHN BERRYMAN, Professor of Humanities at the University of Minnesota, received the Pulitzer Prize in Poetry in 1964 for *77 Dream Songs.* He has written three other volumes of poetry, including *Homage to Mistress Bradstreet.* His *Stephen Crane* was prepared for the American Men of Letters series.

WILLA CATHER, the distinguished American novelist and short-story writer, is best known for her novels *O Pioneers, My Ántonia,* and *Death Comes for the Archbishop.* She was awarded the Pulitzer Prize for *One of Ours* in 1922.

JAMES B. COLVERT is Professor of English at the University of Virginia. He has written several influential essays on the art of Stephen Crane, and is engaged on the new Virginia edition of Crane's works.

JOSEPH CONRAD is one of the major novelists of modern fiction. He was a warm personal friend of Crane's in England.

OLOV W. FRYCKSTEDT, who teaches at the University of Uppsala, has written *In Quest of America: A Study of Howells' Early Development as a Novelist,* and has edited Crane's uncollected writings.

DANIEL HOFFMAN, poet and critic, is Professor of English at the University of Pennsylvania. He won the Yale Series of Younger Poets Award for *An Armada of Thirty Whales,* and has published later poems in *A Little Geste* and *The City of Satisfactions.* He is also the author of *The Poetry of Stephen Crane, Form and Fable in American Fiction,* and *Barbarous Knowledge,* and the editor of *American Poetry and Poetics,* and *The Red Badge of Courage and Other Tales by Stephen Crane.*

GEORGE W. JOHNSON, Associate Professor of English at Temple University, has published essays on fiction in journals such as *American Literature* and *PMLA,* and is completing a book on Crane and Norris.

A. J. LIEBLING, journalist and staff member of *The New Yorker* since 1935, was best known for his continuing series, "The Wayward Press." Among his dozen books are *The Road Back to Paris*, *The Wayward Pressman*, and *The Earl of Louisiana*. *The Most of A. J. Liebling* appeared in 1963, the year of his death.

SERGIO PEROSA, who teaches English and American literature at Ca' Foscari University, Venice, visited the United States as a Fulbright scholar while preparing his major study of Fitzgerald, translated in 1965 as *The Art of F. Scott Fitzgerald.* He is also the author of *Le vie della narrativa americana* and *Il Teatro nord-americano*, and the editor of Italian editions of Emily Dickinson and Washington Irving.

DONALD PIZER, Professor of English at Newcomb College, Tulane University, is the author of *Hamlin Garland's Early Work and Career*, *The Novels of Frank Norris*, and *Realism and Naturalism in Nineteenth-Century American Literature*. He has also edited the literary criticism of Frank Norris.

ERIC SOLOMON, Associate Professor of English at San Francisco State College, is the editor of *The Faded Banners*, a collection of Civil War fiction, and the author of *Stephen Crane in England* and *Stephen Crane: From Parody to Realism.*

R. W. STALLMAN is Professor of English at the University of Connecticut. He has published many studies of Crane and edited Crane's writings, including his journalism and letters. His essays are collected in *The Houses That James Built and Other Literary Studies.*

WILLIAM BYSSHE STEIN has written *Hawthorne's Faust* and many shorter literary essays. He is Professor of English at the State University of New York at Binghamton.

DANIEL WEISS is Associate Professor of English at San Francisco State College. He is the author of several works on Crane, Kafka, and Lawrence, including *Oedipus in Nottingham: D. H. Lawrence.*

PHILIP YOUNG, Professor of American literature at the Pennsylvania State University, achieved fame with his study of Hemingway in 1952, recently revised under the title *Ernest Hemingway: A Reconsideration.* He is at work on *Studies in Classic American Myth.*

LARZER ZIFF is the author of *The Career of John Cotton: Puritanism and the American Experience* and *The American 1890's.* He is Professor of English at the University of California, Berkeley.

Selected Bibliography

At present, despite its omissions and erroneous texts, the major edition of Crane's writings remains *The Work of Stephen Crane*, ed. Wilson Follett, 12 vols. (New York, 1925-27), reprinted in 6 vols. (New York, 1963). This edition has recently been supplemented by two collections: *The Complete Stories and Sketches of Stephen Crane*, ed. Thomas A. Gullason (New York, 1963), and *Stephen Crane: Uncollected Writings*, ed. Olov W. Fryckstedt (Uppsala, 1963). R. W. Stallman and E. R. Hagemann have edited two other collections, *The War Dispatches of Stephen Crane* (New York, 1964) and *The New York City Sketches of Stephen Crane and Related Pieces* (New York, 1966). *Stephen Crane: Letters* has been edited by R. W. Stallman and Lillian Gilkes (New York, 1960). A new edition of Crane's writings, under the general editorship of Fredson Bowers, will appear shortly.

The best one-volume collection of Crane's prose and poetry is *Stephen Crane: An Omnibus*, ed. R. W. Stallman (New York, 1952); the *Red Badge* manuscripts in this volume are supplemented in Stallman's later Signet edition (New York, 1960). Other excellent general editions are those of Richard Chase and William M. Gibson. Good editions of *The Red Badge of Courage* have been prepared by Frederick C. Crews (Indianapolis, 1964), and by Sculley Bradley, R. C. Beatty, and E. H. Long (New York, 1962). The 1893 *Maggie* has been edited by Maurice Bassan (Belmont, 1966). A much needed complete edition of the poems is being issued by Joseph Katz to replace the *Collected Poems* (New York, 1930).

Stephen Crane: A Bibliography, ed. Ames W. Williams and Vincent Starrett (Glendale, 1948), is accurate but now somewhat outdated. It should be supplemented with the annual bibliographies edited by Robert N. Hudspeth appearing each spring in *Thoth* (Syracuse University), beginning with the comprehensive listing of Crane studies 1893-1962 in *Thoth*, IV (Winter 1963), 30-58. The bibliography published in the Stephen Crane number of *Modern Fiction Studies*, V (Autumn 1959), 282-291 is still valuable.

Thomas Beer's *Stephen Crane: A Study in American Letters* (New York, 1923), with an introduction by Joseph Conrad, was the first biography; it contains much original material not verifiable elsewhere. An equally colorful but more reliable biography was integrated with a critical study by John Berryman in *Stephen Crane* (New York, 1950), probably the single most valuable book for the student of Crane to know. There are biographical-critical memoirs by many of Crane's acquaintances, including Willa Cather, "When I Knew Stephen Crane" (1900), reprinted in *Prairie*

Schooner, XXIII (Fall 1949), 231-237; Conrad, noted above; Ford Madox
Ford, *Portraits from Life* (Boston, 1937), pp. 21-37; Hamlin Garland,
"Stephen Crane as I Knew Him," *Yale Review*, III (April 1914), 494-506;
Corwin K. Linson, *My Stephen Crane*, ed. Edwin H. Cady (Syracuse,
1958); and H. G. Wells, "Stephen Crane from an English Standpoint,"
North American Review, CLXXI (August 1900), 233-242. Lillian Gilkes
has written a charmingly opinionated biography of Crane's presumptive
wife, *Cora Crane: A Biography of Mrs. Stephen Crane* (Bloomington,
1961). A major biography of Crane by R. W. Stallman will appear soon.

Daniel Hoffman's study, *The Poetry of Stephen Crane* (New York, 1957),
was a pioneering investigation of the influence of Crane's religious heritage
upon his ideas and his craft. Edwin H. Cady's *Stephen Crane* (New York,
1962) attempts to see Crane through a number of fresh perspectives, all
illuminating. Eric Solomon's *Stephen Crane in England: A Portrait of the
Artist* (Columbus, 1964) sketches Crane among such English peers as Conrad, Ford, and Wells; his more substantial book, *Stephen Crane: From
Parody to Realism* (Cambridge, Mass., 1966), is most valuable for its close
readings of Crane's major works. Other books contain stimulating chapters
or essays on Crane and his work: Lars Åhnebrink, *The Beginnings of
Naturalism in American Fiction* (Uppsala, 1950); Ralph Ellison, *Shadow
and Act* (New York, 1964); Edward Garnett, *Friday Nights* (New York,
1922); Maxwell Geismar, *Rebels and Ancestors* (Boston, 1953); Donald
Pizer, *Realism and Naturalism in Nineteenth-Century American Literature*
(Carbondale, 1966); Robert W. Schneider, *Five Novelists of the Progressive
Era* (New York, 1965); R. W. Stallman, *The Houses That James Built and
Other Literary Studies* (East Lansing, 1961); Charles C. Walcutt, *American
Literary Naturalism, A Divided Stream* (Minneapolis, 1956); Philip Young,
Ernest Hemingway (New York, 1952); and Larzer Ziff, *The American
1890's* (New York, 1966). Recent full-length introductions to Crane for
college students in *Major Writers of America* (by J. C. Levenson) and in
American Literary Masters (by Roy R. Male) are excellent.

Some of the most illuminating general studies of Crane have appeared in
periodicals. These include, aside from those reprinted in this volume,
Maurice Bassan, "Misery and Society: Some New Perspectives on Stephen
Crane's Fiction," *Studia Neophilologica*, XXXV (1963), 104-120; James B.
Colvert, "Structure and Theme in Stephen Crane's Fiction," *Modern
Fiction Studies*, V (Autumn 1959), 199-208; Stanley B. Greenfield, "The
Unmistakable Stephen Crane," *PMLA*, LXXIII (December 1958), 562-572;
Robert L. Hough, "Crane and Goethe: A Forgotten Relationship," *Nine-
teenth-Century Fiction*, XVII (September 1962), 135-148; Joseph Kwiat,
"Stephen Crane and Painting," *American Quarterly*, IV (Winter 1952),
331-338; Russel B. Nye, "Stephen Crane as Social Critic," *Modern
Quarterly*, XI (Summer 1940), 48-54; Neal J. Osborn, "The Riddle in 'The
Clan': A Key to Crane's Major Fiction?," *Bulletin of the New York Public
Library*, LXIX (April 1965), 247-258; Ray B. West, "Stephen Crane: Author

in Transition," *American Literature*, XXXIV (May 1962), 215-228; and Max Westbrook, "Stephen Crane: The Pattern of Affirmation," *Nineteenth-Century Fiction*, XIV (December 1959), 219-229.

Omitting the manifold source studies, the most important statements on *The Red Badge of Courage*, aside from the pieces that appear in this volume, have been the following: James T. Cox, "The Imagery of *The Red Badge of Courage*," *Modern Fiction Studies*, V (Autumn 1959), 209-219; Norman Friedman, "Criticism and the Novel," *Antioch Review*, XVIII (Fall 1958), 343-370; John E. Hart, "*The Red Badge of Courage* as Myth and Symbol," *University of Kansas City Review*, XIX (Summer 1953), 249-256; William L. Howarth, "*The Red Badge of Courage* Manuscript: New Evidence for a Critical Edition," *Studies in Bibliography*, XVIII (1965), 229-247; Eric Solomon, "The Structure of *The Red Badge of Courage*," *Modern Fiction Studies*, V (Autumn 1959), 220-234; Kermit Vanderbilt and Daniel Weiss, "From Rifleman to Flagbearer: Henry Fleming's Separate Peace in *The Red Badge of Courage*," *Modern Fiction Studies*, XI (Winter 1965-66), 371-380; and George Wyndham, "A Remarkable Book," *New Review*, XIV (January 1896), 30-40.

Good studies of Crane's poems are those by James M. Cox, "*The Pilgrim's Progress* as Source for Stephen Crane's *The Black Riders*," *American Literature*, XXVIII (January 1957), 478-487; and Harland S. Nelson, "Stephen Crane's Achievement as a Poet," *Texas Studies in Literature and Language*, IV (Winter 1963), 564-582. On Crane's earlier novels and stories, see Maurice Bassan, "Stephen Crane and 'The Eternal Mystery of Social Condition,'" *Nineteenth-Century Fiction*, XIX (March 1965), 387-394; Joseph X. Brennan, "The Imagery and Art of *George's Mother*," *CLA Journal*, IV (December 1960), 106-115; Marcus Cunliffe, "Stephen Crane and the American Background of *Maggie*," *American Quarterly*, VII (Spring 1955), 31-44; David Fitelson, "Stephen Crane's *Maggie* and Darwinism," *American Quarterly*, XVI (Summer 1964), 182-194; Thomas A. Gullason, "Thematic Patterns in Stephen Crane's Early Novels," *Nineteenth-Century Fiction*, XVI (June 1961), 59-67; and W. D. Howells, "New York Low Life in Fiction" (1896), reprinted in *Criticism and Fiction and Other Essays* (New York, 1959), pp. 271-275.

Crane's later stories have received almost as much attention as *The Red Badge*, but the late novels have been neglected. Important studies include: James B. Colvert, "Style and Meaning in Stephen Crane's 'The Open Boat,'" *University of Texas Studies in English*, XXXVII (1958), 34-45; Caroline Gordon, "Stephen Crane," *Accent*, IX (Spring 1949), 153-157; Mordecai Marcus, "The Threefold View of Nature in 'The Open Boat,'" *Philological Quarterly*, LXI (April 1962), 511-515; George Monteiro, "Stephen Crane's 'The Bride Comes to Yellow Sky,'" in *Approaches to the Short Story* (San Francisco, 1963), pp. 221-238; James T. Cox, "Stephen Crane as Symbolic Naturalist: An Analysis of 'The Blue Hotel,'" *Modern Fiction Studies*, III (Summer 1957), 147-158; Donald B. Gibson, " 'The

Blue Hotel' and the Ideal of Human Courage," *Texas Studies in Literature and Language,* VI (Autumn 1964), 388-397; James Hafley, *"The Monster* and the Art of Stephen Crane," *Accent,* XIX (Summer 1959), 159-165; Thomas A. Gullason, "The Jamesian Motif in Stephen Crane's Last Novels," *Personalist,* XLII (Winter 1961), 77-84; and Eric Solomon, "Stephen Crane's War Stories," *Texas Studies in Literature and Language,* III (Spring 1961), 67-80.

English criticism of Crane, beginning with the essays of Conrad, Garnett, Ford, Wells, and Wyndham, and extending to recent studies by Marcus Cunliffe and V. S. Pritchett, has been acute. Representative Continental criticism includes Jean Cazemajou, "Stephen Crane et Ses Esquisses de Vie New-Yorkaise," *Caliban* (Toulouse), No. 1 (January 1964), 7-24; R. E. Lucky, "Apreciación del Poeta Stephen Crane," *Revista Iberoamericana,* V (October 1942), 317-343; Henry Lüdeke, "Stephen Crane's Poetry," in *The Democracy of Henry Adams and Other Essays* (Bern, 1950), pp. 111-122; Sergio Perosa, "Stephen Crane fra naturalismo e impressionismo" (reprinted here), *Annali di Ca' Foscari,* III (1964), 119-142; and Georges Remords, "Un Précurseur des Romanciers Américains Contemporains: Stephen Crane (1871-1900)," *Bulletin de la Faculté des Lettres de Strasbourg,* XXVIII (March 1950), 190-202; (April 1950), 249-262; (May-June 1950), 351-367, and XXIX (December 1950), 158-166; (January 1951), 182-195. One article in Russian has appeared: O. V. Vasil'evskaja, "Èvoljucija tvorčestva Stivena Krejna," *Izvestija Akademii Nauk S.S.S.R., Otdelenie Literatury i Jazyka* (Moscow), XXIV (1965), 226-236. Among the half-dozen studies by Japanese scholars is an interesting linguistic essay by H. Yoshida, "Stephen Crane's Use of Colloquial and Slangy Words and Idioms," *Anglica,* IV (1961), 59-71.